The Discovery of Competence

Teaching and Learning with Diverse Student Writers

Eleanor Kutz
Suzy Q Groden
Vivian Zamel

University of Massachusetts
at Boston

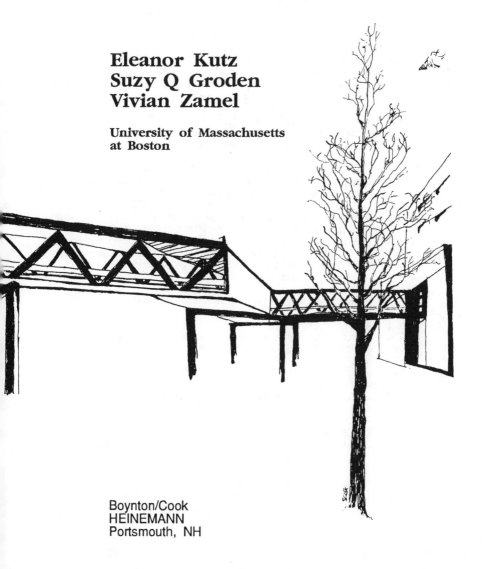

Boynton/Cook
HEINEMANN
Portsmouth, NH

Boynton/Cook Publishers, Inc.
A subsidiary of Reed Publishing (USA) Inc.
361 Hanover Street
Portsmouth NH 03801-3912
Offices and agents throughout the world

© 1993 by Eleanor Kutz, Suzy Q Groden, and Vivian Zamel

Excerpts reprinted with the permission of The Free Press, a Division of Macmillan, Inc. from *Lives on the Boundary: The Struggles and Achievements of America's Underprepared* by Mike Rose. Copyright © 1989 by Mike Rose.

Excerpts from "I Always Called Her Aunt Susie" copyright © 1981 by Leslie Marmon Silko. Reprinted from *Storyteller* by Leslie Marmon Silko, published by Seaver Books, New York, New York.

We gratefully acknowledge the people who have given their permission to include in this book material written for classes they attended while students at the University of Massachusetts at Boston. Every effort has been made to contact copyright holders for permission to reprint borrowed material where necessary, but if any oversights have occurred, we would be happy to rectify them in future printings of this work.

Library of Congress Cataloging-in-Publication Data

Kutz, Eleanor.
   The discovery of competence : teaching and learning with diverse
student writers / Eleanor Kutz, Suzy Q Groden, Vivian Zamel.
      p. cm.
   Includes bibliographical references (p.) and index.
   ISBN 0-86709-323-4
   1. English language—Rhetoric—Study and teaching.
   2. Intercultural education. I. Groden, Suzy Q II. Zamel, Vivian.
   III. Title.
PE1404.K88 1993
428.0071'1—dc20   93-16574
                                                              CIP

Cover designed by T. Watson Bogaard
Cover illustration by Suzy Q Groden
Printed in the United States of America on acid-free paper
93 94 95 96 97 98 99 9 8 7 6 5 4 3 2 1

The
Discovery
of Competence

Contents

Foreword

Midway through his essay "The Origin of Extermination in the Imagination," the writer William Gass tells us:

> When we fail to see whatever is plainly put before us; when we deny the existence of certain concepts, and will not entertain them; when we refuse to draw necessary inferences, and continue to cherish our beliefs long after their infamous, false, and misleading nature has been disclosed; when we are indifferent in our responses, callous in our concerns, capable of counting only half the heads that comprise the company of [hu]mankind and discounting the others . . . then we are polluting, distorting, maiming, killing consciousness, that space which should be most sacred to us. . . . (1985, 232–33)

The accounts in *The Discovery of Competence* remind us of the very failures that Gass enumerates here. In our reading of this book, we feel ourselves lifted up, moved into the scene, and invited to see, hear, know, and feel with students and teachers as they learn together. We know our partially exterminated imaginations are coming to life.

The authors call on readers to acknowledge the stories told here as highly dependent on us as observers, listeners, and interpreters. We must take the words on the pages for actions. We must look within ourselves to see and feel as fully as possible the richness of experience and sensation behind the episodes, engagements, and enlightenments of learning offered in this book.

It is tough to convey wonder on paper; only by the fanciest of typographic plays can we even offer color and texture to the page; the linearity of page following page and chapter after chapter places all presentations of black print on white page on a similar footing. It is tough to shake the status quo, to move out of habituated ways of visualizing, verbalizing, listening, and, perhaps most important, categorizing—of really seeing no more than half of those around us.

This is a book that demonstrates faith that the imagination of all educators has not been exterminated by "teacher-proof" curricular guides, textbooks and teacher manuals, and in-service days of "training." The authors here believe in teaching and learning as conjoined enterprises for students and teachers. They believe that there are imaginative, caring, and intellectually curious learners upon whom this book can depend. Thus the readers offer no prescriptions or blueprints. Deeds, cooperative ventures, and interweavings of oral and written endeavors between students and teachers come through as suitable, wise, and persuasive. Episodes inspire in us awe and caution that we should translate into attentiveness for observing in our own classrooms and during times of reflection on our own learning experiences. The accounts here allow us everything and facilitate much. Unlike too many records of reforms in teaching, restructured alignments within schools, and renewed attempts to engage all students, *The Discovery of Competence* makes it difficult for readers to remain unbidden to try *their own* reforms and to lift themselves above programmed correctives for education.

This book moves beyond such correctives to illustrate the wit, wisdom, honesty, and integrity of teachers and students—and students and students—learning together in both wonder and frustration. Cognitive psychologists now suggest that a certain amount of irritation or disjunctiveness spurs learning on. Social interactionists insist that opportunities to negotiate in socially supportive and reliable contexts instill and reinforce learning. Sociologists and anthropologists observe that, across cultures, a sense of responsibility, engagement, and accountability feed learning and foster a sense of the power to move learning in one context to another scene and group of actors. *The Discovery of Competence* brings these abstract research findings alive and sets us as readers squarely down in the middle of multiple layers of collaboration in the classrooms and administrative structures described here. It slowly dawns on us as we read this book that the authors made a virtue of more, not less, assessment, that they moved the key players in assessment—*students*—to the center of accountability and responsibility. It is eminently clear to us that the course of change is not smooth, but that there are allies we can tap in our efforts. We see here that students helped nudge institutional change along by the very encouragement they gave the innovations of teachers joining in teams across classes, encouraging language research outside the classroom, and linking students around research and writing for real audiences.

We have heard much in the last decade of the twentieth century about teacher research, restructuring, and finding essentials of learning. This book makes clear that any of these reform efforts alone is simply too flat, too narrow, too insular. The key to enduring change rests in the commitment to learning, dynamism, and adaptability of all the players on the team: students, teachers, administrators. The rivulets of change that result as these players discover their competencies come together and swirl around obstacles and temporary obstructions, and pick up other rivulets to converge as currents of change.

Essayist Gass reminds us that "each one of us is an other too, a flesh in flower for a fellow being, possibly" (233). *The Discovery of Competence* never lets us forget both the possibleness and the possibility of such flowering.

Shirley Brice Heath

Preface

This book continues a conversation that began over ten years ago among three teachers of first-year college writing and extends that conversation to a reading audience made up primarily of others who are engaged in similar and related work. It has its roots in the sorts of questions we have asked and the understandings we have developed in our teaching of writing at an urban university. These questions and understandings arose, over time, as we designed courses and programs together, created placement and assessment mechanisms, read essays and portfolios of student writing, and worked with teachers and with students preparing to teach writing at many levels, in classrooms where English was a second as well as a first language. But the book emerges, particularly, from our ongoing conversations about the work of our own students in our own writing classrooms, and it focuses frequently on particular student texts—those that engaged us or puzzled us and that helped us to form key questions at critical junctures in our own teaching.

Despite the knowledge that comes to us from current research in education and language learning, it is still common for college faculty to view entering students more in terms of what they need to learn than of what they know and bring to their education. Typically, faculty complain that students are unable to write complete sentences or coherent paragraphs, or to spell or punctuate correctly. We have tried, instead, to focus on the underlying competence in learning and in using language that our students bring to their work as writers, to find ways to see and understand that competence, to help our students build on it, systematically, in the writing classroom, and to create a pedagogy through which students may discover their own competence. In this effort we have moved back and forth between our students' writing and the theories and research that would improve our understanding of that writing and the process that produced it. The early chapters of the book reflect this movement— our own process of gaining new understandings as teachers of writing—while later chapters suggest the implications of such understandings for pedagogy, for curriculum, for assessment.

We have come to see the ability to write as acquired through a natural process having much in common with the processes of acquiring first and second languages, as connected with cognitive and intellectual development, and as taking place in specific social and cultural contexts. Our own work has been embedded in a particular context—an urban university that is trying to respond in effective ways to the needs of a diverse student body. Our conversations with our colleagues and our students at the University of Massachusetts at Boston have contributed a great deal to the understandings represented in this book, and we would like to thank them all. We would also like to acknowledge the contributions of Shirley Brice Heath to our thinking. Her book *Ways with Words,* which shows how children acquire particular ways of using language in particular community contexts, appeared at a critical point in our own work. For several years, as we researched with our own students the cultural and linguistic practices of the several communities (including the academic community) in which they functioned, Shirley was a frequent contributor to our conversations, helping us to place the discoveries we were making about these immediate communities in a broader context related to her own research. Most important, she reinforced our view that through collaborative inquiry with our own students we could find many of the understandings that we were seeking. Because our aim was to help students gain an appreciation of their own competence, this seemed an ideal form of teaching.

Finally, while this book emerges from our own quest to become more effective teachers of writing in our own classrooms, we believe that both the process of our inquiry and the understandings we have gained have important implications for the work of all writing classrooms in a diverse and multicultural society. They allow us to recast the writing classroom so that it is not simply a place for certifying that some students can demonstrate the linguistic practices of the university but a place where students may build on their competence and realize their possibilities as writers and learners.

Acknowledgments

We would like to thank all the students whose writing contributed to this book, including Edith Agnew, Alison Sharkey Boland, Fukiko Cudhea, Carole Gustely Cuerten, Thao Duong, Ann Jenkins, Shu Kuei Lai, Albert Leneski, Lucy Leu, Antonio Lopes, Helene Lundberg, Tatsu Matsuda, Hung Tan Nguyen, Edwin Perez, Phung P. Pham, Larry Purdy, Deborah Sacon, Margie Sarmiento, Emily Singer, Sook Young Song, Shawn Terrell, Ruth Trytko, Kathleen Vejvoda, Souyan Wong, and Maya Zaitzevsky. We wish to thank Renée Betz, of Central Missouri State University, who suggested the link between assessment and the Latin verb *adsideo*. We also wish to express our gratitude to Ron Thornton, Constance Emmett, and David Goldman, for their continuing support and encouragement.

Chapter One

The Discovery of Competence

We begin with a story told by Suzy Groden.

It was a Saturday morning in early March, and I was about to give a workshop on the teaching of writing, at a conference being held at my college. With my arms filled with samples of student writing, model assignments, and other handouts, I hurriedly entered the catwalk which connects all of the buildings on campus. This catwalk is a structure that is suspended above the ground at second-floor level, constructed of steel and glass, with girders that run from floor to ceiling, forming triangles.

I suddenly realized, as the door slammed shut behind me, that two starlings were trapped in the catwalk. I stood still and watched them. The birds were frantic, flying the length of the structure, trying to escape by flying out through the glass, which they mistakenly interpreted as open air. They kept smashing against the glass, flapping their wings madly, then retreating to the ceiling girders before they began their next foray.

After I had watched for a few minutes, I asked, aloud, "How did you get in here?" "What are you doing in here?" and observed, "You don't belong here." Each bird hit up against the glass several times before I asked—again aloud—"How are you going to get out?" The starlings responded by smashing against the glass, flapping their wings, flying up to the rafters, and then beginning all over again. I looked around, but there wasn't any opening where the birds could have gotten in. I guessed that sometime earlier in the weekend someone had opened all of the doors from outside, allowing the birds to enter. But the route out was extremely complicated, and I knew

1

that even if I opened the doors leading to the hallways, stairways, and out to the fresh air, there was virtually no chance that they would all be left open long enough to ensure the birds' finding their way. I realized that if I wanted to help, I would have to catch them and carry them out.

I found this thought rather daunting. The truth is that I was a little afraid of the starlings—afraid that they'd scratch or bite me— and besides, it didn't look all that easy for me to catch them, since their flight across the ceiling area was higher than I could reach with my arms extended. So, for awhile, I continued to stand and watch, unable to imagine a solution to what I had come to see as our problem. Then, unexpectedly, one of the starlings hit the glass, stunned itself, and slid down the glass wall into a corner that was formed by the diagonal steel girder and the wall! I put down my folders, kneeled beside the immobilized bird, and wrapped my left hand around it. It struggled against me a bit, but I managed to draw it to me, wrap my right hand around it as well, and gently pull it free of the steel beam.

The bird stopped struggling and glared at me over my hands. It was warm and soft, and I could feel its heart beating against my palm. I laughed and said, "The tight spot turned out to be your way out!" I adjusted the pressure of my grip so that it was tight enough to keep the bird from getting free or hurting me, but not so tight as to squeeze it. Then I walked very, very slowly—so as not to shake the bird or frighten it—to the building I'd been heading for originally. I managed to pull open the heavy door with my pinky, though it was stuck at first, and my pinkies aren't very strong. Then we moved—still very slowly and steadily—across the second-floor hallway, down a flight of steps, through the first-floor lobby, and out two more sets of heavy doors, to the plaza. I walked to a raised lawn and opened my hands. The starling hesitated a second, then flew up past a tree, around a building, and out of sight.

My satisfaction was short lived, because I remembered the other bird, still in the catwalk. I decided not to look at my watch, realizing that, regardless of the time, I wasn't going to give up at this point. I marched back indoors, up the stairs, and into the catwalk.

The second starling was now even more frantic, probably because of several additional smashings into the glass wall. I started talking actively now—telling the bird to let me help it—telling it that it could trust me, that I wasn't going to hurt it. But it would have none of me, and kept flying away from my outstretched hands, hitting the glass, flapping wretchedly. I was at a loss to imagine a successful solution. But, as I moved, speaking and reaching out to catch it, the bird moved ahead of me, and I noticed that in this way we were approaching another corner. Then, miracle of miracles! the second bird hit the glass, slid down the wall, and became wedged in the angle between the girder and the corner! This time I knew how it would go. I slid my left hand in first, drew the bird up far enough so that my right hand could wrap around it, pulled it toward me, adjusted the pressure of my hands so that they would hold the bird firmly without causing pain, and started my stately walk through the catwalk, into the building, down the stairs, and out. This time I felt feisty enough to stop at the spot where I'd caught the first starling and gather up the folders I'd set down there. Then I resumed my progress, with this paraphernalia tucked against my side and the starling in my hands, pulling open the resistant door to Wheatley Hall (using the now familiar pinky action), and proceeding to set the bird free.

It is not irrelevant, I believe, that as we walked I brought the bird's head up to my face, touched it to my cheek and kissed it. It glared at me sharply, but the act gave me a remarkable sensation.

What does Suzy's story have to do with the learning and teaching of writing and the discovery of competence? Actually, quite a lot. It suggests some of the problems facing the students who enter our classrooms, particularly the first-year college students who find themselves faced with the new conventions of a new community. And it suggests ways in which teachers can begin to work toward solving these problems: by drawing their students into the academic community and helping them to discover their existing competence as thinkers and writers and the relationship between what they know and what and how they will come to know.

Consider the plight of the birds. By acting as they had always done, they got themselves into a place that was somewhat elevated and looked like the space they understood. But it was not what they thought it was. What they saw as open sky was an invisible glass wall, a boundary, which they couldn't conceive of, and which, when treated as if it were what the birds *imagined* it to be, constrained and hurt them. Left to struggle in this situation—misinterpreting the space, having no understanding of the system of doors, hallways, steps, and so on—they couldn't discover how to use their ability to fly in order to get out through the doors that would be opened as people passed back and forth. Acting only as they knew how to act, lacking an understanding of where they were and how they should move through these particular spaces, they would probably have hurt themselves, perhaps so badly they would not have been able to fly again.

Then consider Suzy's first response—Suzy, who understood the space with a deep familiarity. She came upon the birds acting in their desperately inappropriate way and immediately felt afraid. Her initial response was to tell them they didn't belong. She then tried to help them briefly, using strategies they couldn't take advantage of, given their own sense of what was going on, and she and the birds became locked in a futile exercise. If they had continued in that fashion, of course, Suzy would finally have had to walk away, sighing and leaving them to their fate. She would have felt grief for them, but also helplessness in the face of her inability to communicate with them. Remember, too, that she had her own obligations to meet that morning.

Then, take the rescue. Suzy and the birds accomplished it in a remarkable collaboration. At first glance, it seems that it happened through a lucky chance. But a closer analysis of the process reveals that it came about through a strange combination of misinterpretations, engagements, and responses within a specific physical context. The birds were confused by the space and by Suzy, stunned by their smacking into the glass walls. But then they became caught— engaged—through their unexpected encounters with a structure of supports and walls and corners.

Finally, consider the evolution of Suzy's role—the process she had to go through. Despite her fear and her inability to see an immediate solution, she did care enough to wait and worry and watch. This eventually made it possible for her to respond to events as they unfolded, to do things she had never done before, which, it turned out, were the very things that had to be done.

Suzy's first response is the one she is least proud of: "How did you get in here? You don't belong here!" Then she tried to deal with the problem in a way that had nothing to do with the nature of the birds as birds, and experienced feelings of helplessness and hopelessness. But what saved Suzy is the fact that she did not keep walking. She did not give up, even though at first she had no idea how she might be of help. She stayed and watched and, happily, recognized the opportunity created by the starlings and the catwalk structures.

What happened then seems particularly instructive for our current enterprise. Suzy put down the things she was carrying, things that had nothing to do with the birds and, in this case, would only have gotten in the way of her helping them. She let their plight—their confinement between the steel supports and walls—help her and reached in, first with one hand, tentatively, then with the other, to draw them to her. She consciously adjusted the pressure of her grip so that she would neither stifle and hurt them nor lose hold, and she carried each one separately, held close, feeling its heart beating, watching the glowering, outraged eyes, assuring it of her good intentions, to that place where she could let go and it could fly. When Suzy was holding the birds in her hands, her progress had to be slow and steady, although once she was sure of herself she was able to gather up and carry with her those papers and materials she'd laid down temporarily.

This episode suggests some of what it seems to us that teaching is about, including that flood of affection Suzy felt once she had learned that she and the birds could succeed. As teachers, we often find ourselves in Suzy's situation: a great deal has to happen before we can get to the point of seeing our students "fly" by using the powers of language and thought they *bring with them,* but don't *realize* they have. We have to help our students recognize and confront a world of at first unfamiliar and incomprehensible values, questions, relationships, and forms of communication and evaluation. And we discover that we must engage in a long and often frustrating process, overcoming the impulse to deal with the students in ways that have little to do with who they are and what they need, and overcoming as well our (often unconscious) fear of them as "outsiders" whose attitudes, assumptions, behavior, and language all seem alien and threatening to the world we know.

As teachers, we have to be willing to set aside, for a time, the "stuff" we are carrying and take these students up where they are, as individuals, using everything that comes to hand and providing supports and structures that allow them to find their way within this community—to engage with ideas, texts, and issues and to communicate their thinking without becoming shattered by multiple failures. We have to have the patience to allow their development to proceed as slowly as necessary, and the courage and imagination to work out new routes, new curricula, through which we can draw them into the world of learning and inquiry, holding them firmly without stifling their capacities, and offering them the means to learn actively, to explore problems and questions, and—most important— to discover in these enterprises their own competence as observers, thinkers, critics, creators. We have to expend the efforts needed to open doors that would otherwise constrain progress. And we have to remember to pick up our "stuff" again, to share with our students what we consider most cherishable about learning and the process of systematic inquiry. While all teachers within an academic community must share in these efforts, much of the work that is critical typically falls to the teacher of composition, and in this book we will focus first on that work or, more precisely, on the ways in which we think that work needs to be reconceived. Too often it is the first-year composition teacher who is expected to serve as gatekeeper to the community: to provide all of the "skills" that students need in order to fit in and to restrict the entry of those who do not. And many students do not fit in. National statistics indicate that almost half of every entering group of first-year students at public institutions of higher education have dropped out by the end of the first year, and the figures are comparable for populations of nontraditional students at private institutions.

There are many ways of describing what is wrong, particularly with the students: "they can't think," "they can't write," "they don't know what a sentence [or noun, or verb] is," "they don't know what a university is," "they don't know how to set standards, do research," "they can't even speak English," to quote a few of the comments made regularly by our colleagues, who are in despair over their inability to teach or understand their students, who need to vent their sense of helplessness and frustration at discovering that their lectures are poorly understood, their students' papers hard to read. It is as if they were shocked at the inability of the starlings to comprehend and deal with their situation: "Can't they see it's glass? Why don't they stop smashing up against it and fly out the way they got in? Why are they acting like this?"

To some, the solution lies in better gate (or door) keeping. And since the values and culture of the academic community, like those of any other community, are represented in its linguistic practices, in its ways of using language, most of these gatekeeping efforts focus on those practices, on ways of ensuring that students learn the linguistic forms of the academic community *before* they can become a part of it. This is the argument for remedial programs that "quarantine" the increasingly large numbers of students entering public higher education institutions each year who have not mastered the linguistic conventions of an academic discourse community. It is the institutional response to the disturbing presence of "starlings" who don't belong. These "starlings" may be learning English as a second language, or they may be native speakers of English whose social and economic backgrounds differ sharply from those of traditional students and faculty. They are likely to have had precollege schooling that prepared them in limited ways for limited educational and life expectations. Seeing only what the entering students *don't know,* colleges have created a variety of "Learning Centers," "Resource Centers," "Writing Centers," "Developmental Studies Programs," and "Reading and Study Skills Courses" as isolated enterprises that disconnect the study of these linguistic practices both from the community that uses them and from the knowledge and competence students bring from other communities. Such efforts reflect a lack of understanding about how an individual is drawn into a community, and into its conversations, as an active participant.

What these efforts also fail to recognize is that people learn the ways of the new communities they enter not from being contained, as in an "immigration quarantine center," "a remediation corral," but rather through an authentic immersion in the community. Students become engaged, functioning participants in the intellectual and social life of their educational communities by speaking, listening, reading, and writing with other participants about the issues that burn at the community's heart; by being listened to, having their words read, being held accountable for the ideas they express; by being responded to with honesty and care. Everyone agrees that language is the key to helping outsiders become insiders. The question is how best to invite people into a new linguistic community.

Our desire, as teachers of writing, is to foster our students' ability to use writing in natural and forceful ways to engage authentically in the conversations that form the life of the academic community. In order to achieve this, we see ourselves as having to help these students to understand the nature of the questions people ask in this community, and to discover, in their own already established modes of questioning, seeing, interpreting, and articulating experience, the competence that will provide the foundations for their ability to acquire new modes, including those most useful and recognized in the academic community.

These foundations exist in the language our students already use in their homes, families, and communities, in the ways they construct and share knowledge through stories, riddles, and arguments, in the problems they solve and the events they interpret and analyze, and in the rich and varied cultural perspectives they bring to our classrooms. The acquisition of new ways of using language in order to enter into new conversations happens through a process that is analogous to the way children acquire their native languages and enter into the conversations of their families and communities.

One major focus of this book, then, is the nature of language and its acquisition—the nature of linguistic and communicative competence, the ways in which new competence is acquired, and how teachers of writing can help their students acquire the new ways of writing and speaking demanded in the college classroom by building on their existing competence with language.

The students who find it so difficult to enter the academic community are members of other communities—of families, peer groups, neighborhoods, churches, workplaces—communities in which they have engaged successfully as full participants. They have learned how to talk, to behave, to interact in order to be accepted as members by others in the group. Much of what they've needed to know they've acquired unconsciously and gradually through their interaction with other members of the community. Some rules of the community's code have been pointed out to them for their conscious learning ("Look at that nerd wearing sandals"; "Boys don't cry"). But both the unconscious and the conscious process of coming to know how to be a member of a community begins, for children, with their earliest experiences. These experiences, like later ones, are rooted in and represented in language. And so, in order to grasp the nature of the problem of how individuals learn to interact in a new community and to discover potential solutions to this problem, we should look at the one experience of learning in which almost all human beings, regardless of social class, race, or culture, are successful: the learning of their native language.

For all of the reasons mentioned, language acquisition is a good model for what we are seeking to understand about learning and teaching, and we will draw on that model throughout this book. What we know about language acquisition suggests not only that language and language learning lie at the core of all the learning that our students must do, but also that there are striking analogies between the acquisition of language and the particular forms of learning that our students must do. This is the case because the process of acquiring a language entails coming to be able to use not only the systems of phonological, lexical, and syntactic rules that govern that language, but also the systems of paralinguistic and sociolinguistic rules for using the language to communicate in a variety of social contexts. The process of acquiring a language is also the process of acquiring the culture in which it is embedded.

So, a second focus of this book is the relationship between acquiring new uses of language—such as writing within an academic context or within academic disciplines—and the cultural perspective represented in those uses.

Like the members of any community, the members of the academic community share a sensibility. Despite intense and endless disagreements among them about what knowledge is, how it may best be acquired, and what sorts of activities are significant, they tend to agree on the acceptable *forms* of disagreement, persuasion, refutation, and proof. They share at least a basic understanding—one that must be construed by the newcomer—of how one engages in inquiry and debate, of the kinds of issues and themes that are important enough to be researched and debated, and of ways to talk and write about them. The student entering the academic community must be familiar with these aspects of its cultural norms, practices, and definitions. She has to be an insider in order to know what to say, to whom, and how. The practices of a community change as its members change, and the students who have become part of the academic community may alter, question, or resist its practices. But those who are perceived as outsiders will be ignored or misunderstood.

While all normal human beings have successfully acquired their native language and have become full participants in at least one linguistic community, many have acquired another language as well through processes that are remarkably similar to those involved in first language acquisition and to those involved in learning how to use one's native language in new ways within a new community. The movement into any new language community is a difficult one. It requires the individual to move out from what is comfortably known—to cross a boundary—and take risks by trying new ways of representing ideas, of communicating. Because the processes of acquisition in any context are similar, by understanding the nature of these processes we can discover new ways to understand and extend the linguistic competence our students bring to our classrooms. And because the processes of acquisition are similar for first-year college writers encountering new uses of their native language and for second language learners encountering a new language, studying the experience of the English as a Second Language (ESL) learner can help us to see learners of all new forms of discourse in new ways.

In her autobiographical account of her experiences adjusting to a new country and culture, appropriately entitled *Lost in Translation,* Eva Hoffman painfully recollects what acquiring a new language in adolescence represented for her.

> Every day I learn new words, new expressions . . . but mostly, the problem is that the signifier has become severed from the signified. The words I learn now don't stand for things in the same unquestioned way they did in my native tongue. . . . This radical disjoining between word and thing is a desiccating alchemy, draining the world not only of significance but of its colors, striations, nuances—its very existence. It is a loss of a living connection.
>
> What has happened to me in this new world? I don't know. I don't see what I've seen, don't comprehend what's in front of me. I'm not filled with language anymore, and I have only a memory of fullness to anguish me with the knowledge that, in this dark and empty state, I don't really exist. (106–8)

Hoffman's account gives us some sense of what it means to learn to live in the world of a second language and helps us understand the complexities, confusion, loss, the "verbal blur," as she puts it, that many of our ESL students have had to face and continue to face in their own acquisition of English. It also offers us insight into what many of our native speakers face as they too are confronted with the new expectations of our first-year writing classrooms. It suggests that what is lost with the movement away from a known language is not just a set of words but a whole way of thinking about the world, of constructing meaning from it. With the acquisition of a new language, of new linguistic practices, comes new ways of knowing. And these, too, are embedded in culture and acquired through participation in a community that uses these new ways.

A third focus of this book is the relationship between the development of writing and other uses of discourse on the one hand, and the development of new ways of thinking on the other.

All students face new demands when they enter the world of schooling, for they are now being asked to enter yet another community, one with its own set of expectations, assumptions, and conventions, and to acquire those new "ways with words," to use Shirley Brice Heath's oft-quoted title, as well as the ways of thinking that are appropriate to this new school culture. In fact, when the City University of New York adopted an open admissions policy in 1970, the students who flooded the classrooms seemed to English professors like Mina Shaughnessy very much like speakers of another language. In *Errors and Expectations*, Shaughnessy characterized the difficulties her nontraditional students were experiencing, difficulties with language that made it seem as if they had come from a different country. This group, according to Shaughnessy, "contained true outsiders . . . strangers in academia, unacquainted with the rules and rituals of college life, unprepared for the sorts of tasks their teachers were about to assign them" (2–3).

In working with these students, Shaughnessy tried to set aside the filter of her expectations and look instead at the evidence she found in her students' writing of the ways that they were thinking about the task they were undertaking. Her work was shaped by the understanding that students themselves can be the sources of our ability to appreciate the challenges they are facing as they enter our classrooms. That understanding leads, by extension, to a fourth major theme of this book.

For students who are learning new modes of discourse, engaging in active inquiry into the nature of language allows them to discover for themselves—and to use—many of the aspects of language that are the object of traditional (and often ineffective) composition instruction.

Over the years we have gathered many accounts from our students of their own experiences in entering college, and we feel that we can learn much from these descriptions of their experiences as "strangers in academia." Here is an account by a Chinese student of the agony she endured trying to meet what she took to be the expectations of her professor for a term paper.

> Last semester I spent eight hours in all writing one of my term papers and got only one paragraph, six to seven sentences. I told my classmates the next day. No one believed me. Was I exaggerating the fact? No.
>
> It was the first time in my life to write a six-page-long paper in English. I went to the reading room in the library, and hoping that no one would come. I started with the first sentence of the first paragraph which had already in my head. The only thing I had to do is putting the idea on the paper. But, it was not easy at all. The first sentence took me more than two hours. It was changed and revised again and again, sometimes because I was not sure whether the sentence was grammatically correct, or whether it was "pure English" (not Chinese English), and sometimes because I thought it was probably not suitable to be the first sentence of a long paper. I wasted lots of paper on which were only a few words.
>
> I wished I had been an American. If I had been an American I would have been able to write down everything in my head in a very short period and correctly. I was envious of my American classmates. I thought at least they did not need to worry about grammar.
>
> Another six hours was spent on the following five to six sentences of the rest of the first paragraph. While I was working on them, I began to worry about the next paragraph about which I didn't have exact ideas. It was such a big burden.
>
> Finally, after eight hours, the first paragraph was finished up, not because I was satisfied, but because there was no much time for me to write. the paper was finished hurriedly and submitted in the last minute. When I was handing it to the teacher, something came into my mind at once. "God! I forgot to put that point in the paper." But it was too late. That point cost me a lot. (Min)

What can we learn from reflections such as these? We can discover a great deal of what this student thinks about language, about writing, about thinking, and about the relationship between them. Min does not at first anticipate that she will encounter the difficulties Hoffman faced. She has acquired English, and she can think in it. She has "the idea" and only has to put it on paper. But that task proves to be "not easy at all." Min is strongly aware of the outside constraints of the discourse situation she finds herself in—the constraints of a particular task within a particular community. She (rightly) assumes that correctness according to the standards of "pure English" will provide the most weighty measure of whether she has accomplished that task. She suggests a relationship between language and culture as she (wrongly) assumes that if she were an American she could handle the task easily. And she responds to the task, the constraints, and her own limitations as she perceives them with a particular set of strategies—getting the first sentence right both grammatically and in terms of its suitability as the first sentence of a long paper.

Our prevailing theories of composition offer us, as teachers, some critical perspective on this student's writing process. But her process in this instance is dictated by her perceptions of the cultural context in which she is writing. She is an outsider to that context not just because she is not an American but because she is a first-year student in her first college writing course. Her uncertainties and responses are echoed by native speakers as well. To help her expand her repertoire of processes and to encourage her to work in ways more appropriate to the larger task before her, a teacher must alter that context in a way that is analogous to what Suzy did when she contained the starlings in the clearly defined space made by her hands so they would not keep hitting the wall of glass. That altered context can provide an environment in which it is safe to take the necessary risks to learn new strategies and new ways.

A fifth theme of this book is that responsive curricula can provide this altered context, offering both support and encouragement, both structure and room to grow.

As long as our students are allowed to remain outside or on the fringes of our community—trapped in the catwalk, as it were—they will share the plight of the starlings: they will remain unable to interpret in a meaningful way the requirements and approaches we are using or to adopt them as their own. Their own efforts will continue to be directed in inappropriate ways, and they will grasp little of what we think is patently obvious and significant. They will study what their instructors feel are the wrong things, answer what turn out to be the wrong questions, and go on missing what their teachers see as the point of what they are reading and hearing, smacking up against invisible but nonetheless impassable walls and becoming part of the appalling attrition rates that plague our public higher education institutions year after year.

But what of students who are insiders, who know their way around the university and understand the work that goes on there? When we ask such students to reflect on their writing, what do we find? One upper-division English major describes it in the following terms.

It usually takes me a week or so after getting an assignment to sort out the direction I want to go in the pursuit of the topic. Topic choice is the most difficult . . . that is, narrowing down the professor's suggestions to an engaging issue. I can't even attempt to begin writing until a topic "grabs" me. This often backs me up until I'm close to panic. The anxiety begins NOW and doesn't disappear until the writing process starts. The funny thing is, that the butterflies are fluttering continuously up to the point of composing. They hibernate while my fingers engage with the computer keyboard, but as soon as I walk away, they begin fluttering again. (But this is a different kind of anxiety, because I know the paper will be completed. The act of *beginning* confirms eventual closure.) (Margie)

Deborah, another advanced student who is preparing to teach English, offers this report on *her* writing process:

At the beginning of the process of a new paper I sometimes feel as if I am a blind person in that I can't see the direction I am heading as I search for "words" and search for "ways to use these words" when I am composing. Eventually though, as I work my way into the text, I gain a higher sensitivity to the things around me and I can say more, as the sightless person can sense more, than the sighted one.

Also, in the beginning stage of a paper writing, it is difficult to focus my intention on anything specific because I don't know what my intentions are yet. I mold my topic as I go along. Sometimes the ideas in my head which I transfer to paper come from nowhere, and I think that they are unrelated to each other or to the larger topic that I sense is evolving. This not knowing where I am going creates a sense of anxiety, until I can see development of "form" and ideas that work together to prove a point or several points.

Getting to the stage where things start to fall into place occurs after hours of fits and starts as I read, reread, and reinterpret the things I've said. At times this process is very painful and I feel as if I will never get through it.

I have tried some invention strategies to get me out of the anxiety mode of starting a paper—generally they have not been successful in that I resort back to the journey out method where I begin nowhere and end up somewhere—eventually.

These students, expert as they are, are also voicing their anxiety as they begin the task of writing a particular paper. But they know themselves as writers, as learners. They know what to expect next in their own idiosyncratic processes. And they see the shape of the whole project. They can trust that they will "end up somewhere— eventually." They are lost in the process, but only temporarily, and they can trust in the now-familiar experience of being lost and eventually finding a way out. They know, after all, that if they smack up against an obstacle, there are other passages. There is none of the sense here, which we found in Min's account, of hours, paper, words, being "wasted." These students are patient with their own methods of negotiating ideas, concepts, and language and thus can take some pleasure in them despite their intermittent bouts of anxiety. They are not afraid to take risks, to try new intellectual routes.

This is the most important difference between them and the students who are still outsiders, who, like the starlings, don't know the way out, feel trapped and lost, unable even to see the walls that inhibit them. These insiders know their own competence. They discovered it long ago and *rediscover* it in the process of writing and thinking about each new paper. These papers—explorations of top-ics—are *theirs*, chosen, thought through, and crafted in processes that ultimately afford them considerable joy.

Of course, this does not mean that they have no need of us as teachers. It is true that they know how to gather information, read difficult texts, and write papers, and it is sometimes difficult to see ways in which they need us. But although they are insiders in the academic world, they need intellectual challenges, the chance to collaborate on serious, engaging work that pushes them to their limits and suggests some of the new routes they can consider exploring. We need to be aware of this and to be ready to draw *these* students into our intellectual lives, even to use *them* to challenge and push *us* and other students.

Thus, in the case of both insiders *and* outsiders, we have the responsibility to find ways to guide our students into intellectual work that will afford or heighten for them those pleasures we know to be the potential outcome of our joint educational enterprise. We need to envision new kinds of relationships with students, ones that make it possible for teachers and students to engage simultaneously in dynamic, reciprocal processes of learning and teaching. From the students' point of view, such processes can provide support and stimulation, instruction and knowledge. They can draw students organically toward an increasing engagement with the world of ideas, problems, relationships, and phenomena, and toward a deeper sense of their responsibility to know, interpret, understand, and respond to the world. Even more important, they will open the way for students to a recurrent and thoroughly pleasurable discovery of their own capacities. From the teachers' point of view, these processes can provide new opportunities for engagement in meaningful investiga-tions in association with people who can be expected to bring to the work fresh attitudes, questions, and approaches. They can afford teachers the chance to rethink their assumptions and to sharpen and expand their understanding of the processes of learning and of inter-

preting data as well as the opportunity to experience the enjoyment
that comes from being able to draw students into the worlds they
know and care about. Through the students' eyes, teachers can come
to see these worlds in new ways and discover new facets of familiar
objects of study.

This way, both students and teachers can come to discover their
competence as learners who know *what* they know, know *that* they
know, and know *how* they know. They also come to understand that
new kinds of knowledge, new areas of competence, are needed for
new situations but that these new kinds of knowledge have a direct
relationship to the knowledge they already possess. Students who
enter our first-year writing classrooms need to discover their competence as writers and language users and to see how that existing
competence will support their acquisition of the new forms and uses
of language they will need in their academic enterprise. Teachers too
discover their competence by reflecting on what they know about
teaching and learning, what they know not to be true, and what they
don't yet know as they encounter new learners and new situations.
As teachers and students extend their existing competence to these
new contexts, they will acquire new words to represent them and the
new "ways with words" they need in order to participate in them.

In this book, then, the concept of linguistic competence becomes
a metaphor for that competence as learners, thinkers, writers, we
must help our students discover in themselves. It draws heavily on
our experiences with our students and on our own discoveries as
teachers of writing. The early chapters will explore the relationship
between language and learning and knowing, the evidence that students' writing can offer about their competence in these areas, and
the ways in which teachers can build a safe framework of responsive
and yet challenging curricula through which they can support students' learning. Later chapters will draw more directly on the specific
contexts of our own writing classrooms, on the ways in which learning and teaching and "content" intersect in classrooms focused on
writing and inquiry. We will identify some of the implications of the
relationships among language, thought, writing, and knowledge for
the assessment of student learning and writing. And finally, we will
explore the implications of all of this work for creating in our first-
year writing courses an environment that is deeply multicultural—in
the ways in which it draws on the perspectives of diverse students
as well as in the focus of its inquiry.

We see the work described in this book as part of what we hope
will turn out to be a promising new direction in education: the
creation of genuinely new forms of curricula that respond directly to
the dramatic changes in the populations of students who are entering

our institutions of higher education. We are setting out to address the problem that Mike Rose, who has written extensively about his experiences teaching writing to diverse groups of students, has identified in *Lives on the Boundary:*

> How much we don't see when we look only for deficiency, when we tally up all that people can't do. Many of the students . . . display the gradual or abrupt emergence of an intellectual acuity or literate capacity that just wasn't thought to be there. This is not to deny that awful limits still exist . . . : so much knowledge and so many procedures never learned; such a long, cumbersome history of relative failure. But this must not obscure the equally important fact that if you set up the right conditions, try as best as you can to cross class and cultural boundaries, figure out what's needed to encourage performance, that if you watch and listen, again and again there will emerge evidence of ability that escapes those who dwell on differences. (1989, 222)

We see our work as an attempt to achieve what Rose calls for in that book:

> an orientation to instruction that provides guidance on how to determine and honor the beliefs and stories, enthusiasms, and apprehensions that students reveal. How to build on them, and when they clash with our curriculum . . . how to encourage a discussion that will lead to reflection on what students bring and what they're currently confronting. (236)

Chapter Two

Aspects of Competence I
Language Acquisition

All students come to the classroom as competent speakers of a first language, and perhaps of others. Certainly they have much to bring to the mastery of another language or other uses of language (like writing), and they can tell us a great deal about what they bring and what, like Mike Rose's students, "they're currently confronting." Just as Suzy's story of her encounter with the birds helps us to define issues in our teaching, and our students' accounts of their own approaches to writing give us new perspectives on writing instruction, our students' accounts of their own language learning experiences can help us to "discover" much of what we—and they—know about language learning and teaching. Edwin's account is typical:

> I still remember that my English class, in my first grades, was almost like the later classes. First you learn the basic words like mother, father, etc. Then they start you with the grammar. But as nobody likes grammar I think that the learning of English slow down a lot. As you going in higher grades the system of teaching was about the same. You learn a few more words and grammar. They never make you write which I think would be a great idea.
>
> When I started in this university my first papers were very superficial because I thought that what I was writting were silly or that nobody cares. I also used to think that if my writting were short I wouldn't have many grammar mistakes. As i was getting more practice and feedback I learned that the professor was more concern in my ideas and next the grammar. Also as I wanted to writte better I learned grammar but in a different way. The grammar that I'm learning is not from a book but from my own mistakes.

I think that this is better way because I'm learning two things together.

Edwin's account of his early English classes is echoed in the journal entries of many other students, confirming that his experience of the English classroom is a common one, both for ESL students and for native speakers. In these classrooms the essence of language has been fragmented into what is assumed to be its constituent parts, "words" and "grammar," and there is little sense of how or why language is genuinely acquired. The goal is to have students demonstrate mastery of discrete and isolated features of the language on the assumption that with enough practice and repetition of these parts, they will acquire the whole of language. The mechanistic nature of such an approach becomes particularly striking when these classroom accounts are contrasted with accounts of language acquisition as it takes place in naturalistic settings.

The anthropologist Margaret Mead (1964) describes a very different language learning experience:

> I am not a good mimic and I have worked now in many different cultures. I am a very poor speaker of any language, but I always know whose pig is dead, and when I work in a native society, I know what people are talking about and I treat it seriously and I respect them, and this in itself establishes a great deal more rapport, very often, than the correct accent. I have worked with other field workers who were far, far better linguists than I, and the natives kept on saying they couldn't speak the language, although they said I could! Now, if you had a recording it would be proof positive I couldn't, but nobody knew it! You see, we don't need to teach people to speak like natives, you need to make the other people believe they can, so they can talk to them, and then they learn (189).

Mead's account of her entry as a participant-observer into many different language communities tells us much about why formal classroom approaches are generally so unsuccessful. Instead of drawing on whole and meaningful conversations about events that are important to people, they most often focus on parts of language and the teaching of these parts in an order determined by preconceived notions about what appears to be easy/basic and difficult/complex, rather than by actual use. These approaches ignore what we know about the process of language acquisition and those conditions that enable that process to get underway. They organize sequences of language items and call for repetition of these sequences in ways that have little to do with how we internalize language. They fail to recognize that language acquisition has little to do with mimicry and performance; rather, it is driven by the need and the desire to make meaning and fulfill genuine purposes. It involves active engagement in a community. Like Margaret Mead, successful language learners understand that language is embedded in the contexts in which it is used—in an understanding of "whose pig is dead"—and they focus on whole chunks of language that are related to these contexts, not on noun forms from a declension chart. For language learners in natural settings, underlying competence is far more critical than any particular outward demonstration of a correct form.

Acquiring Language

For educators like us, who have been dissatisfied with the outcome of traditional language instruction either in second and foreign language classrooms or in high school English and college composition classrooms, it has made sense to look to the places and times that enable people to acquire language successfully, most strikingly to their acquisition of a first language. In fact, much that researchers have come to understand about the nature of language acquisition derives from their observations of children learning their native language. Since the 1960s, linguists, psychologists, and anthropologists have increasingly turned their attention to studying how children acquire grammatical structures and an understanding of how to use language effectively in particular social situations, as well as the ways in which this acquisition is embedded in a cultural context. Much of what they have learned has immediate relevance here.

Children acquire their language through an unconscious process, unaware of its complex rules or the acquisition process itself. For them, the process of language acquisition is embedded in the context in which it takes place, just as Mead's was: children make guesses about the way the language they are using works in order to accomplish something or to communicate. They make these guesses, in other words, in order to interact meaningfully with someone or something in the immediate environment: to get a drink of water, to tell about an exciting experience, to refuse unwanted food and get the food they prefer, to ask for an explanation. Their attempts, often viewed as ingenious by their parents and welcomed with delight, are not explicitly corrected, for parents intuitively understand that with further exposure to the real uses of language, and experience with it, their children's early attempts will come to approximate the correct forms.

In *Child's Talk,* the psychologist Jerome Bruner follows the prelinguistic and linguistic interactions of two children with their mothers from the time they are a few months old until they are about two. Through early games like peekaboo and through the formats that develop around particular speech acts such as requests, the children gradually expand their linguistic repertoire, learning how to use language appropriately while they learn its grammar. When Richard holds out his cup and says "More," his mother's response focuses on the appropriate condition for such a request, that it must be for something he doesn't already have: "You've got some. You can't have more" (102). Bruner finds that a third of the mothers' responses to their one-year-old children consist of such speech act lessons, while none focus on grammatical structures. At the same time, the mother extends the child's utterance, providing a "scaffold" on which he can build more language. Bruner concludes:

> Children learn to use a language (or its prelinguistic precursors) initially to get what they want, to play games, to stay connected with those on whom they are dependent. In doing so, they find the constraints that prevail in the culture around them embodied in their parents' restrictions and conventions. The engine that drives the enterprise is not language acquisition per se, but the need to get on with the demands of the culture. (103)

Over time, the child formulates hypotheses about the grammar of the language and its uses, tests these out, receives feedback about whether her constructions make sense to others (whether, for example, she gets the desired response to her request), and then revises them. Furthermore, these approximations are not random but often reveal a good deal of logic and intelligence and an appreciation for the systematic nature of the language.

Children's hypotheses about language may initially be erroneous. The fact that they often use language in ways that they have never heard to create new constructions ("upside over") or new forms ("bringed") demonstrates that acquisition is not a matter of merely imitating language that has been modeled; it is an active process, one often called a process of "creative construction." Adults who try to correct children's language are often surprised or dismayed at their resistance to such correction, at how they can keep responding "Yes, I bringed my book" no matter how many times the adult says "No. You *brought* your book" with no sense of why the adult seems displeased. In fact, children's erroneous but systematic patterns of language use, and their resistance to attending to explicit surface correction, reflect the central roles that meaning and the construction of rules, rather than the surface features of form, play in the child's learning process.

Studies of young children's use of language show that even the emergence of grammatical categories arises from the ways in which they view the world and interact with others. The linguist Dan Slobin (1989), for example, reports that children use subject pronouns to refer to themselves when they are expressing desires or intentions ("*I* want it, Mummy") but their own names to show that something belongs to them ("*Tommy* has a red car"). These are not grammatical distinctions that are made by adults; rather, they are generated by the child in a systematic and meaningful way (15).

Although it's clear then that children acquire their first language by using that language to interact with the world around them, attending to meanings rather than forms, second language acquisition for adults is often assumed to be fundamentally different. It is, after all, being undertaken by individuals who are more mature, who have already developed competence in one language, and who have therefore developed some awareness of language, so it seems that it might be most efficiently promoted by the study of the new language's systematic features. (And some research suggests that focusing the learner's attention on certain formal features of language does have an impact on the learning of those features, although it has little effect on the learner's overall competence in the language.) Given the instruction that takes place in most foreign and second language classrooms, the underlying assumption seems to be that language has to be formally taught and consciously learned. However, as numerous accounts written by second language learners indicate, most learners who have been exposed to a second language only in the classroom don't gain much real mastery.

In part, it is the overwhelming evidence of the failure of our second language classrooms that has raised serious questions about the extent to which classroom input can become genuine intake, that is, the extent to which what typically gets taught in formal language courses is incorporated into anyone's language repertoire. Stephen Krashen (1982) has proposed that we see language learning and language acquisition as "two distinct and independent ways of developing competence" in a language (10). For Krashen, *language learning* involves the conscious knowledge of rules and explicit attention to form, and it accounts for learners' ability to monitor their own accuracy and correct their first attempts at an expression, but only under certain conditions: they must have a lot of time, their anxiety has to be low, and they must already know the relevant rule. (A student in a second language classroom who feels relaxed, who already knows the rule, and who has sufficient time to work on a piece of writing may be able to produce or correct the form of a verb so that it agrees in person with the noun—the boy sing*s*—although the same student may often omit the *s* in a fast-moving conversation.) *Language acquisition,* on the other hand, has much in common with the way children acquire their first language and accounts for the development of fluency and underlying competence. It is also supported by the provision, by those around the learner, of "comprehensible input"—language that extends what the learner can already produce in terms the learner can understand (much the way parents extend their children's early phrases into full sentences).

Like first language acquisition, second language acquisition is driven by meaningful interaction, by attempts to make sense of and respond to the world. It, too, involves unconscious and informal learning. Second language learners construct for themselves a rule-governed system that reflects their current understanding of the target language. (This system is often referred to as an "interlanguage" because it represents neither the first language nor the second, but a language system that is somewhere between the two.) While erroneous when measured against formal standards, this system shows the learner's active attempts to approximate the target language. It also reveals an impressive logic, giving us insight into the learner's creative constructions. Learners often create, for example, a new subject-verb agreement rule in English that calls for an *s* to be added to all plural nouns and to their accompanying verbs—"The mens sings." Or they may deliberately omit the *s* on verbs when adverbs indicating time—"always" or "never," for example—are included. The learner keeps making further efforts to determine what does and does not "work," testing out alternative hypotheses about the language, and, on the basis of these trial and error experiences, formulating new rules. It is this ongoing, incremental, and cyclical process (a process that is analogous to learning in general) that eventually leads to the acquisition of a second language.

But such acquisition—the ongoing creation of a linguistic system that more and more closely approximates the target language—requires that the learner have opportunities to hear and use the language for real purposes in meaningful contexts. Such opportunities are provided too infrequently in our classrooms. Without the need or desire to use language to make meaning, learners are motivated to make very few attempts—too few to have much impact on their underlying understanding. This helps explain why typical classroom language instruction, with its focus on formal features of language or languagelike behavior—the kind most of us experienced in high school and college foreign language classes—does little to facilitate language acquisition and why language acquisition "in the field," as experienced by Margaret Mead, seems to be much more effective. Meaning is what drives genuine acquisition. Yet in most instructional settings the focus is on the language itself, not on using it around a meaningful activity that engages the learner's interest and intentions in the same way that getting more juice engages the child's, and little of what is taught in these settings gets internalized. Evidence of the failure of most classroom instruction can be seen in learners' seeming inability to make use of the language they have practiced in their classrooms in less structured, genuine communicative situations. Students of foreign languages in American schools, with virtually no exposure to the target language outside the classroom, are notoriously weak in their ability to use their new language to communicate, no matter how well they may score on achievement tests.

The following account, written by a graduate student recollecting her own second language experiences, captures the distinction between learning and acquisition:

I'd had two quarters of Italian—horribly taught at UCLA using the professor's own antiquated text, romantically entitled *Basic Italian*. In fact, there was nothing at all basic about it. We were force-fed as many as three verb tenses per week! (I found my old textbook when I was home in March and was appalled at how it was all grammar, grammar, grammar, and not real meaning-oriented.) I'm a foreign language buff in the truest sense. They come very easily to me, with hardly an effort, and yet I learned little from this teacher. When I arrived in Italy the first time, I spoke few words. What sentences I was able to paste together were due to my fluency in French. I would simply "Italianize" the French that I knew. Anyhow, I found myself in a little village where I went to visit a friend. When I stopped at the "ufficio postale" to buy some stamps, I went up to the window and asked the clerk for some beautiful stamps. We chatted briefly—I rather haltingly, as my Italian was so "limitato." So began a sixteen-year correspondence between Mario and me. He spoke no English, no French, no German, so the only means of communication was his beautifully articulated and "espressivo" Italian and mine.

It has only been during the last five years that I learned to appreciate Mario's letters on a deeper level, for I'd always valued them. Their arrival had sent me running for my "dizionario" and textbook, and if it took me three hours to answer his letters, I answered them in the best Italian I could muster. The vocabulary I used was perforce that which was important to me, and I used his letters for their "ispirazione" as well as for their rich didactic characteristics. He writes, I realize now, now that my Italian is so much improved, a lexically rich, poetic, assolutamente bellissimo italiano. His letters are very descriptive (of feelings and places and things) and concise, and I now can appreciate how grammatically correct they are. (That's important to me, because I have a "thing" about speaking idiomatically and correctly.) He was a frequent letter and "cartolina postale" sender, so I got lots of practice. (Carole)

Because the letters this student received were meaningful, they provided "comprehensible input," a factor that seems to foster both first and second language acquisition. What children are offered by the adults around them in the form of "caretaker speech" is language that is often adapted or modified. For example, adults will restate the same thing in several forms, providing for redundancy, and they will refer explicitly to the content of the child's utterance, making a connection between language and meaning. The mothers in Bruner's study responded to each vocalization made by their children ("Oh, what do you have?"), repeating (or guessing at) a key term ("A book?"), elaborating on the child's utterance ("Are you bringing another book for Mummy to look at?"), and, in the process, providing rich linguistic cues about the language. These modifications help children make guesses about the way the language works and thus shape and enhance their acquisition process. But adults make these modifications when they are talking with children for the purpose of real communication. They refer to the immediate content and context of their interchange and negotiate meanings that are accessible to both. Different cultures have different patterns of adult-child "caretaker" talk, but most have some.

Like caretaker talk, "foreigner talk," the kind of language native speakers use with nonnative speakers in genuine communicative situations, is similarly modified and adapted in order to take into account the needs and intentions of the nonnative speaker. Such talk also provides input that is comprehensible and meaningful, the sort of input that informs the learner's developing competence. Again, we can distinguish between caretaker and foreigner talk on the one hand, and the kind of talk teachers use in language classrooms on the other, and understand why so much classroom language does not serve as "comprehensible input." Most classroom language is based neither on the immediate real-world concerns and interests of the learner, nor on her real grammatical needs. The *Basic Italian* text that Carole had studied from has chapter titles that suggest those real world concerns: "The Telephone," "The First Day of School." But the topics listed under these titles show the real focus of the book: "subject pronouns, conjugation of verbs, the present indicative of the first conjugation, the present indicative of the second conjugation, interrogation, forms of address, and negation" for Chapter 2. Most classroom language study is based on a predetermined, hierarchical organization and presentation of language features and structures that all students are expected to learn at the same time and pace. It does not necessarily take into account students' individual interlanguages or their underlying approaches and goals, and the focus is typically on language as an end in and of itself, rather than as a means to an end. For these reasons, classroom language learning as organized by most textbooks is a poor substitute for real input.

The focus of typical classroom instruction may, in fact, be more harmful than helpful to the process of acquisition. Because of the attention it places on the accuracy of formal features, learners become overly conscious of errors and their need to avoid them. This in turn affects attitude and motivation, raising anxiety and lowering self-confidence, creating psychological conditions that undermine language acquisition (as they do all learning). Instruction that creates such adverse psychological conditions activates what Krashen (1982) calls the "affective filter," interfering with what the learner can take in, and constraining and hampering the acquisition process.

In the following account, a Korean graduate student describes the impact this focus on errors had on her husband's written attempts in English:

> My husband took English language courses because it was a required course for all foreign students. There were a lot of homeworks including writing. My husband wrote essays, which was not an easy job for him. But when he got back his essays and found out that they were full of red marks, he was very discouraged. He had not thought that his English was so bad. I saw carefully the red marks. Most of them were grammatical corrections and I think it's all right. He did mistakes and he must know what he did. But the teacher often marked, 'What do you mean by this sentence?' or 'What are you trying to say?' What he wanted to say about was quite obvious to me, though the sentences might be a little awkward to the native-speakers. I suspected she pretended not to understand the sentences because they were not perfect sentences. I felt a little angry with the teacher. It was his first year in America. What did the teacher expect from him? After a couple of writings, my husband came to a conclusion that he should write only very simple, correct, clear sentences avoiding complicated expressions. He thought the teacher preferred the simple, clear sentences without any error more than the long, delicate sentences. Naturally, he couldn't put into his essays all that he wanted to talk about. Is this really an effective language learning or teaching? (Sook Young)

And in the following passage, a Chinese student recollects the stress associated with her experience of writing in a foreign language:

> We students lost all confidence in writing because of our disability to write successfully. We felt shamed when submitting our writings to the teacher and we were afraid of going to the next writing class, though we had to in spite of our unwillingness because we knew we would be severely scolded and badly criticized by the teacher. . . . That year was a nightmare to me and from that time on I refused

to do any English writings, which I regarded as a good way to escape
from being struck down by the lousy writings I did. Of course I didn't
read any books about writing skills and composing to improve my
writing ability either because I didn't have the courage to reface the
defeat writing brought to me. (Shu Kuei)

Given the conditions that are associated with classroom instruction,
it is not surprising that some in the field of second language acquisition, like S. P. Corder (1981), question whether or not language can be
taught at all: "We cannot really teach language, we can only create
conditions in which it will develop spontaneously in the mind in its
own way. We shall never improve our ability to create such favorable
conditions until we learn more about the way a learner learns and
what his built-in syllabus is" (27).

Language and Social Context

Another reason to question the possibility of teaching language stems
from our understanding that language is embedded in context and
that context attaches to language its meanings, functions, and conventions. Thus, while we may generate individual interpretive systems about how language works as we are acquiring it, we deduce
these systems from our experience of the way language is used and
constructed by a particular community and its members. As a number of significant studies have shown, language does not exist apart
from the social context in which it occurs. Perhaps the best known
of these is Shirley Brice Heath's ethnographic research reported in
Ways with Words. Heath's work makes obvious the extent to which
language is inextricably tied to how people use words to make sense
of their particular worlds. Her study of three different communities
in the Piedmont Carolinas underscores the relationship between
their ways of being and knowing, their norms and values, and their
"ways with words," and points to the central role each community
plays in socializing children into these language practices. While
members of all three communities speak the same native language,
English, they use it in ways that are different enough at times to
prevent mutual comprehension. Even so basic a form of expression
as narrative is used differently in these communities. For example, a
child from the white rural community Heath refers to as Roadville is
likely to come into the Maintown school believing that any fiction is
a "lie," and even that "story" means "lie," as in the parent's admoni-
tion: "Don't you go telling stories now!" This meaning fits with the
community's belief in a truth that is god-given and biblical and its
practice of ending accounts of current happenings with a moral that

will fit with god's meaning. For a child from the black community of Trackton, a "true story" refers to a clever fictional elaboration on a real-life event, a way of showing the cleverness of community members in imagining ways to overcome the real-world obstacles that they often face. Both children are likely to be puzzled by a Maintown teacher's request to "tell the story of the Mayflower" in a classroom where stories can be narratives recounting factual information and historical "truth" as well as fiction.

Heath's work illustrates that language is embedded in the social practices of the community and that language acquisition is fostered as a natural extension of those practices. Second language learners, then, often find themselves faced with disjunctions in cultural practices even as they acquire the words and grammatical structures of a new language. Helene, a Swedish student, describes this realization:

> Speaking English, I find that I do not always sound like myself. My tone of voice changes and is much higher than when I speak my mother tongue. I also notice that I say things in another language that I ordinarily would not say in Swedish: I have to adapt to the behavior that goes along with speaking in a different language. This has become very obvious to me while living in the United States. When I had just moved here, it was difficult to understand the kind of polite conversation most people have. I was, for example, very bothered by people who asked questions like "How are you?" and "How are you doing?" all the time. To a Swedish person, it seems insincere to ask how somebody is, as you walk away and don't hear the answer. After a while, I understood this way of talking, and I began to like the idea of addressing strangers, just to lighten things up a little. Soon it felt natural to talk the same way. I broaden my personality by expressing myself differently than what is habitual for me. I do not learn to translate all my thoughts from my mother tongue, but I develop a new way of thinking and being.

Helene's "new way of thinking and being" is inseparable from her developing competence in English, a competence that, as she recognizes, has to do with her ability to "adapt to the behavior that goes along with speaking in a different language." This certainly helps explain why the decontextualized practice of using language items like "How are you?" outside contexts in which they might be used, a practice that is all too representative of language instruction, falls short.

Given the meaning-driven nature of language acquisition, the creative and active role we play in that acquisition, the extent to which language form and function are interrelated, and the ways in which language and context are intertwined, it's not difficult to understand why schooling, with its narrowly conceptualized conventions and expectations, may not be a conducive language acquisition environment for many learners. Heath's work has demonstrated that this is the case even for children who share the same first language yet have different "ways" with that language. When children enter the world of schooling with an entirely different language, their frustration is understandably exacerbated. In *Woman Warrior,* Maxine Hong Kingston refers to her experiences as the "misery of silence" and recollects how the thickest silences occurred at school where, because she could not speak English to anyone, she "flunked kindergarten." In *Small Victories,* the journalist Samuel Freedman describes the experience of Carlos, a boy from the Dominican Republic, as he is confronted with the culture and language of the inner-city elementary school he enters:

> English confounded him, with its incongruous grammar and its devious diction, ar even in bilingual class, he needed to repeat himself three or four times to be understood. He pronounced "people" as "pay-oh-play" in the Spanish style, "yes" as "yez," and "is" as "ees," and when he erred too often, the teacher commanded him to write the troublesome word on the board one hundred times. One escape was art class, where he needed no language, where he could draw sports cars and Hercules and drift back to Cibao. The other was the bathroom, to which he repaired frequently to think and study and unscramble his brain. After months of futility, he earned 100 on a spelling test, proceeding without pause through "come" and "went" and "left." The teacher inscribed his name on the board, and "Carlos Pimentel" remained there in chalk for a full week, until the next test. He walked past it every morning, a war hero admiring his monument. . . . But with one swipe of the eraser, Carlos was returned to the familiar frustration. (282)

And in *The Hunger of Memory,* Richard Rodriguez describes the painful ordeal of trying to acquire the language of school, where language is so often about language and thus is so different from the private language of home, where language is used for communication (or as Rodriguez puts it, "self-expression").

> I easily noted the differences between classroom language and the language at home. At school, words were directed to a general audience of listeners. Words were meaningfully ordered and the point was not self-expression alone, but to make oneself understood by many others. The teacher quizzed: "Boys and girls, why do we use that word in a sentence? Could we think of a better word to use there? Would the sentence change its meaning if the words were differently arranged? Isn't there a better way of saying much the same thing?" I couldn't say. I wouldn't try to say.

> Three months passed. Five, a half year. Unsmiling, ever watchful, my teachers noted my silence. They began to connect my behavior with the slow progress my brothers and sisters were making. (20)

These childhood experiences speak to the problems these learners confronted because they did not share the language or the perspective, framework, and reference system that are subsumed by schooling practices. For Kingston and Rodriguez, for the young boy Carlos, not only has language in school been severed from that which gives it meaning, not only is the focus on language for its own sake, but because the classroom offers no fuller context to draw upon, this decontextualized language becomes the only means through which learning can take place.

Language and Literacy

The alienation depicted in the above childhood experiences obviously pervades all forms of school encounters. But perhaps in no situation is this experience of "not belonging" as acute as in the acquisition of literacy, yet another form of language, with its own sets of conventions and rules. And, again, although this acquisition process is a challenge for all learners (since it is focused on making sense of decontextualized language), when students bring with them a language whose cultural norms and values clash with those of schooling practices, the acquisition process is often subverted. Heath's study demonstrates what happens when children's home language practices are incongruent with the literacy practices of school. While children from the mainstream community succeed at school because school uses, in effect, an extension of their home ways of knowing, children from Trackton and Roadville, the non-mainstream communities, are not successful because they are not used to looking at and experiencing language and literacy in the decontextualized ways called for in school. The expertise with language they bring to the classroom is not recognized or built on, and their knowledge is seen as deficient rather than different.

Similarly, in their rich and detailed study of language and literacy among the Athabaskans of Alaska, Ronald and Suzanne Scollon (1981) reveal the extent to which discourse patterns are tied to a culture-specific worldview and help us understand why a change in these patterns involves the adoption of a radically different perspective. The Athabaskans do not, for example, value the display of an individual's abilities, and school-based literacy expectations for the display of knowledge in speech and writing are thus incompatible with Athabaskan assumptions.

While Mina Shaughnessy's (1977) seminal work with beginning writers was not informed by these studies, it arrived at similar conclusions about the population of students entering college for the first time as a result of open admissions. As we saw in Chapter 1, on the basis of her analysis of their writing Shaughnessy characterized these students as representing a different culture, as true "outsiders," and concluded that the difficulties they were having in writing courses derived from this difference. Mike Rose (1989), too, addresses the extent to which the nature of academic literacy confounds and disorients students, particularly students who bring with them a set of conventions that are at odds with those of the academic world they are entering. In describing his work with Lucia, a Hispanic student, who experiences particular difficulty with her course work in psychology, he makes it possible for us to see that Lucia's difficulties stem from her unfamiliarity with certain frames of mind on the one hand, and the ways in which her own belief system and personal history conflict with what she's expected to know on the other. As Rose says:

> Students like Lucia are often thought to be poor readers or to have impoverished vocabularies (though Lucia speaks two languages); I've even heard students like her referred to as culturally illiterate (though she has absorbed two cultural heritages). It's true there were words Lucia didn't know *(alchemy, orthodoxy)* and sentences that took us two or three passes to untangle. But it seemed more fruitful to see Lucia's difficulties in understanding [the work of psychologist Thomas] Szasz as having to do with her belief system and with her lack of familiarity with certain ongoing discussions in humanities and social sciences—with frames of mind, predispositions, and background knowledge. (184)

Lucia's difficulty, in other words, comes not so much from an inability to engage with the texts or from the linguistic complexity of the material she is expected to read as from the fact that her classes require her to think and act in ways that are incompatible with her current knowledge and views of the world.

To understand that the acquisition of literacy is in many ways analogous to the acquisition of a language points to the limitations of models of instruction that predominate in writing classrooms. Like the foreign language teaching described earlier, traditional writing instruction too often reduces the whole of writing to an assemblage of structures and removes it from a socially constructed context that gives it value, purpose, and meaning. It ignores the ways in which different attempts to use language—like reading and writing—contribute to one another, and it fails to take into account the underlying understanding and "built-in syllabi" of learners, viewing their nonstandard and idiosyncratic attempts as deficient. On the other hand, to see literacy acquisition as analogous to the acquisition of spoken language suggests that we adopt an approach implied by the findings of studies of first and second language acquisition in naturalistic settings. Rather than focusing on decontextualized forms that are practiced and drilled for their own sake, rather than stressing the rules/patterns to which writing should conform, rather than emphasizing the need to monitor written attempts and evaluate these attempts against some absolute standard, these studies underline the importance of establishing an environment in which "acquisition," not just "learning," can take place.

An acquisition-rich writing environment reorients priorities so that *meaning* becomes the end of instruction and written attempts are simply the means to that end. Students in this kind of environment are encouraged to use writing to make sense of the world around them, to learn, conceptualize, and inquire and then to communicate this sense to themselves as well as to others. They are provided with opportunities to use language in multiple ways so that their writing, reading, and speaking voices give rise to one another. Their continuing efforts to make meaning are fueled by their engagement with the content of these efforts and the context in which they take place. They are supported by the meaning-focused and accessible feedback they receive. Their attempts at writing are understood the way Rose understands Lucia's attempts at reading, as serious and well-intentioned approximations, even when they are unconventional.

Writers in an acquisition-oriented classroom become active learners. Rather than learning a list of *dos* and *don'ts* or practicing received formats, they formulate hypotheses about the expectations and norms of written discourse. In testing out these hypotheses, they discover when to revise them and test out new ones. This trial-and-error constructive process applies not only to global discourse features, but to issues of lesser concern, such as surface features of language. Given the almost universal tendency of writing teachers to attend to nonstandard features of language use, it's important to note that in writing as in speaking, standard surface features are most likely to be acquired in the context of creating meaningful discourse.

This change in how we view the process of language acquisition has important consequences for how we approach instruction in our writing classrooms and how we read the writing our students produce. Instead of looking for errors and deviations from standard patterns and rules, we can begin to look at what the writer is bringing to the task and try to identify changes that may point to growth. Several studies published in the 1980s illustrate this shift in approach, in which writing began to be read as an approximation of the target language of the college writing classroom—"conventional written discourse." In "The Study of Error," David Bartholomae (1980) analyzes the text of a basic writer, modeling a kind of reading that he calls a "misreading." Bartholomae draws attention to the text's complexity, its underlying logic and coherence, and its attempt to use language to create meaning despite its mechanical flaws. He views the nonstandard features that are evident throughout the student's text not only as inevitable but as helpful to the teacher, offering evidence about the rule-governed system that underlies the student's written effort. Such features speak to the hypotheses about texts that the writer is formulating and testing out, and they offer insight into the writer's individual strategies and intentions. It is this kind of reading that helps Bartholomae understand a text as a performance rather than as an indication of underlying competence, and it suggests the dangers of drawing conclusions about a student's knowledge of language and writing on the basis of individual written texts.

Our own collaboration led Eleanor Kutz (Ellie) to apply second language acquisition theory to her work in composition. In a 1986 article, she suggests how such theory can shape pedagogical practice and our evaluation of student writing. She describes the ways we were all working to create contexts in which students are challenged to explore and raise questions about rich and engaging subject matter, to make their own observations and generalizations, and to draw meaning from them. Viewing writing as language use, she describes how students can be invited to participate actively in this constructive process, so that their approximative attempts are validated and they are encouraged to take risks. Like Bartholomae, she looks carefully at the language students produce and examines what they can do, borrowing the term "interlanguage" from the field of second language acquisition and using its concepts to help her resee her students' writing so that she can locate in a student's text the approximations of (or foundations for) the very features of academic discourse she wants her students to develop.

The concept of *interlanguage* is helpful in this process of seeing what is contained in students' writing because it emphasizes several characteristics of the developing language that can be found there: it will necessarily contain features that do not occur either in the students' spoken language or in the target language of academic discourse; these unique features are developmental, representing necessary stages in the acquisition process; they are systematic, rule-governed, and predictable (though transitional); and they are a necessary part of constructing and testing hypotheses about the new language. Although an interlanguage is not correct from the point of view of the target language, it is a valid linguistic system and can allow its user to communicate competently.

Ellie discovered such competence in her students' texts as she began to look for evidence of the features of academic discourse she wanted her students to develop: fluency, coherence, logical structuring, autonomy, elaboration, and complexity. One advanced ESL student, Antonio, was enrolled in the freshman studies seminar that Ellie and Suzy team-taught. (We'll say more about the work of that seminar and look at other examples of Antonio's writing in later chapters.) In response to the first out-of-class assignment to "observe someone working," Antonio produced the following text:

> The ill interest to work is shared among everyone in this working place near lunch break and breaks, especially end of the day break. They pass the time with breakaways to the Rest Room, for 10 to 15 minutes, or slowing down the production. Those who weren't interested in putting in a good 8 hour day got even lazier when it was close to break time. They keep moving about lazily and sometimes doing nothing but trying to entertaining themselves until it was time to stop working.
>
> Among those blue collars worker's who didn't I found not contribute much sweating eye-brow to their paycheck was a man who looked like a chinese and Hispanic cross-breed. In my opinion, A misfit, attempting to go straight, and earn an honest living. He's a short sleezy bearded Fatu look-a-like, much taller though.
>
> He started the morning in a fearly desent pace. But as the day lingered, his enthusiasm desapated to a point where he just goes around, 5 minutes here and there bringing up conversation, Making time go by faster. finally after finishing, He proceeded to the second phase of his duties. At this point of the working day He starts doing his carefree thing. He slowly drags a misplaced piece of lumber, dusts of his wrangler, blows dust off his plastic shoe, He casually goes to the Rest Room for 15 minutes, stops and talks a little with his pal. All of a sudden, It's close to lunch break. He takes a leisure walk around the plant, trying to look busy while the boss is looking. It's lunch break.
>
> He comes back starts the second half of the day as loosely as he finished. And continues to work in that laqedazical pace, until it's time to clean-up, taking his time. does what he can do in that depressing pace. he checks his watch; it's almost time to leave. He picks what he swept, dusts off and joins his friend until the whistle blew. Another dollar another day.

And this is what Ellie (1986) saw in Antonio's text:

Beneath the surface of this error-laden text lies the work of a writer already competent in many ways. The text is *fluent,* as measured not simply by overall length but by the extended sentences and paragraphs which show the expansion and extension of each idea. It is *coherent,* focusing on one worker who is representative of the larger group, and unified, with effective closure, ending not only with the end of the observation but with a statement which sums up the attitude implied by this worker's activities: "Another dollar another day."

In terms of *logical structuring,* an initial, generalizing assertion is made ("the ill interest to work is shared among everyone in this working place"), and then supported with the specific example of this worker. The ordering principle here is one of simple chronology, but temporal connectives are not the explicit "first," "second" which one would expect at this level: they are far more subtle and implicit: "as the day lingered on," "at this point of the working day." The paragraphs represent clear units of thought.

The opening passage places the reader in a context *(autonomy).* While the workplace is not specifically named (and that ambiguity effectively allows the reader to associate what follows with any number of workplaces), a general frame is established in the first paragraph before the focus moves in onto one particular worker. Individual statements are expanded and *elaborated:* "At this point of the working day He starts doing his carefree thing. He slowly drags a misplaced piece of lumber, dusts of his wrangler, blows dust off his plastic shoe," etc. And they contain effective and imbedded modification: "He's a short sleezy bearded Fatu look-a-like" versus "he is short and sleazy and looks like Fatu." And overall *sentence complexity* is demonstrated by other embeddings: "Among those blue collars worker's who didn't I found not contribute much sweating eye-brow to their paycheck was a man. . . ." (394–95)

Ellie concluded that "this is the paper of an already skilled language user, who will be able to transfer much of that skill to the mastery of academic discourse."

As a freshman, Antonio was invited by Ellie and Suzy to develop as a writer in a course designed to support his full participation in an academic community. Too often, however, interest in academic discourse and discipline-specific discourse communities has led to pedagogical approaches that reduce academic discourse to a set of generic forms and formulaic models, that invite students to learn through imitation rather than participation. The more student populations are viewed as lacking experiences with academic discourse, as is the case with basic and ESL writers, the more this is likely to occur. The problem with these approaches is again one of focusing on academic practices and conventions in artificial and decontextualized ways, ignoring students' own connection making and experimentation, failing to provide recursive experiences in which academic discourse develops, and misunderstanding and discounting their evolving views, perspectives, and frameworks. These instructional approaches keep students from committing themselves to an idea in writing and from taking an active part in interpreting and (re)constructing texts. Academic models of writing are separated from the genuine kind of participation and collaboration within a community that gives rise to its discourse, and the context-dependent nature of discourse (of all language processes) is kept hidden.

But can an academic discourse that is genuinely representative of the language of intellectual inquiry, which we take as our work, be developed within a classroom community? We think so. We must first discover what that language is. Peter Elbow (1991) describes as central to his conception of academic discourse "the giving of reasons and evidence rather than just opinions, feelings, experiences; being clear about claims and assertions rather than just implying or insinuating; getting thinking to stand on its own two feet rather than leaning on the authority of who advances or the fit with who hears it" (140). Elbow is pointing to ways of thinking as well as talking and writing, and we will explore the sort of thinking that underlies academic work in the next chapter. But inviting students into an academic community also requires recognizing their perspectives and experiences and giving them opportunities to grapple by themselves with these new ways of conceptualizing and knowing. The following excerpt was written by a graduate student (a nonnative speaker of English) who was reflecting on her process of reading and understanding a difficult assigned text:

> While reading, I'm saying to myself, I understand what he's saying, but if you ask me exactly what I agree with, I don't know yet. I think I have to write it out myself before I can internalize the points I agree with. . . . By writing it down I internalize the meaning in my own words to make ideas real to me—so that I own the words. (Souyan)

We need, then, to sustain and extend students' ways of "internalizing" what they are learning and create a dynamic context in which their understanding can develop.

For ESL students, in particular, that classroom context must value and foster the alternative rhetorics that they may bring with them, rhetorics that reflect the cultural contexts in which they were learned. Fan Shen (1989), an English composition teacher whose first language is Chinese, describes his own experience of learning to write in English:

> Looking back, I realize that the process of learning to write in English is in fact a process of creating and defining a new identity and balancing it with the old identity. The process of learning English composition would have been easier if I had realized this earlier and consciously sought to compare the two different identities required by the two writing systems for two different cultures. It is fine and perhaps even necessary for American composition teachers to teach about topic sentences, paragraphs, the use of punctuation, documentation, and so on, but can anyone design exercises sensitive to the ideological and logical differences that students like me experience—and design them so they can be introduced at an early stage of an English composition class? (466)

Fan Shen asks for exercises, but he himself has discovered what he knows about his two cultural identities by speaking, listening, reading, and writing with others in a community, for it is in this way that we learn the conventions of a particular community and its ways of using language. He has also constructed for himself a mode of inquiry, a "game" in which he lists features about writing associated with his old Chinese self and with his new English self and then pictures himself getting out of his old identity and into a new one. This strategy helps him "to remember and accept the different rules of Chinese and English composition and the values that underpin these rules" and to reconcile his "old cultural values with the new values required by English writing" (462). Fan Shen has formalized his knowledge about the discipline of English composition by doing the work of that discipline—by writing—and by inquiring into his own processes as he does that work. In succeeding chapters we explore how writing development is supported by these two activities: acquiring new forms of discourse by using them in meaningful context, and engaging in inquiry that helps what has been acquired become consciously known and understood.

Chapter Three

Aspects of Competence II
Development of Thought

The students who enter our classes are entering a new discourse community. Like those who have moved from Beijing to Boston or from rural Alabama to New York City or from the high school classroom to the loading dock of a local trucking company, they must learn how language is used—its forms and its purposes—in that community. But the college or university writing classroom is not only the entry point into a particular sort of discourse community, it is also an intersection of many such communities that have as their common culture a concern with knowledge and the making of knowledge. And the classes that will bring students into this community must necessarily focus, in a conscious way, on the students' development of new ways of thinking as well as their acquisition of new uses of language.

In the field of composition a lot has been written about how to foster students' thinking through their writing and writing through their thinking. (Ann Berthoff's *Forming/Thinking/Writing* is a good place to begin to think about techniques to use in writing courses that will help students actively make and discover meaning through their writing.) But our focus here is somewhat different. We want to look at what students bring, as thinkers and as language users who have functioned competently in other discourse communities, when they enter this one. We also want to identify the ways of thinking and using language that are privileged in this community. And then we want to explore the ways in which the academic community's larger enterprise—the building of new knowledge and new ways of knowing—can itself be used as a bridge for students' development of thought and language.

In looking at what our students bring to our classrooms we have to consider what we as teachers bring as well. In this chapter we will consider some of the writing (and thinking) done by students in our composition classes for ESL students and for native speakers of English. But we will also be tracing the development of our own thinking about this writing. By the time of Suzy's encounter with the birds in the catwalk, the three of us had been working together for about ten years, reading placement essays and writing proficiency exams, designing courses and programs, team teaching, and presenting workshops for colleagues and at conferences. The various forms of our collaboration arose because each of us was profoundly interested in discovering all we could about our students as writers and learners and then figuring out how to support them in our own teaching and in shaping our institutional structures. Our work with students became the locus of our own ongoing inquiry, and each piece of writing they produced contributed to the body of data that would help us understand their development as writers. We became, in effect, what would now be referred to as teacher-researchers.

We will begin by looking at the writing of two students in a basic writing class. Then we will consider several areas of research that have contributed to our understanding of the relationships between thought, language, and writing and how our own developing schema helps us see students' texts in new ways.

Two Students

Alison and Jean were students in Ellie's class several years ago, at a time when we were first beginning to look carefully together at the work of our freshman writers. Both were from the inner "suburbs"— really a ring of older cities surrounding Boston that provided a first step away from the ethnic enclaves of the city itself. Although one was from a public high school and the other from a parochial school, both had been placed in the university's basic writing course. What stood out about them was that they were always together, whether walking in the halls or seated in the classroom—the sort of students it's hard to keep separate at first because they talk and dress and sound so much alike.

But there was also a lot that was different about Alison and Jean, and it showed up very quickly in their writing. We can see some of these differences in the first day's entry in a journal students in the class were keeping that semester. The assignment was to "tell about

one of the earliest incidents that you can remember from your childhood." This was Alison's entry:[1]

> One of the first and most frightening things I remember as a child
> is when my mother got sick.
>   first we have to start from the beginning. my mother has asthma
> So I was already used to her bein sick sometimes and not being able
> to breathe. But it never stopped her from doing anything, and if it
> did it didn't stop her for long.
>   Well the day that I remember she was very sick and had been
> for about five days or so. I just thought it was another one of those
> times and she would be fine in another day. What did I know I was
> only about seven. well that night she got worse and I remember
> standing at the bottom of the stairs and watching my brother carry
> my mother down the stairs.
>   I couldn't believe it my mother who always could do just about
> anything—was being carried down the stairs.
>   Well I was very confused but after awhile I went to see my
> mother in the hospital, and found out she would be fine and would
> come home.

And this was Jean's:

> I was part of a very serious motorcycle accident at the age of eight
> years old. One day I was playing on my street with my girlfriend
> when her sister Ellen and her Boyfriend Randy drove up beside us
> and asked if we wanted a ride. I ran to ask my parents and they first
> said no because I was too young but I begged and pleaded with them
> till they said yes. It was the first time I was ever on a motorcycle so
> Randy was only going to take me around the block.
>   As we were riding around the corner on to Gallivan Boulevard,
> Randy had lost his helmet and turned to look for it. When Randy
> turned his head he hit the Median on the Boulevard and that's when
> I blacked out. When I woke up I was on the other side of the highway
> and I saw Randy a few yards away from me. I panicked and started
> to run, I didn't feel any pain as I did and that's when a man had
> stopped me. I was comforted til my mother came and she then came
> with me in the ambulance to Carney Hospital. I ended up having 2nd
> degree burns on my body but was released that night.

Alison's entry is clearly the work of a basic writer: what she has written
is relatively brief and unelaborated, with little subordination; there are
many intrusions from oral language that are less appropriate to written
language; and the punctuation, capitalization, spelling, are erratic.
These features are at the surface—they're the sort of thing that used to

1 Alison's texts are also discussed in E. Kutz and H. Roskelly, *An Unquiet Pedagogy:
  Transforming Practice in the English Classroom,* Portsmouth, NH: Boynton/Cook,
  1991.

discourage us anew each time we faced a new class. However, in working together we had begun to see how to look below the surface.

Because we believed that form and correctness are internalized through communication in a meaningful context and that they are acquired in the attempt to express clear meaning rather than learned through conventional instruction, in our discussions of Alison's writing we focused not on error, but on what it could tell us about the way she was thinking—about written language itself and about the world. And because we knew that acquisition of new competence in language would depend on extending and elaborating present knowledge, Ellie tried to use her understanding of what Alison could do on the first day of class to find ways of extending that ability throughout the semester.

Jean's entry, on the other hand, appeared to be the work of a more accomplished writer primarily because her text showed fewer errors. But as the semester went on, she was the student who made less progress in her development of the sort of extended written discourse that would be needed in her other classes. In fact, just before the semester ended, she decided to leave UMass/Boston and take a secretarial job that had been offered to her. Five years later, Alison had graduated; Jean, to our knowledge, did not return.

In retrospect, it is easy for us to see, even in these first entries, some of what Alison brought to UMass/Boston that would help her find her way and what it was about Jean's writing that made her seem less ready to engage in academic work. What's remarkable to us is that over that very semester, as we met to share our students' texts and to puzzle out new ways of looking at them, we were already struck by the characteristics that soon became so salient.

Prompted by the first day's assignment, both Alison and Jean told stories about events that had happened to them. Ellie was beginning her course by eliciting narrative accounts from students, not because, as is often the case in composition courses, she was planning to take the students through a progression from "easier" narrative and descriptive tasks to "harder" exposition and analysis, but because narration is such a fundamental human activity that everyone would have done a lot of it. Thus students would be engaging in the sort of familiar activity that can show a great deal about the language they use and the ways that they use it to understand familiar events and to communicate that understanding to others. If, as the linguist James Gee (1985) suggests, "one of the primary ways—probably *the* primary way—human beings make sense of their experience is by casting it in narrative form" (11), then we can see in our students' narratives how they go about doing something that they already know how to do.

A key element in the way people make meaning through narrative is their evaluation of the events they are telling about. In conversation, each speaker is expected to follow understood rules of turn taking; a speaker who takes a longer-than-normal turn is expected to justify the length of that turn in some way, to indicate to the listener just why the turn should go on for so long, answering the listener's implied question, "So what?" Narrative accounts typically require long turns compared with ordinary conversational exchanges, and the narrator is expected to make it clear why this account is important. Narrators with different cultural experiences will have different ways of showing why the events recounted are meaningful, but, as the sociolinguist William Labov's (1972) research on narrative syntax in the stories of urban adolescents shows, the narrator's evaluation of the events being recounted will appear somewhere, whether embedded in the action of the story or, as is often the case with middle-class narrators, stated explicitly, usually at the beginning or the end.

A second element that becomes important to narrative meaning is the frame of reference. Most conversational narrative takes place between people who know each other and who can assume some common knowledge about the world and some common ways of looking at it. The events in stories told in families or by friends are likely to be evaluated in a familiar style, with much more implied than stated explicitly, and according to shared norms. The linguist Deborah Tannen (1982) has recorded narrative accounts by friends at the dinner table. One speaker, telling of a young girl's precocity, says "she's just so . . . ," and then squeals and wiggles. This teller is conveying a clear message about what she thinks the child's behavior means and assumes that the others will find the same meaning. But a visitor from California doesn't get the point—that the child is too sexually precocious for her age—until it's stated explicitly, and he doesn't necessarily share in that meaning or interpret the child's actions within the same frame of reference. A narrator can't always assume that others will share the values and meanings that provide a framework for the evaluation of particular events.

If the classroom writing task were really a naturally occurring incidence of narrative, Alison and Jean would face several challenges in telling about an event from their childhoods. They would have to tell a coherent story—one that would orient the listener (reader) and set the scene, that would give the listener a clear picture of the sequence of events and the sense that these events are related and relevant. They would have to make it clear why they thought their stories were worth telling and, in effect, what they thought these stories might mean. And they would have to decide what an appropriate frame of reference would be for convincing a particular audience that the story *is* worth telling and that it means what they are suggesting it means. But this classroom narrative event was not a natural one, and so they were faced with the additional challenge of *imagining* what might be worth telling to an unfamiliar audience and how to make what they knew about telling a story mesh with the assigned task. They responded to these challenges in different ways, and those ways suggest a great deal about how they will approach the other meaning-making tasks that will be asked of them in college.

Both Alison and Jean tell coherent stories that have a beginning and an end, a logical sequence of events, and relevant details. Both have chosen to tell of a significant event that had happened to them, in language that reflects both their familiar telling of their story and their sense that they are now *writing* of these events for a new audience. Both students evaluate the events: Alison is recounting one of the "most frightening things" she remembers; Jean writes of a "very serious" motorcycle accident. But the ways in which they evaluate these events and the frames of reference they use in their evaluations are quite different. Let's look at their accounts in more detail.

Alison begins with a generalization that sums up what she sees as the meaning of the event she is about to recount: "One of the first and most frightening things I remember as a child is when my mother got sick." She goes on to tell her story in support of that generalization and shows conscious attention to the explicit ordering of details ("first," "from the beginning"), reflecting her awareness that she is structuring her telling of these events in a particular way. Her story is generally coherent, although her focus shifts from her response to the event to the outcome of the event. Paragraphs form meaningful units: paragraph 1 presents her generalization, paragraph 2 describes the existing state of affairs at the time of the incident, paragraph 3 tells of the change that took place with this event, paragraph 4 tells of her response, and paragraph 5 concludes with the outcome. Alison is also aware of her audience, and her opening generalization places the reader in relation to the event. She then holds the reader with oral forms (the repeated "well") that demonstrate her attention to the need to connect with her audience, although these might seem intrusive in a written text. In all of this she is using her existing linguistic repertoire to engage meaningfully in the task of recounting, and reseeing, an early memory.

Another feature that is particularly noticeable (but that might seem intrusive) in Alison's text is her repeated references to her own thinking. It is these references that tell us just *how* she is thinking. "I just thought," "What did I know," "I couldn't believe it." Alison is conscious of the ways in which she evaluated these events at the time they were happening and of the limited framework of experience she had as a seven-year-old for working out their meaning. The event she has chosen to tell about is worth telling precisely because of its meaning to her at the time it happened. Her mother's sickness was a significant event to *her* because she found it frightening.

Jean, on the other hand, has chosen a "big event," a motorcycle accident that would seem to be impressive to others as well as salient to her. But she doesn't offer the reader a framework that suggests its significance. The event had no apparent impact on her life, and although she offers a beginning and an end with a story in between, the beginning is simply a statement that the event happened rather than a generalization that would place it in such a framework, and the story ends with the end of the event, not with a conclusion about its importance or effect. Because Jean makes no larger point about the incident, we have no way of determining whether the details she chooses to include (such as pleading with her parents) are relevant. Her story strikes us as clear but strangely flat. The "So what?" is left unanswered.

When we look at Alison's and Jean's responses to a formal mid-term essay assignment on Anne Frank's *The Diary of a Young Girl,* we find that the patterns that emerged in their early journal entries continue. Their assignment, building on the idea that particular events have a larger significance, was to "find an incident from the diary that impressed you as important and retell that incident to illustrate something about Anne, her life, or her situation." Here is part of Alison's response:

> In reading the diary of anne frank, I was impressed at how mature she was and how she handled the changes in her life. In one part of the book Anne talks of how she is frightened by the bombing and she goes in and sleeps with her farther. She says in the book that she is acting like a frightened little child. I think that just by recognising that she was acting like a child that it showed how mature she was. Because if you are immature than you really can't recognize when you are acting immature, but if you are mature than you can recognized when you are being immature.

Alison has again chosen an event that is evaluated by the narrator—this time Anne Frank—as frightening, and she is again interested in the framework that supports that evaluation. But her own framework for this essay focuses not on the frightening events themselves but on how they are perceived. She notes Anne's ability to step out of a particular event and to evaluate her responses to it, to see that she was "acting like a frightened little child." But she also redefines Anne's evaluation, teasing out the difference between acting like a child and seeing things from the perspective of a child, defining for herself the concept of maturity. She contrasts two different interpretations of these events, hers and Anne's, showing the logical consistency of her new interpretation and using terms that signal these logical relationships ("*because if* you are immature *then* you really can't recognize when you're acting immature, *but if* you are mature *then* you can recognize when are being mature"). And her "I think" now marks her own, differing view, as she takes time (discussing in the longer paper several representative incidents) to work out each of her ideas.

Jean's response to the assignment on Anne Frank is quite different:

> This is the only book that has ever touched me emotionally and I enjoyed being part of what Anne felt because it brought myself back to a few incidents I've been through and I really felt for her. I knew what Anne was going through at times. The one incident I want to write about is the one where she discovers Peter. I feel that this was an important stage where she felt love and how to be loved. Living in the Secret Annex for three years and dying a short time after that didn't give her a chance to know how important it is to love and share with a special person in your life She didn't get that chance to grow and feel how really special and important she was in this world and share it with other people.

Jean has also chosen an event in Anne Frank's life that she sees as important to Anne's growth and that connects with her own life. But her response seems to us to be *wholly* personalized. She doesn't show that she can see Anne's life at all but seems rather to see only her own; because love is currently the most important thing in her life, it must be in Anne's. She doesn't show two points of view, hers and Anne's, but seems to assume that Anne's must be the same as hers, that there is only one way to see an event. In fact, she doesn't seem conscious of consciousness itself, of point of view. Finally, she doesn't enlarge her frame of reference and therefore doesn't begin to interpret events and texts actively in ways that take into account the needs of an audience of readers.

In her final journal entry, Alison reflects once more on the concerns she has been probing throughout the semester by looking back at the event she wrote about in her first entry. (Jean left the university before the semester ended and made no final journal entry.)

> Well I am now nineteen and just recently my mother went to the hospital for her asthma. It was quite a different situation from the last time. This time I wasn't even home when she went to the hospital, I was at a friends house and didn't find out that my mother had gone to the hospital til the next day. But I remember feeling the

same way as I did when I heard about the last time. At first I was scared. But this time I was able to understand more and I didn't have all those crazy ideas that she would never come home or die. I knew this time that she would be fine and the doctors would help her. Also this time I was thinking more about her than about myself. Last time all I could think of was, "what will I do without her." This time I thought "What can I do for her" I feel I have matured and can look at things like this much clearer.

Alison's knowledge is not fixed or static. She is actively thinking and inquiring, trying out and testing ideas, as she moves through successive course activities and assignments. Along with new ways to use language, Alison is acquiring some new ways of thinking, and she is doing so in systematic ways. In her final entry she contrasts the events of two different time periods ("last time" versus "this time"), seeing the relationships between two whole sequences of events, and she can not only prove a larger point but can do so inductively, moving from a set of observations to a concluding generalization ("I have matured"). She is also able to interpret events and see their significance—to see that one incident can represent a whole perspective on life—and she shows that she is able not only to maintain a consistent perspective or point of view, but, in this third excerpt, to contrast two different perspectives, that of the child and that of the young adult. Comparing what Alison accomplishes at any one point with what she's accomplished earlier, we can see changes in the ways she represents her ideas.

Language, Thought, and Writing

As we looked at our students' writing, we kept returning to a larger question: "How can we describe the underpinnings, the kinds of competence, necessary for students to produce writing in academic contexts—not in language alone, but also in the thought that it represents and makes possible?" We began to look for the answers to this question by studying the data of our students' speech and writing, and we drew on the theoretical and research perspectives of several fields to help us understand what we found there.

We wanted to know more about what might be characteristic of the thinking of students like Antonio and Alison and Jean who were entering college as young adults. We were beginning to think of the development of new ways of thinking as a process somewhat like the process of second language acquisition—one to which learners brought existing strategies they would build on until they approximated the new ways of a new community. As with language acquisition, studies of children helped us identify important aspects of intellectual development, although here the differences between child and adult processes seemed greater. In addition, much of the important early work in cognitive psychology had not adequately formulated the role of language and had excluded reference to social or cultural context. Nevertheless, there was much we could learn from the literature on cognitive and intellectual development, so we turned next to that work as well as to related work in literacy and in narrative.

Studies in a number of areas have contributed to our understanding of intellectual development as it applies to our work with first-year writing students. Much of the study of children's cognitive development, beginning with the work of Piaget, has focused on the development of the kinds of logical thinking that underlie our study of the natural world—our scientific and mathematical thinking. Piaget saw the development of a child's thought as an active, constructive process that is linked to a growing ability to perceive the physical world, to operate in conjunction with it, and to predict the outcome of those operations. Piaget found that by adolescence, children can think systematically about difficult abstract concepts like space and time. They can also think about larger questions from more than one perspective (consistently imagining how all aspects would be arranged from each perspective), and they can think hypothetically about ways to solve a problem.

These kinds of "formal operations" (as Piaget termed them)—hypothesis creation and testing, logical deduction, and abstract conceptualization—are central to advanced study in many disciplines and provide the core of what students are expected to learn and do in college. The tendency to use hypothetical reasoning allows the student to interest herself increasingly in problems that go beyond her immediate experience. Alison shows such interest in the problems of Anne Frank when she reflects on Anne's reaction to the bombing that goes on outside her attic hiding place. The student becomes interested, too, in the nature of thinking itself, in the nature and the problems of communication, and in the presentation and representation of ideas and concepts. This interest results in an improved ability to do various types of assessment: of the logic of arguments, of one's own learning processes, and of the effects and effectiveness of particular acts of representation, including the writing the student has done or is reading. (We'll see Alison's assessment of her own development as a writer in Chapter 8).

Clearly one type of thinking that is needed for effective study in college courses is precisely what Piaget characterized as formal operational. But in order to give form to abstract conceptualizations, the propositions, proofs, and "representations of representations" Piaget identified as the hallmarks of this stage of cognition must be organized and articulated in language. In college today, to a very considerable degree this means that they must be written. Writing requires, in its turn, many of the intellectual capacities already identified with formal operational thinking. A writer has to be able to imagine a reader, a consciously defined audience: the reader's purpose for reading and relationship to the writer, the reader's knowledge about the world in general and about the topic under discussion in particular. Experienced writers know they must define their reader in order to determine the extent of contextual background needed, the register in which to conduct the discussion, and the terms in which they can most appropriately develop the argument. Inexperienced writers may begin this process, as Alison does, by drawing on their immediate experience with listeners. Others, like Jean, may not succeed in imagining an audience at all when they find themselves in a new context, and their writing may at first show little sense of the needs of a reader.

Another aspect of cognitive development comes into play in order to make this kind of hypothesizing possible for the writer. In Piagetian terms, the writer must have emerged from what developmentalists refer to as "childish egocentrism." Piaget described development as the progressive emergence of the self from egocentrism, and this seems to have at least as much importance to the development of one's ability to write as does the use of analytic and hypothetico-deductive thinking. Piaget saw development as a process through which successive egocentrisms replace one another. The individual becomes more able, with each cycle, to differentiate increasingly varied aspects of self and others, and through this process to conceptualize about relations and categories, ideas, theories, values. From this perspective, Alison's thinking is less egocentric than that of Jean, who sees others' experiences only as a reflection of her own. Alison's final journal entry, in which she comments about how she is now thinking about her mother as well as herself, marks her own awareness of this change.

An "emergence from egocentrism" is important to an individual's ability to write because it makes the working out of the particular elements and forms of a piece of writing possible. Choosing phrasing or register, judging the order in which ideas should be represented, imagining the understandings and needs of a reader, revising, refining an argument—all of these require the ability to consider the point of view and knowledge of another person. This aspect of development, as described by Piaget, thus enables the writer to assess her own writing and decide whether it is appropriate, useful, and accessible to another, or whether it needs to be changed.

Although Piaget's concepts were useful to us in thinking about our students' writing, the study of mature adult thinking suggests that some of these concepts, particularly formal operational thinking as Piaget envisaged it, might actually be inadequate to the realities of adult life and that the years following adolescence can be expected to produce quite different structures of thought and ways of gaining knowledge.

Some studies of intellectual development have focused specifically on the development of thinking during the college years. William Perry (1970) followed groups of students at Harvard through a process that he saw as integrating ethical and intellectual development in nine successive "positions." He found that while freshmen were likely to see the world in terms of absolutes ("right" and "wrong"), as they progressed through their college years they came next to an understanding that things could be seen in different ways from different perspectives and that all positions could be accepted as valid (making it hard initially to choose among them—"She's entitled to her opinion"). Toward the end of their college years, Perry found that some students attained a different state of mind, which he called "commitment in relativity," that enabled them to make reasoned choices about ethical positions and serious commitments to those positions, even as they recognized that others, in different circumstances, might still make different choices.

Another Harvard researcher, Lawrence Kohlberg, focused on the development of moral reasoning, finding a "highest stage of moral reasoning" that linked ethical choice making to the ability to think abstractly and analytically and enabled an individual to arrive at a decision about a problem with certainty, reasoning to the solution from an articulated moral principle.

Such theories of development, for good and ill, have been extremely influential in educational practice as teachers have attempted to modify their instruction to accommodate the developmental stages they assumed their students to be working within. (We've seen presentations on college writing courses that purported to take students through all of the levels of development that Perry found for the college years in a one-semester sequence of writing assignments.) Much criticism, questioning, and refinement of these theories have been generated on several grounds: that stages of development cannot be rigidly defined in the ways that these theories suggest; that they don't consider the contexts in which people operate (most children and adults in fact operate in different ways in different areas of their lives and in different physical, social, and emotional contexts), and that they don't take into account differences based on culture or gender.

Certainly, while these studies of cognitive and intellectual development could contribute to our own thinking about these issues, they could not provide a complete picture. Our students were not going to fit into a simple model of development: they were of varying ages and backgrounds (the youngest were eighteen-year-old freshmen like Alison and Jean, often from the Boston area, while one of the oldest was a seventy-nine-year-old man who had spent his early years as a sharecropper in Mississippi); they came to us speaking different languages and dialects; and they brought the perspectives of different cultures. To better understand their learning, we needed theories of development that would be contextually based and culturally sensitive in ways that much of this work was not.

In considering the social element of thought, the effect of social context on the ways that our students had developed as thinkers, we turned to the work of the Russian psychologist, Lev Vygotsky, whose studies were conducted during the years immediately following the Revolution. Like Piaget, Vygotsky emphasizes the active ways in which people construct an understanding of the world, build theories or models or schemata of how things work, and then test these against available evidence. But Vygotsky focuses on the social environment as well as the physical one, seeing the development of thought and language as a social as well as an individual process, since the individual is embedded in a society and a culture. For both the child and the adolescent, development is shaped by the social world:

> [The] thinking and behavior of adolescents are prompted not from within but from without, by the social milieu. The tasks with which society confronts an adolescent as he enters the cultural, professional, and civic world of adults undoubtedly become an important factor in the emergence of conceptual thinking. (1962, 108)

In Vygotsky's work, the role of language becomes particularly important, for it is language that mediates between the learner and the world, shaping and extending thought. As people acquire language, they acquire a culture's ways of looking at the world—in a society where the adults have a single word for green and blue, the child can speak of a color that English speakers have to struggle to describe ("greenish blue"). Even the words we use to represent our thoughts to ourselves are words that are necessarily drawn from a social context. As Mikhail Bakhtin, the Russian literary critic working at the same time as Vygotsky, points out, they come weighted with the meanings that others have given them, so that even in talking to ourselves we are always engaged in a conversation with others.

Cross-cultural studies like that of the Scollons (1981), while not focused on intellectual development per se, also point to the intersection between people's ways of thinking and knowing and their social and cultural context. They show clearly that the characteristics of fully developed adult cognition as they have appeared in Western contexts are not necessarily those valued for adults in other cultures. Among the Athabaskans, according to the Scollons, "the higher order structures that are organized to integrate very different or essentially irreconcilable events and views are rejected . . . in favor of lower order structures," at least partly because of "the need for the individual to internally integrate his own knowledge" and thus to reject outside knowledge that cannot be easily integrated (102). Similarly, Fan Shen found that he had to wrestle with a very different logical system in order to shift from writing in Chinese to writing in English, for rather than moving from the premises of an argument to its conclusion, what is most valued in Chinese thinking is *yijing,* a nonlinear recreation of mental pictures in the mind of the reader (464). Our students may come from cultures that value aspects of cognition that are quite different from those seen as "most adult" in Western society.

Within Western society too, new empirical and theoretical inquiry into the nature of adult intellectual development points to the different ways that people come to know and the different sorts of knowledge they value. Some of this work has focused on women's development. Carol Gilligan's *In a Different Voice* shows that women tend to make moral judgments that take into account particular circumstances as well as abstract principles; this does not mean that they are less morally developed than men, as Kohlberg's work might suggest, but that the patterns Kohlberg found for white men at privileged institutions are not universal. Similarly, Belenky et al.'s *Women's Ways of Knowing* questions the path of intellectual development described by Perry, emphasizing the importance of women's embeddedness in particular social contexts and relationships and the essential role that this embeddedness plays in the development of their thinking over the college years. (If we had begun with this perspective, we might have seen better how to work with Jean and her focus on love.) These studies question the image of development as a steady progression toward increasingly abstract thought, the image presented in earlier research.

The new picture of adult thinking that emerges from these perspectives allows for the possibility that the very abstract thinking traditionally seen in the academic world as most highly developed, and the kind of embedded and situated thinking more often valued in other contexts and cultures, need not be seen as irreconcilable.

This picture has informed our understanding of the ways of thinking that our own diverse students bring to our classrooms and suggested four qualities of adult thinking that have particular importance for writing: (1) a view of knowledge as understanding, personally constructed and susceptible to influences from the context in which it is constructed, rather than as a set of absolute, universal, and unchanging facts; (2) a sense that such knowledge emerges as the product of a process whereby alternative interpretations of experience are exchanged, a process that involves communication with others; (3) a tendency to see things "dialectically," which among other things allows for the acceptance of opposition and contradiction; and (4) a way of thinking about issues and problems that integrates analytical and logical approaches with figurative, metaphoric, and analogical ones. We see some of these aspects of adult cognition operating in Alison. She is sufficiently decentered in her thinking to be conscious of her own construction of knowledge—to define terms for herself and to do so in the context of an ongoing conversation with others in her class. Her classmates' interpretations, like those in the books she reads, help her shape her own. She has also started to identify contradictions between her own earlier interpretations of events, for example, and her current one.

One other area of research that has influenced our understanding of the thinking our students build on in our classrooms has focused on narrative. We've already talked about the ways in which the underlying narrative competence that students bring to our classrooms has provided one means through which they can order, interpret, and question events—engaging in the kinds of thinking that we have been describing here. While narrative provides a basic way of understanding and interpreting the world, it has most often been seen as demanding a less developed form of cognition, one that students should leave behind as they move into "higher," more abstract forms of reasoning. As a cognitive psychologist, Jerome Bruner (1986) has reconsidered the place of narrative in our repertoire of ways of thinking. He suggests that people use *two* primary ways of thinking to create possible models of how the world works: one is the logical or "paradigmatic" mode, but of *equal* importance is the narrative mode, which focuses on particular contexts, on the details of ordinary experience, to create "possible worlds" through "the metaphoric transformation of the ordinary and the given" (49).

Narration accounts for a large part of the way we make sense of our world, and we use it not only in our most mundane conversations, but also in our most significant texts of literature, history, and religion. When we select details from the flux of experience and shape them into a story, we are also engaged in naming, abstracting from, and restructuring the raw data of the physical world, and in finding its patterns of meaning. And it is in our stories—like that of Suzy and the birds—that we embed our understanding of more abstract concepts like pedagogy. It is most often, then, through the stories they tell that our students have connected particular details with the larger and often abstract meanings associated with advanced cognition. So we have come to see self-generated or self-selected narrative as both an analytical and an interpretive act and to see in our students' narratives many of the underpinnings of their thinking, including those of the logical or "paradigmatic" mode that is more explicitly demanded in academic settings. Since academic writing rests on the understanding that the significance of events or facts will be seen and reported, and that an answer to the question of why something is important will be stated explicitly, one indication that a student is ready to think (and write) in ways necessary to academic settings is often that the student begins to discover her own meaning in the events she writes about and includes in her writing some indication of her own sense of the significance of what she is saying, as we see Alison doing in her narrative accounts of her mother's illnesses.

Ways of Thinking

Thus, several kinds of thinking are necessary in order for our students to make any kind of sense of what goes on in their classrooms, of what they're hearing when they attend lectures and discussions, of the kinds of assignments they get, and of the writing they are required to do in their courses. Some of these kinds of thinking they do consciously on a regular basis in their daily lives; others they have not had the chance to develop actively because there hasn't been much in their lives that required them. In all interactions, but particularly in the classroom, people tend to move back and forth between different kinds of thinking, which we have come to group in particular ways.

One kind is *analytical.* It includes the kind of thinking Bruner refers to as paradigmatic, the sort of formal operational thinking Piaget described as first appearing in the thinking of adolescents, the kind of thinking most often seen as central to college courses. It allows students to appreciate the nature of a proof when it is offered to them. It allows them to identify things in terms of their categories, to do "classificatory thinking" as Piaget calls it. It enables them to see the implications of the things they are reading about and learning about—in scientific experimentation, for example, or in political

arguments. It allows them to see the importance of providing explanations and, conversely, to appreciate the fact that they are being
offered explanatory material when they read. It allows them to conceive of the nature of theories and to take critical stances with respect
to them: to identify the elements of an argument, to recognize which
parts are premises and which conclusions, and to see the relationship
of evidence to those conclusions. It enables students to devise strategies for solving problems.

A second kind of thinking is *dialectical.* It allows people to see
one position in relationship to another, to see from different perspectives, to respond to different contexts, and to tolerate ambiguity and
multiple meanings. It encourages an appreciation of complexity and
controversy, of challenge and dialogue. It also supports reflexivity
and an awareness of the self as knower. It allows an individual not
only to analyze a situation, to stand back and think abstractly and
hypothetically about it, but to behave reflectively and see himself as
part of a context while also imagining himself as a participant in
other contexts, providing, in Bruner's terms, a "landscape for thinking about the human condition." Context sensitivity—the sort of
sensitivity that Carol Gilligan and others have found to be characteristic of women's mature intellectual development—is one of the most
important aspects of this kind of thinking. The term "dialectical" in
part implies a recognition of the intrinsic contradictions in things
and a tolerance for the kind of conflict that characterizes most situations offering any sort of complexity or interest. It's this sort of
thinking that ultimately allows a person to develop a sense of irony
or to see growth as the result of loss. And it makes it possible for
students to step back from what they've written to anticipate the
needs of a reader—to provide context for the reader and definitions
of terms a reader might not understand—so that they are less likely
to produce writing that seems to float without background, without
explanation, without being linked to anything. It reflects a sense of
reciprocity in the reading-writing situation, a sense of the importance
of the reader and the reader's mind, and a consciousness of another
way of thinking that makes it possible for a writer not only to
structure a piece of writing but to write well.

A third kind of thinking can be termed *figurative,* or *metaphorical.* It is this kind of thinking that is closest to what Bruner
describes as the narrative mode—seeing particular events or things
as pointing to something else (Bruner uses James Joyce's phrase
"epiphanies of the ordinary")—although such thinking is not represented *only* in our narratives. It is also present when people see
things as significant—see that what they read, what they experience, and what they perceive require interpretation in order to be

understood. Figurative thinking is what we do when we dive beneath the surface of experience and pull out meaning. It can be seen as an integrated version of analytical and dialectical thinking, but it involves a more intense concern with the nature of consciousness, with the nature of language, and with the ways that consciousness and language are related to one another. When students become comfortable with this sort of thinking, they are able to work very closely with a text. Corrections and comments about their own texts become meaningful and useful to them. But the big difference between this kind of thinking and the others is that it is problem *finding* in nature, rather than simply problem *solving.* Diving below the surface to find new questions and complexities becomes part of seeing texts and of seeing life.

It is all too easy to see only analytical thinking as true higher-order thinking and to undervalue the others. But that is to ignore the power of the particular and the concrete to inform understanding. Both science, with its reliance on the inductive method, and poetry, with its necessary immersion in the details of human existence, require the particular for insight into the universal.

The ability to think, solve problems, and generate new questions outside the context of one's own immediate experience, to be self-reflective and aware of one's own thinking and ways of acting, and to respond to the world with an interpretive stance are all important to the work of the college classroom. Education facilitates the shift from thinking that is personal and context-based to thinking that is more abstract and varied. But our ability to learn depends on our being able to link specific details—of our lives, of the lives of others, or of our observations of the physical world—with more abstract concepts that can pull these details together into a larger, more coherent model of how things work. The more richness of detail we bring to our model and the more flexibly we work with it, the more we will understand.

Our students come into our classrooms with ways of thinking and ways of using language that derive from their families and communities as well as from their past schooling. In the classroom they will be exposed to new perspectives—those of other students, the teacher, the books they read. Some students, like Alison, will eagerly engage in the work of this academic community. Others, like Jean, who have different priorities and values, will choose to leave it. Still others, like Antonio, will move between work and the university, between their native language and English, shifting their worlds and their ways of thinking and of using language, and in the process seeing these worlds in ways that are continuously new.

For all these students it is full participation in the work of the academic community that will enable them to learn to think and write in the ways that are valued there. Ideally, this work will also allow them to gain a new consciousness of the other communities in which they are participants and of the uses of language and the thinking that are appropriate to those contexts. We would argue, finally, that just as it is not through memorizing forms but through engaging in meaningful conversation that people acquire new ways with words, it is not through learning facts but through thinking, working with others, and having the opportunity and the need to perform certain intellectual operations and see things in new perspectives that people come to value their own knowledge and to acquire new ways of thinking.

Chapter Four

Teaching as Inquiry

We create the world we know not through direct encounters alone but by negotiating and interpreting what we take from those encounters. As Jerome Bruner (1986) says, "The world that emerges for us is a conceptual world. When we are puzzled about what we encounter, we renegotiate its meaning in a manner that is concordant with what those around us believe" (122). That conceptual world is mediated by culture, which can itself be seen as a forum for negotiating and renegotiating meaning. Bruner describes the stance of a learner in such a world as "negotiatory," and he uses the term "transactional" to refer to the kind of thinking we have been describing as "dialectical." We would argue that this stance must be the stance of both the teacher and the student. Only by taking on an interpretive or dialectical relationship to the world and to that part of the world our students represent can we redefine and reconstruct our role as teachers in appropriate ways.

Such a stance begins in inquiry of the sort we have engaged in as we have looked at the texts of students like Alison and Jean to see what we could understand about their negotiations with the world. It is a stance not unlike that of a language learner in an ideal, meaning-rich and risk-allowing setting, where constructions can be created, tried out, and altered in communication with others. And it stands in opposition to the stance that approaches knowledge as fixed and nonnegotiable, one often accompanied by a similar stance toward "proper" language. (Followers of E. B. Hirsch [1987] and Allan Bloom [1987] are likely readers of "language police" Edwin Newman and William Safire.) Yet even those who see knowledge as something constructed rather than fixed may not recognize and encourage their students' active construction of linguistic systems.

For some of our colleagues whose real interests lie outside the realm of writing instruction, any nonstandard forms of discourse students use, any divergence from expected formats and organizing structures, are experienced as distractions, as simply messes to be cleaned up (preferably by a tutor) before a paper can be turned in. But the excitement of our work as teachers of writing has come from our ongoing discovery of the shapes and forms of our students' linguistic and communicative competence. Proceeding as researchers might (as linguists, for example, who define as grammatical anything the speakers of a language produce and use these data to infer the grammatical system underlying those utterances), we use whatever our students produce as a means to understand more about their systematic knowledge. We have learned, most of the time, to be excited by the new data we find in our students' writing, rather than appalled by its apparent distance from what is expected of college writers. (Mina Shaughnessy pointed the way to this change in perspective in *Errors and Expectations,* but the change has been slow to spread, although it is vitally important to the enterprise we are describing here.)

Engaging in inquiry is the first step in evolving the stance we propose, and in this chapter we would like to continue our inquiry into student writing and ways of seeing it. Our approach is analogous to that of the anthropological field worker: it is as if we were stepping into a new culture and learning how to look at what we see there in the terms presented by that culture.

Clifford Geertz (1973) describes his anthropologist's stance toward studying culture not as "an experimental science in search of law but an interpretive one in search of meaning" (5). He characterizes the ethnographer's method as "thick description":

> What the ethnographer is in fact faced with . . . is a multiplicity of complex conceptual structures, many of them superimposed upon or knotted into one another, which are at once strange, irregular, and inexplicit, and which he must contrive somehow first to grasp and then to render. (10)

Geertz is describing the interpretive stance we propose to use in order to understand what we find in our students' writing. Yet we recognize that there is a problem with our anthropologist analogy. Margaret Mead and Clifford Geertz stepped as outsiders into functioning communities, hoping to become participants in the life of the community. But as Geertz tells us of his time in Bali, he was reminded that he was still a "nonperson," "a gust of wind" (413). One effect of beginning "to doubt whether you are really real after all" is to become quite certain that those in the community you are studying are very real, to begin to see the world increasingly from their perspective until, like Geertz, you act more like an insider, with the same fears, concerns, and interpretations of events. As teachers, however, we continue to be the insiders who define the classroom community, and no matter what stance we try to maintain toward our students, their language and ideas and writing will not present the same coherent picture of competence to us that they would if we were to enter into their communities.

One way to shift our stance is consciously to take on the role of learner as it is experienced in a different setting. Ellie had this experience:

> After I had been teaching for about ten years, I began to play the recorder. I had grown up in a musical family—my grandfather was a professional violinist, and he had lived with us, selected my piano teachers, and supervised my practicing until he died, when I was twelve. After that, my interest in playing, and particularly in practicing, declined sharply, and by the middle of my high school years I played only because it frequently got me excused from doing the dinner dishes. But I came to the enterprise of learning to play the recorder with some existing knowledge—I could read music—and with the confidence that came from having had some success at learning another instrument. So, when some recorder-playing friends gave me a recorder for a present one Christmas, I worked my way through the beginner's book, learning the fingering and figuring out how hard to blow.
>
> My friends were attending a recorder camp that summer—a camp at which amateur recorder players gathered and under the direction of professionals played together in ensembles. The minimum requirement for admission was that one could read music and could play all the scales on either the soprano or the alto recorder. I was barely at that minimum, but I thought I could play, and I was eager to learn more.
>
> My experience at the camp reminds me, at this point, of the stories I hear from my students. When I am teaching classes for people who are preparing to teach, I usually ask my students to reflect on their own early experiences as learners in school settings, particularly in learning to read and write. One student, Sally, told of going to school thinking she could read, telling the teacher she could read, being called on to read, and then stumbling over a word and being told "That is a baby word. You can't read. Go and sit with that other group—the crows." Now the teacher's words may not have been so harsh, the nonreaders were probably not called crows (though they often were), and Sally may or may not have been able to "read" in the sense of being able to decode words from a page of unfamiliar text. But what is clear from this account is the emotional

effect of this experience on a learner who was confident that she could read but was told that she could not—who was moved from being an insider to the work of that first-grade classroom, a bluebird, to being an outsider, a crow.

I too thought of myself as someone who could "read." I did know how to play an instrument and how to read music. I was confident in my knowledge thus far of the world of music, as Sally was of the world of books, and like her I was eager to expand my existing knowledge and to use it in a new context. But the "reading" was done differently at this summer music camp. We were playing in groups, while I had always played piano alone or with one other person. We were reading music that looked and sounded different to me—Renaissance music without bar lines and with parts for a variety of squawky-sounding instruments. My rudimentary skill at fingering the soprano recorder worked as long as I was playing familiar music alone or with my friends. But in this new and threatening context it left me entirely, and I fumbled along letting out real squawks and finally no sounds at all. My instructor, like Sally's, was surprised at my initial self-confident assertion that I belonged in this group at this music camp. I could not perform in this situation and by her standards it was my actual performance, not any underlying competence that I brought to this work, that mattered.

Soon I began to question that I had any knowledge about music at all. I had confidently signed up for the camp chorus, since I had always sung in choruses and had performed some difficult music. But now I worried about whether I was reading the music correctly. I was certain that I was making mistakes and that the director was glowering at me, and I sank silently into the back rows, following along with other voices occasionally but not trying out anything on my own and not really mastering the music.

Ellie survived her week at music camp, though she never went again. Over time, in other settings with other people, she learned to play Renaissance music on the recorder. But the most important thing she learned at music camp was not about music but about learning itself. As a successful student, she, like most teachers, hadn't had much experience with failure in school. And as a teacher, she had sometimes been stymied in her efforts to help students who were unsuccessful because she was unable to fully imagine what it must be like to fail. But now that she had known the profound humiliation of being what she calls "a twentieth-century crow in a world of fifteenth-century larks," she began to see the experiences of her own students from a new perspective, to understand the effect that context has on performance, to realize that seemingly incompetent performers are not necessarily incompetent learners with nothing to bring to the enterprise in which they are engaged.

Of course, as teachers, we are also continually learning about ourselves, our underlying competence as well as our "performance" in this role. We would echo the concern of another anthropologist, Mary Catherine Bateson (1984), the daughter of Margaret Mead, to "avoid mistakes and distortions not so much by trying to build a wall between the observer and the observed as by observing the observer—observing yourself—as well, and bringing the personal issues into consciousness" (161). We are in a constant process of negotiating meaning, and we would have our classrooms be a forum for such negotiation. But we are also participants in a larger community, negotiating with one another as well as our students and recognizing that everyone brings both personal strengths and personal issues to this negotiation.

Stance and Language

Our stance toward the world, and the language in which we express it, is both personally and culturally based. Some theories of the relationship between language, thought, and culture, like that of the linguists Edward Sapir (1921, 1949) and Benjamin Whorf (1965), have held that the language we speak significantly delimits the ways in which we think—that we cannot think the things for which our language provides no words. A more moderate position acknowledges, as Vygotsky (1962, 1978) does, the strong, shaping influence of sociocultural context—of the beliefs and values of a society and the language that represents them—on the things members of that society notice and pay attention to and the ways they think about those things, but it would not limit the possibilities of thought to the boundaries of a particular language and culture.

What is true for a culture and a language as a whole seems to be true to some extent for the various discourses of communities within the larger society. When we associate ourselves with a particular community, for example, a profession like law or medicine or psychotherapy, we tend to view the objects of our ongoing inquiry about the world in the terms that community provides, even as we signal our membership in the community by using its language. For many children, school provides the first significant exposure to a new discourse community, and some research, like that of Sylvia Scribner and Michael Cole (1981), highlights the common effects of schooling, across many cultures, on people's ways of thinking and using language.

James Gee (1989), in exploring the ways that language shapes experience, uses the term "Discourse" to encompass ways of thinking, ways of using language, and the cultural frame of reference that informs them (all that we've been describing in Chapters 2 and 3). He distinguishes between a primary discourse, "our socioculturally determined way of using our native language in face-to-face communication with intimates," and secondary discourses, those that involve social institutions beyond the family and require communication with nonintimates (22). Gee defines literacy as "control of secondary uses of language" and argues, as we do in Chapter 2, that literacy is mastered through acquisition, not learning, and that it requires exposure to models in natural, meaningful, and functional settings. But he also considers how acquiring new discourses may affect one's thinking about the world, providing a perspective from which it is possible to gain larger understandings about the nature of discourse and to critique and even change the discourses one has already been using. For Gee, this perspective on discourse is more important than perfect mastery.

Our experience as teachers lends support to Gee's argument. Our ESL students, engaged in the process of acquiring a new language, often give voice to new understandings about language and its uses. They may discover, as Helene did in the journal entry quoted in Chapter 2, that words alone give little sense of how an expression is actually used: that "How are you?" is embedded in expectations about social interaction that cannot be learned from a textbook. Or they may learn, as Carole did, that for a language learner, a genuine correspondence with a native speaker of the language is more effective than textbook exercises. Students who are encouraged to reflect on their learning of new discourses—on their process of writing or learning to write, for example—may come to see, in Gee's terms, "how the Discourses you have already got relate to those you are attempting to acquire, and how the ones you are trying to acquire relate to self and society." For teachers, ironically, learning a new discourse about a world in which they are already expert is harder. In the rest of this chapter, as we look at the work of students who are learning new uses of language and acquiring new discourses, we will also explore the process of a similar movement for us as teachers of composition moving from the discourse of error and deficit to the discourse of learning and possibility.

Shifting Stance

Shifting our own stance as teachers has not been neat and linear. It has evolved in association with two ways of defining our role, one based in inquiry and one in curriculum. The first gave us new ways of looking at our students and the kinds of competence they bring to our classes, the second gave us new ways of looking at our teaching and the kinds of meaningful work we should provide to support our students' acquisition of new intellectual and linguistic discourses. Although we treat these two approaches to our teaching in separate chapters, they have become increasingly enmeshed.

Our inquiry has had several aspects:

- We have been working to discover more about our students' processes of reading and writing, their responses to their past and present learning, and their knowledge of their own competence. This sort of inquiry draws heavily on students' journals, on their concurrent or retrospective accounts of their work.

- We have been looking for evidence of our students' knowledge and competence, for their developing systems or interlanguages, and for the underlying development of new conceptualizations of self and world. For us this process began with seeing our students' texts in new ways. In previous chapters, we have introduced the beginnings of this approach by looking at the work of Antonio, Alison, and Jean. The rest of this chapter will focus on such evidence in more detail. (We have also been working with students on more structured and formal assessments, so that the evidence we are looking for and their perceptions of themselves as learners and writers intersect, and we'll say more about that in Chapter 8.)

- We have been inquiring into other areas of our students' lives as learners and language users—into the language of other courses and classrooms, of their homes and communities, of their workplaces—and the relationship between those discourses and the ones they are acquiring in this new context. This sort of inquiry is based on collaborative research, and it has become the basis for the sorts of research-oriented curricula we will be describing in succeeding chapters.

In this kind of inquiry the all-important first step has been to see our students' writing differently. Seeing our students' texts in a new way has been an important part of our work in understanding their underlying competence and systematic development, in part because the production of written academic discourse is the explicit goal of the writing classroom and because the assessment of such discourse provides an external measure of our students' success or failure. To persuade others to see evidence of underlying competence and developing systems of language and thought in our students' writing, we've had to begin by showing them that such evidence exists. We have found ourselves looking for three sorts of evidence:

- Evidence of systematicity in the acquisition of new discourse structures appropriate to written academic discourse. These discourse structures include an awareness of orthographic as well as stylistic features (such as nominalizations or universalizations through the removal of first person references). Students often overgeneralize the rules for using these features, sprinkling their papers with semicolons and layering on relative clauses, thus committing one of the worst offenses in the academic world—writing the "academese" that seems to mock it. A common response to overgeneralization in the use of these developing systems has been the generally unhelpful mandate: "Just write as you speak." But such overgeneralizations can tell a great deal about a student's assumptions about the linguistic system and strategies for approximating it.

- Evidence of our students' use of new conceptual structures. This includes language that points to the sorts of thinking we described at the end of Chapter 3:

  - *Analytical*—providing logical structuring, coherence, and sequencing; making and supporting propositions or generalizations, providing explanations, seeing implications, solving problems, and generating larger theories.
  - *Dialectical*—describing relationships between things, presenting the complexity of issues, elaborating where necessary, taking on different perspectives, showing a sensitivity to context, taking a stance, reflecting on oneself as knower.
  - *Metaphorical*—explicitly interpretive, showing how small events or particular examples can represent larger patterns, finding and inquiring into representative problems.

  Again, we expect to find evidence that a student is developing systematic sets of responses and strategies for handling the sorts of conceptual tasks required by the academic world, even though these may be only approximations of those used by "insiders."

- Evidence of our students' development of new evaluative structures, of shifts in the ways they place themselves in relation to the world and evaluate their own experience. This is related to the stance taking of what we have described as dialectical thinking, but here we want to focus on a more extended and extensive use of different knowledge bases. These reference frames are based in part on the language and culture of the family and community, in part on expanding knowledge of a wider world. For instance, as learners gain factual knowledge about the establishment of apartheid in South Africa, or of the interaction of chemical compounds, or of normal patterns of children's development, they gain a new base for interpreting events that may have seemed isolated or idiosyncratic, or may even have passed unnoticed. Anyone who has functioned successfully in any context has had to learn, for that context, how to use knowledge and what knowledge to use in order to render meaningful any object of investigation or concern. As the curriculum provides new information and new ways of seeing and using that information, students gain many interpretive options to draw on, and begin to shape a larger framework that integrates them. We look, then, for the ways in which the conceptual process of recognizing and taking a perspective intersects with students' ability to draw on different frames of knowledge.

Evidence of these various aspects of our students' underlying and developing competence are interwoven in all of their work. Here, to elaborate on our own developing system of looking at that competence, we will highlight some examples that have helped us see the errors and problems and "mess" of a student's writing as evidence of development.

Discourse Features: Seeing the Surface in a New Way

In changing our stance as teachers, we need to begin at the surface of our students' writing, seeing, as Mina Shaughnessy did, the errors that point to the inexpert status of "basic" writers as signs of their systematic acquisition of a new target language. Earl, a classmate of Alison's and Jean's, recounts an "early memory" of a school outing:

> It was a glorious day and my school had planned a trip to Holbrook, MA. All the school was invited to a public cook-out and family outing at the expense of the town's people. Sort of a city meets country gathering . . .

Earl goes on to detail his experiences, how he wandered off and got lost, how he met another lost student and made an unexpected friend. He contrasts his city expectations with country realities:

> But soon I realized my instinctions are far more appropriate in the big city rather than the country. Out here there are not streets of signs, unforatunately. Luckily I met up with Lisa who happen to be in the same predicamet. Somehow we found our way back to the main campground just as the bus began to pull off.

Earl's text can be seen in terms of its logical structuring—its organizational strategy in the classifying of city ways versus country ways and the fact that he is able to hold two different points of view in a dialectical relationship. But Earl's text can also be seen in terms of its errors: spelling errors, shifts in tense, sentence fragments, and, in this excerpt, the invented word "instinctions." The appearance of a few errors in one text may offer few hints of an underlying system. But the recurrence of particular types of errors tells us more. Here is a selection from Earl's midterm essay on Anne Frank:

> Anne Frank's life was centered around many different emotional complexities. Nonetheless she dealt with these conflictions by giving it her all and accepting those challenges with dignity. But the most important feature aspect of Anne's life was the overwhelming strive to achieve conquest of maturity. Young Anne had become a young woman inspite of Germany's quest to rule or the harsh sometimes inhuman living conditions in which she had to reconcile to so that the hope of being accepted as a person and not a Jew would not peerish.

Here the number of discrete errors has increased, new problems have appeared, and others have persisted. But the very persistence of a form like "conflictions," when seen next to Earl's earlier production of "instinctions," shows us the systematicity of his creative approximation of academic discourse. Having picked up, unconsciously, the sense (confirmed by discourse analysis) that one key feature of academic discourse is its large number of nominalizations—making verbs into noun forms (like "nominalization") wherever possible—Earl systematically creates long noun forms in his writing. And having acquired the form "tion" to be added to verbs in the creation of nouns, he applies it wherever possible, even to existing nouns. These constructed terms don't, in fact, interfere with his meaning or his ability to communicate that meaning, but neither do they exist in the target language that he will eventually come to approximate more closely. Other errors can also be attributed to Earl's more extended attempts to construct academic discourse. He has acquired forms like "nonetheless," but he has also created overblown rhetorical constructions like "to achieve conquest of maturity," and syntactic knots like "in which she had to reconcile to."

By comparing different texts, we can see Earl in the process of entering a new discourse community. He is acquiring its forms by hearing and reading them, trying them out, creating whatever he needs that will approximate them. As he becomes a more practiced participant in this community, he gains a sense of some of the features of its discourse—nominalizations, infinitive phrases—and begins to sense as well the need for elaboration and specification that these features support. With continued participation in this community, his approximations will come closer and closer to the target; in the meantime, attempting to untangle a specific knot or to explain the rule for a specific construction (as Ellie tried to do for "instinctions"), will have little effect.

When we look at Earl's writing using the discourse of possibility instead of the discourse of error, we see that his errors increase with the complexity of his thought as he tries to juggle many things at once and to experiment with new forms to express new ideas. In his essay on Anne Frank, Earl is trying to provide a larger framework for Anne's life—"emotional complexities"—and to identify and focus on one part in relation to that whole—Anne's growing maturity. He cannot yet neatly sort out the pieces, and the paragraph is muddled (as is the larger paper). But the appearance of "complexities" is a sign of growth. We push students whose work is always superficial and clean to probe their ideas until they find the muddles. It is only by working into and through what they don't already know that our students learn.

Earl is a native speaker of English (of Black English Vernacular). The ESL students in Vivian Zamel's section of freshman writing showed similar systematicity in their approximations of appropriate conventions for written academic discourse in English. The following paper shows Vito, a native speaker of Italian, to be focusing particularly on rules for capitalization and punctuation in English. Vito overgeneralizes these rules, creating more errors in his concern for correctness. At the beginning of the semester, Vivian asked her students to tell something of their background. Vito responded:

> The story, that I will be writting, is based on
> My father's life.
> To start, I think it would be best to say, that
> My grandfather dies when my father was
> Seven years old. As a result, my father had to
> Stop attending school, after his fourth year
> Of elementary school.
> When he was ten years of age, he got his
> First job. His first job's duties were, pick the
> Leaves from the tea trees, there he worked
> For three years, then with the help of his
> Older brother he was hired by a small wood
> Work shop.
> . . .
> Today we are living reasonably well, but there
> Are a few words that he always tells me and

Those few words are "I never enjoyed my infancy"
I know that it was not because he had to work
When he was ten or because he did not go
To school after he was ten, but that it's because
He had no father. Those words tell me alot.

The surface of Vito's first text shows some errors in spelling and some tense shifts that may or may not recur systematically. But there is striking systematicity in one orthographic feature: the capitalization of the first word of each line. Vito has hypothesized a rule for English capitalization that is quite likely, although incorrect for prose. Were he to call this text a poem rather than an essay, what appears as error from one perspective would no longer be seen as error at all.

Conceptual Underpinnings: Seeing Below the Surface

Vito is a mature and experienced student who is able to pay close attention to form because many of the conceptual tasks being asked of him in an academic setting are familiar. In his first paper, after telling his father's story, he repeats and interprets his father's words: he offers one possible interpretation, rejects that, and offers another, finally asserting the significance of his father's words for *him*. He is comfortable with dialectical, interpretive thinking. For Vito, careful experimentation with form leads quickly to essays (written at home, with time for him to monitor what he produces) that display not only the discourse conventions of formal academic writing, but the expected conceptual approaches as well.

> Marjorie Shostak is an anthropologist who visited a tribe in Botswana, Africa. The objective of her twenty month visit to that tribe was to study the people who lived in that tribe and who were known as the !Kung. During the first few months in the field, she didn't communicate with the people, for she couldn't speak their language. Therefore, she spent those few months following the !Kung on hunts, gathering vegetables, and eating with them. While she observed the !Kung she studied their manners. However, she felt there was information that could only be captured by talking with the !Kung.

From the opening paragraph of this second paper, we can see that Vito is already a participant in the academic discourse community. He uses appropriate vocabulary in discussing Shostak's work (her "objective"), he presents logical relationships, pointing out cause and effect ("therefore") while following and reproducing the logic of Shostak's research. Because he understands the nature of the enterprise Shostak is engaged in, he can restate the objective of her study, her method, and the problems this method presents. He sees the dialectical nature of Shostak's relationship with the !Kung and the ways in which her understanding of their perspective is inhibited by her inability to talk to them. He can also imagine the perspective of his own readers and provides the information that will bring them smoothly into the frame of reference that Shostak has provided.

Among ESL students we see some of the differences in ways of conceiving and responding to the work of the writing classroom that we saw between Alison and Jean. When Vivian asks her students why they came to this country, Bertha answers in the following way:

> Why did I came to this country?
> I came to the United States in 1980, I was 13 years old. the reason that I came to this country was because of political problems in my country Nicaragua and because my family and myself risked the danger of get kill specially my father because he used to work for the Zomosa's government. However, I have some good and bad images in my mind according to what some members of my family, who live in California and who were visiting Nicaragua, by the time that I was preparing myself to come to the United States told me—that the United States is a very rich country with a high technology. Also that, I have a lot of good opportunities for study and work if I really work hard for it and I look for it.
> During all this years Living in Boston, I am able to believe what the member of my family told me about this country before I came here.

Here Bertha answers the question "Why did I come to this country?" with a string of facts about her life, with a logical statement of how the dangers of her country and the image of the United States as rich and full of opportunities led to her family's decision to emigrate. She hints at a more complex picture, at the "good and bad images" in her mind, but at this point she does not look below the surface to explore those images. Like Vito, she is experimenting with orthographic conventions like capitalization as well as constructing a systematic pattern of tense and person markers, and she will continue to move closer in her approximations to her target of standard written English. But she is not yet (at least in her school writing) beginning to question, interpret, take on different perspectives, and engage in the active construction of multiple meanings.

In contrast Winnie, another classmate, does probe below these surface images of life in the United States, and in the process engages in the sort of figurative or metaphorical thinking that underlies much sophisticated inquiry. She too uses approximations of the forms of standard written English that do not yet completely match her target language. But she begins her response to Vivian's question by systematically examining the metaphor that embodies her former image of the United States—"Gold Mountain."

> "Gold Mountain" what a fancy name is: This is the most popular name for the U.S. in Hong Kong. According to the name I could think of that American people were very rich. There was easy money in the country. I was told that U.S. was a good chance for education since colleges in my country were scarce and I was hardly having any opportunities.

On one level Winnie confirms that image with a logical examination of the evidence, and the paper could have ended there.

> Are American people really rich? Compare with my country's people, perhaps they are. Americans have higher living standard. People live in big houses in which they share their own rooms . . .

But she goes beyond the surface to find another interpretation, from another point of view, dialectically. She then rejects the first metaphor and substitutes a new one—working machine.

> In my eyes, America is not a gold mountain at all but a working machine. Everyday, people work hard for their money. They are so busy that they don't have time to communicate with their friends.

To a student like Winnie, no object of inquiry yields simple answers. The world is complex, and assumptions about it must be explored and interpreted. Like her teachers, she is trying to see below the surface.

Evaluative Frameworks: Defining the Terrain

Let's return, finally, to the work of Antonio, the student in Ellie and Suzy's freshman studies seminar who wrote the workplace description we saw in Chapter 2. Even within our early framework for seeing the strengths in our students' writing, Antonio's competence was apparent. But Antonio, who described himself as a "bad writer," saw himself in the terms of deficit that had been the discourse of his earlier schooling. (Unfortunately it continued to be the discourse of his later schooling; his composition teacher for the next semester saw his work only as—to use her particular terms—"impossible," "a mess.") Because we were working on taking a new stance toward the writing of students like Antonio, looking for their developing system or interlanguage, for their ways of conceptualizing, as we've been describing here, we couldn't see Antonio's writing as a mess despite its surface problems. As we began to look at it more closely, we realized that Antonio was not at all the "basic" writer that he had been labeled, but that he was eagerly trying out a variety of complex ways of conceptualizing self and world. Here is his response to the "early memory" assignment:

> In my darkest memory as a child, I remember being in my father's workshop. He was a shoemaker. He had a little shop a short distance from my house. This particular day my father was nursing me because my mother had to runan go somewhere. I was brousing through the dusty and leather smelling room. Being a child, naturally I was touching things. On the shelves. I wasn't satisfied with just playing with the stripes of leather on the floor. I want to touch and play with the heavy tools. As I was touching tool, I came upon a sharp knife. I wanted to get it so I can do my own cutting, but I couldn't reach it. My final measure to reach it was to Hit it with a stick, so it can drop down and I'll have my ways with the stripe. But as I was doing it, I accidently Hit it too hard. The knife blindly flew up in a relentless spinning motion. I tried to get away from it but I couldn't. It as a result landed on my finger, and created a deep sharp cut. I kept on screeming loud and sharp until my father came. He said what happen. I told him in antisepation of pety. But he got and declaire never again will he allow me to be in the shop again. I cry and cry all night that day and promise myself never to think of him as mentor against my hero again, or show interest in his work as my future career.

For this account, Antonio has selected a seemingly minor event, the cutting of his finger in his father's workshop, but one he knew was of major importance in defining or transforming a significant relationship. In making this choice he shows that he is able to see beyond the appearance of events to an interpretation of their meaning. He begins with an evaluation of "my darkest memory," then tells his story to show not only what that memory was but why it was so dark. As he tells his story, we can see that he is also aware of the reader's frame of reference. He creates a common framework and a common basis for a shared evaluation of these events as he moves from the general circumstances of his father's life and workshop to the specific events of this one day, including appropriate explanatory details: "This particular day my father was nursing me." He uses terms ("mentor") that are specific to the conceptual framework he is constructing and exploring (much the way that Alison probed the word "mature"). And that framework gives him a basis for evaluating his father's actions and the meaning of this event in his own life. Antonio's text (unlike Alison's early entry) contains a real conclusion; he explains why this event is significant—that it marked a real change in himself and in his relationship to his father. Not only is he able to see and interpret this early event from his present perspective, but he is able to place the entire event within the framework of his later understanding, to make a final statement about its meaning.

Antonio used the opportunity his courses provided to expand and extend the framework with which he had been examining his own life, to participate in what Bruner describes as "reflective intervention" in knowledge—to use what he was reading and learning for his own purposes, and to share and negotiate the results. In this process he increasingly placed himself within a larger community of writers and thinkers, drawing on the framework presented by their work to extend his own. At midterm he turned in a five-page essay that sensitively analyzes the central conflict of Chaim Potok's *The Chosen*. The carefully ordered essay presents a proposition and offers arguments to prove it. It shows Antonio's ability to analyze and interpret, to take on the perspectives of the central characters, to take into account the needs of his own readers. It also shows many of the syntactic knots, unorthodox but systematic features of punctuation, and misuse of words and phrases that are characteristic of someone acquiring a new discourse ("[Danny's father] literally reined on the hassid community like a king"). But what is most striking about his essay is the way Antonio explores not only the conflict of the son and the father (a salient conflict in his own life), but also the question of where knowledge lies. Of Danny, he tells us:

> Being the first son, Danny was the heir apparent to the throne. The expectation that the whole community, the Hasids, had was naturally for Danny to succeed his father. But his mind craved for more than just being the future absorber of their pains. His mind was too potent to be one demential. He had to absorb knowledge other than that of his religion. He had to know where the world stood in terms of religion. He had to know how radical his religion really was from the perspective of the outside world, which he saw with psychology, Freud, and the other literature he read in the library. . . . The consequence of following the two extreme opposites, psychology and religion, was one reality he had to face sooner or later.

Antonio finally sees Danny's conflict as an internal as well as an external one, arising specifically in questions of how one knows, how one evaluates the meaning of events and decides on a course of action. With his acquisition of a critical perspective on different ways of knowing comes an understanding that life is complex and that people arrive at different interpretations depending on the framework they use to explain and evaluate their experiences. After a careful and detailed explication of this conflict as it appears throughout the text, his essay concludes:

> With all [Danny's] genius, his father raised him in a state of unas-
> surance. He couldn't make his own mind up, what was best, psy-
> chology or his religion. The system which was going to make him
> a sound human being couldn't help him come to a decision.

Here Antonio offers not only a sophisticated look at two conflicting interpretive systems through which meaning might be constructed quite differently, but a sensitive look at the consequences for the individual.

Antonio's essay helped us articulate an understanding that we had been groping for, a way of making sense of the role of curriculum in providing opportunities for students to acquire a new linguistic and conceptual repertoire and for helping them understand, use, and critically examine the interpretive frameworks their college curricula would provide. It is the consequences of that understanding for the courses we construct, for the work we do with students, and for the ways we define our role as teachers that we explore in succeeding chapters.

Chapter Five

Curriculum as a Framework for Discovery

In shifting our stance as teachers, we had to begin to discover our own competence—to see our own work critically and to take on new responsibility for all that shaped teaching and learning in our class-rooms. Because we had come to understand that new uses of lan-guage and thought are acquired through active, constructive, interdependent processes and shaped by social and cultural contexts, we wanted to create writing courses that would provide opportuni-ties for inquiry and discovery—for the learner's personal construc-tion of knowledge—and take into account both the contexts our students came from and the new contexts they were entering. But before our teaching could fully reflect these insights, we needed to examine the assumptions implied in the ways we might read student texts and those suggested by course materials, by writing assign-ments, and by grading practices. We had to explore the implications of the most common elements of the freshman writing course to discover whether they were congruent with what we knew about language and learning. And as teachers who were bringing into the classroom our own backgrounds, and our own relationships to soci-ety and the institution as well as to the academic field of composi-tion, we had to examine our own assumptions as well.

Our own experiences show how aspects of our practice can conflict with what we think we know. Vivian, for example, came into the teaching of composition to ESL students with a graduate degree that was supposed to have prepared her for the classroom. Courses in linguistics, cross-cultural issues, pedagogy, curriculum, and the ways in which these areas of study impinge on working with non-

native speakers of English provided her with a theoretical and philosophical basis for understanding how to promote language acquisition. A course on composition research and theory had pointed to the
limitations of traditional approaches to ESL writing instruction. And
a number of courses, as well as the research she undertook as a
teaching assistant, focused on the importance of describing classroom events, analyzing classroom discourse, and examining the language of the classroom in order to understand teaching and learning
(years before such work had come to be known as teacher research).

Despite this theoretical orientation, despite the questioning
stance this graduate work implied, it is telling that Vivian's early
teaching ended up being shaped as much by the textbooks available
to her as by the constraints she felt when she began to teach. She
recalls:

> As I was about to enter the composition classroom for the first time,
> I was directed to examine an array of composition textbooks in
> order to determine what to do, what my goals ought to be. At the
> time, these textbooks were organized by a rhetorical models
> approach, an approach that focused on particular formats, each
> presented one at a time. This lockstep approach paralleled and was
> congruous with the focus on language forms, a focus which, at the
> time, predominated ESL teaching; like this approach to ESL, it too
> had as its goal the ability to produce predetermined models of
> language, but this time at the discourse level. That this approach
> was at odds with the fundamental principles of the graduate course
> on composition studies and my research on classroom description
> was not problematic, so convinced was I that these textbooks,
> written by teachers who had far more experience than I, teachers
> who seemed to embrace a uniform conceptualization of writing,
> reflected what I needed to and was expected to do.
>
> For two years my teaching was shaped by my parallel concerns
> with correct language forms and correct discourse formats. And
> there was no reason to question these concerns. Students wrote
> compositions that imitated what I viewed as properly organized
> texts, and I was able to evaluate these pieces on the basis of how
> closely they approximated the models presented in their books, how
> closely they reflected standard language use. At the end of one
> semester, however, a student who had consistently written what I
> considered at the time well-organized and developed compositions
> made a remark that surprised me as she turned in her final course
> evaluation: "I thought you were a good teacher," Sabena said, "but
> it's too bad you didn't find out anything about what we were
> thinking." Sabena went on to say that she wished she'd been able to
> write about her own thoughts, about issues that were of concern to
> her. What surprised me about her comment was my conviction that
> this indeed was what I had asked students to do. But clearly, students

like Sabena realized that the real agenda (conventions, forms) transcended my invitation to write about issues that mattered to them, about their observations and realizations. At the surface level, I stated that writing was for exploring and examining deep issues, but it was obvious that at the deep level, the focus of my teaching was still on surface features.

As I reflect back on that time, Sabena's comment seems to mark a turning point in my teaching. I was struck by the realization that engagement, posing questions, and meaning making played only peripheral roles in my classroom and that this was as true for my own work as it was for the work my students were undertaking. I, like my students, was following someone else's predetermined blueprint. Like the students who completed the grammar exercises assigned, I too was filling in the blanks. Even I, as a teacher, was excluded from active engagement by the dominance of the curriculum, and this attitude had been passed on to my students. Sabena's remark revealed my real priorities and led me to question this stance. And once I gave myself permission to question, to approach with uncertainty what others had recommended, to observe closely and inquire into classroom events, to integrate my graduate preparation with my own teaching, I was able to pass on this reflective stance to my students as well. Just as I became more open to learning about my teaching, I welcomed what my students could tell me about what they could do and what they were still struggling with. Sabena's comment was the beginning of my learning to teach and teaching to learn.

For each of us there have been moments like Vivian's that called into question our assumptions about our teaching and led us to ask again: "How can we teach writing most effectively?" For the most part, our answers to that question have not been found in our formal study or in the new textbooks that flooded our desks at book-ordering time. Instead, new questions have come from our classrooms and our students, and it is through taking those questions seriously that we've found, not a single, consistently satisfying answer, but the sorts of underpinnings and directions that we've been discussing here.

Like many teachers faced with the inappropriateness of much formal theory for the real lives of our classrooms, we have sometimes responded by tuning out that theory and trying to see, from a fresh perspective, what Alison and Antonio and Sabena have to tell us. But of course, what we see in our students' words and their work is still shaped by the understandings we bring to them, by some interpretive framework, whether it is one that we are taught or receive with a textbook and leave unexamined, or one that we create anew as we seek new answers to the questions that emerge from our classrooms. As teachers we have a responsibility always to reexamine the assumptions that shape our pedagogy and our curricula, to consider their implications and consequences, and to reconstruct those pedagogies and curricula repeatedly as our students change and as we change.

We have been engaged thus far in delineating our interpretive framework for approaching the teaching and learning of writing in an academic context, a framework that began to emerge from the conjunction of our knowledge, interests, and questions about our students and their writing some years after Sabena made her comment to Vivian. The framework we have been building has drawn in large part on two areas of inquiry that we have found useful but that as disciplines have tended to remain quite separate: the study of language acquisition, especially second language acquisition; and the study of cognitive and intellectual development, especially adult development.

In curricular practice either focus can lend itself to the skills-oriented drill of decontextualized forms: to the teaching of formats for greetings or for opening paragraphs on the one hand, or for syllogistic reasoning and other critical thinking skills on the other. But focusing on language acquisition and intellectual development, particularly when these perspectives are integrated in a context-sensitive curriculum, can also lead to education that engages learners in meaningful inquiry, builds on their existing competence, and situates their competence and their new learning in the real social contexts of the academic world and the larger world. Such learning is more likely to result when it is based in a model of education that stresses the integral relationship of language and thought.

Theory and Pedagogy

Theories of writing instruction have led to different pedagogical consequences largely based on the relationship they assume exists between language and thought. In one direction, language is seen as shaping thought. Whether this conclusion arises from the extreme linguistic determinism of the linguists Sapir and Whorf, who argued that what an individual can think or know is determined by the language she uses, or from postmodern, intertextual theories of discourse, which argue that words always come so weighted with the meanings and the uses of others that they effectively eliminate the individual knower and language user, in the end it leaves little room for the critical, reflective thinking that is done by an individual.

The most traditional approach to writing instruction requires students to practice forms of discourse using formulaic models in a

paradigmatic manner. This approach may come from the not alto-
gether unfounded sense that people who have the power to articulate
their ideas in language that is marked by complex syntax and a highly
literate vocabulary are also most commonly able to think about things
in complex and sophisticated ways. It's easy to fall into the trap of
seeing the thinking as arising from the language, and of assuming that
by providing the linguistic forms you are also providing the logical-
ity, the complexity of thought. But research on children's thinking
and language suggests that the developmental process, at least, is not
one of language giving rise to thinking, but rather of actions and
engagement with others giving rise to both thought and language.

Efforts to change a child's thinking about a problem, for example,
by teaching her to use more sophisticated linguistic forms have not
made that child more able to think maturely or effectively about the
problem. Nor, for that matter, have they influenced the child's natural
use of more sophisticated language. The educational researcher
Eleanor Duckworth (1987) tells of a study, conducted in the 1960s at
the Piaget Institute in Geneva, in which attempts were made to teach
children who were less accomplished at dealing with certain
Piagetian tasks to use the language patterns of children who were
more cognitively advanced. It turned out to be very difficult to get
the less advanced children to adopt the language patterns of the more
advanced ones. Even when they did manage to use the more sophisticated vocabulary and syntactic routines, their thinking about the
tasks was not noticeably improved. Duckworth reports that, in the
end, the researchers were forced to see the development of a child's
linguistic abilities as dependent on her level of cognition, not the
other way around.

> The pedagogical implications here seem to be fairly clear-cut:
> Teaching linguistic formulas is not likely to lead to clear logical
> thinking; it is by thinking that people get better at thinking. If the
> logic is there, a person will be able to find words adequate to
> represent it. If it is not there, having the words will not help. (25)

In college composition curricula, the "language shapes thought"
position too often leads to the imitation of rhetorical models. It
also leads to just such teaching of linguistic formulas, to sentence-
combining exercises, for example, which are based on the assumption
that if students practice making complex sentences from simple ones
they will learn to see relationships in complex ways. In ESL, in
particular, despite a shift away from this position, the focus on
practicing language forms with the idea that such practice will lead
to better performance in English continues to be a dominant concern
of instruction.

The opposing position is that thought shapes language, that ideas are formed first and then words are found to express them. An extreme version of this position denies the power of a society to make things salient through language and the more reciprocal relationship that Vygotsky, among others, found between language and thought. And pedagogies that follow from the extreme view treat language only as an abstract and transparent symbol system that can be made to represent ideas logically, uncolored by the socially influenced nuances of the words themselves. Writing is then seen as ideally decontextualized, wholly removed from the complex contexts that still muddy up meaning in conversations, and the writer is expected to be able to state all terms in such a way that any reader, at any time, can follow the logic of the argument. David Olson (1977) describes the "western essayist tradition" as following from this assumption that meanings can be wholly and clearly represented in texts and suggests that with the rise of literacy in European civilization, the writer's task became "to write in such a manner that the sentence was an adequate explicit representation of the meaning, relying on no implicit premises or personal interpretations" (95).

While the language-shapes-thought position leads, in the extreme, to linguistic exercises, ironically, the thought-shapes-language position can have the same result. If it is assumed that thought is transparently represented by language, then it is possible to conclude that where the linguistic forms expected by the teacher are not present, the thinking that is desired is not there either. The extreme consequence of this position is Thomas Farrell's (1983) argument that speakers of Black English Vernacular, a system in which various forms of the verb *to be* are systematically deleted (a feature of the grammar of the language), are not using the words that show states of being and must therefore be capable of thinking only about actions. Farrell argues that BEV speakers will be incapable of abstract thought until they are drilled in the "full deployment of the verb 'to be'" (479). Of course that position is absurd—BEV makes regular deletions where "standard" English allows contractions, and no one has suggested that those contracted forms represent con-stricted or abbreviated thought—and responses to Farrell's article energetically countered his argument. But the consequence of the view that one's meaning must be wholly represented in the text is often the assumption that if it is not, if a student doesn't present the ideas so that the teacher understands them (or, more to the point, as the teacher would present them), the student "can't think" and "doesn't belong in college." Students who do not adequately repre-sent their ideas in the language expected in the academic world are seen as not having any ideas, as being incapable of doing academic work, and they are encouraged in subtle (and not so subtle) ways to leave it.

A more appropriate position recognizes that language and thought are related and interwoven in complex ways, and that the development of new ways of thinking and new uses of language (including writing) are deeply interactive. This position leads to instructional approaches that support students as they develop new understandings and new ways of expressing complex ideas through careful, patient reflection in an exchange with others. This position and pedagogical approaches that follow from it marked our thinking at the time we were first looking analytically at the writing of Antonio and Alison and Winnie. We saw writing as necessary to the sort of careful reflection and interpretation we wanted our students to engage in, to the sort of dialectical and metaphorical thinking we hoped to foster. And we saw that sort of thinking as related to the development of writing in the ways we discussed in Chapter 3.

Freshman Writing and the Academic Discourse Community

These positions on the relationship of language and thought have corresponded to paradigm shifts in the field of composition over the past ten or fifteen years. Early process approaches tried to support the integrated development of language and thought by focusing on the individual writer, on expressive writing, on finding one's own voice. But such approaches often failed to meet the needs of students who were entering the university from diverse backgrounds and without conventional academic skills. At most institutions these students were relegated to basic skills programs that were based on deficit models of student learning and built around the narrow sorts of language and writing exercises such models imply. But a second, more thoughtful response took into account the nature of language acquisition and the existing linguistic and cognitive resources of students. Based on an interactive model of the relationship between writing and thought, it focused on social and cultural context, on the cultural differences between the "academy" and the communities from which an increasingly diverse body of students was coming. Grounding their theories on insights drawn from the fields of anthropology and linguistics, composition scholars began to speak of the differences between an academic discourse community and the discourse communities of their students' families and hometowns, and to reconsider the work that was required to move from one to another. Students were increasingly seen not as entering the university without thought or language but as needing a period of careful acculturation to a new community with new practices. As David Bartholomae (1986) defines the problem,

> the students have to appropriate (or be appropriated by) a special-
> ized discourse, and they have to do this as though they were easily
> and comfortably one with their audience, as though they were
> members of the academy, or historians or anthropologists or econo-
> mists; they have to invent the university by assembling and mim-
> icking its language, finding some compromise between
> idiosyncrasy, a personal history, and the requirements of conven-
> tion, the history of a discipline. They must learn to speak our
> language. (5)

As Bartholomae looks at the texts of the students struggling to appropriate this discourse, he repeatedly finds that they have "entered the
discourse without successfully approximating it" (8). The consequence is that as "students assume privilege by locating themselves
within the discourse of a particular community . . . learning, at least
as it is defined in the liberal arts curriculum, becomes more a matter
of imitation or parody than a matter of invention and discovery" (11).

Our own thinking about these issues during this period echoed
Bartholomae's concerns. In a 1985 presentation the three of us gave
at the Conference on College Composition and Communication, we
offered an analysis of several types of change in our students' writing.
To the changes in various ways of thinking and of using language, we
added a specific category of "culture" or acculturation. But we have
grown increasingly aware that while our students are entering a new
academic culture, that culture and its discourse are not fixed or
unitary. As Peter Elbow (1991) discovers when he looks at the discourse of our own field,

> I can't tell my students whether academic discourse in English
> means using lots of structural signposts or leaving them out, bring-
> ing in their feelings and personal reactions or leaving them out,
> giving evidence from the poet's life for interpretations or leaving
> that out, referring to the class, gender, and school of other interpret-
> ers, or leaving that out. . . . In short, it's crazy to talk about academic
> discourse as one thing. (139–40)

Thus in shaping a theory of writing instruction we find ourselves
with a much harder and more complicated task than the one framed
in terms of development or of acculturation to a fixed community with
its agreed-upon set of ideas, truths, methods, and ways of speaking.
We cannot simply talk of our students "developing" new ways of
thinking or "approximating" new forms of discourse, as if the movement is all in one direction, as if the goal is clear and there is some

looked only at a student's performances on a particular task—and to develop others—encouraging discussion, assigning journals and other exploratory modes of writing, and using portfolios to evaluate a semester's work. But what were the implications of our evolving theory of instruction, based as it was on the integral relationship of language and thought, for our development of a curriculum? Theories of instruction or pedagogy focus on what teachers *do.* Curriculum is most often seen as what they *have to do*—or what they have to do it about. It is a term we associate first with high schools, where teachers are often responding to mandated curricula that typically focus on coverage or on skills as defined by limited behavioral objectives: "The student will be able to identify. . . ." The university has most recently claimed the word curriculum in "writing across the curriculum." Here curriculum appears as a collective container for a variety of disciplinary courses, each discrete but all requiring a common skill with written language. "Curriculum" provides a structure within which diverse parts of a larger enterprise can be seen. The work of Toby Fulwiler (1986) and others has made clear the degree to which writing is an important part of knowing in all areas "across the curriculum." An emphasis on using writing for learning and not just for evaluating learning has begun to influence the way other disciplines are taught: process journals, for example, give evidence of students' thinking about math or science that can't be ignored by concerned teachers.

In redefining the nature of freshman writing and its teaching, we found ourselves more and more seeing writing not as a tool with which to support the curriculum but as a means of transforming that curriculum and our students' relationship to it and to the academic community.

How is learning presented in the introductory courses that freshmen traditionally take to gain a "general education" and an introduction to the disciplines from which they will eventually be choosing a major? In a typical course, students are assigned reading from textbooks that summarize the knowledge of the discipline, introduce and define key terms, and present in capsulated form the categories of questions the discipline addresses and the methodologies it uses. Some attention may be paid to the history of the discipline and its relationship to others in the spectrum of sciences and humanities; sometimes its controversies are examined; often the significance of its approaches and findings is asserted. The texts for such courses— usually peppered with exquisite four-color photographs and cleverly worked out charts, cartoons, and graphs—present a picture of academic work as orderly, rational, and productive, but, to the student who is reading her evening's assignment, singularly unexciting.

Knowledge in such texts is divided neatly into easily absorbed chunks, often with the most significant statements presented in shaded boxes outlined by a colored border so that the student reader simply has to note them.

Students in introductory courses studying from books like these have little chance of guessing at the true nature of scholarly work or knowledge. They cannot imagine the entangled difficulties that characterize the actual collection of real data, nor the exhaustion, frustration, confusion, disappointment, exhilaration, and argument that are experienced by anyone engaged in attempting to ask a new question, test a hypothesis, or prove an interpretation valid. Some students—those who arrive with previously established goals and some familiarity with the ways of the academic community—quickly choose a field and focus on it. They may get to do honors work or go on to graduate school, and there, finally, they get to experience the ambiguities and complex processes involved in constructing an understanding as opposed to receiving information. As a reward for having endured nearly a hundred hours of classes in which they were told what other people were doing in the field and had come to know, they finally get a chance to do some research themselves.

We have been trying to reverse this process, to engage all students, particularly those who have been outsiders to academic communities, in the more complex, messy, and demanding process of asking the questions and looking for evidence, of constructing their own knowledge in relation to a discipline. We have endeavored to integrate this learning with the acquisition of writing so that the learning of new modes of language and new modes of thought can influence one another. When we conceive of curriculum in this way, writing becomes a means through which students keep track of their perceptions, questions, proposals, explanations, trials, discoveries, frustrations, and conclusions—a means, not an end in itself. The end remains the ideas, the questions, the interpretations, and the understandings toward which students move through the curriculum, and language is the primary medium for constructing, developing, and exchanging thoughts. The more writing students do as part of their learning and working with others, the more effectively they will engage in the processes of discovery, struggle, and intellectual growth and the more they will be able to articulate what they take out of this process. Finally, if they feel confident of their capacity to think and express themselves logically, creatively, and fully as students, they will go on as workers and citizens to recognize problems and illogicalities and to articulate these insights; to arrive at personally satisfying understandings and communicate these to others; to construct knowledge and understanding; to engage with others in productive exchanges about problems, issues, ideas, theories, interests, and projects; and to use these capacities to make meaningful choices about how they live their lives.

We see an effective freshman writing curriculum, then, not as one that is focused on writing as a discrete skill but as one that is intimately bound up with the rest of a student's learning and life. The curriculum for one course provides one moment in this learning, but it is part of the larger life enterprise—a *curriculum vitae.*

Within this framework, we have been approaching curriculum not as a set of things to be learned but as an *environment* in which students can develop. Clearly we don't see curriculum as a list of important titles, historic events, cultural landmarks, famous names, or significant discoveries that students must know about. When we use this word we think of a classroom that is the context for the student's exploration of ideas: a structured, challenging, exciting world in which students can engage in active inquiry about a variety of phenomena and, in doing so, discover problems, ask questions, propose theories, test those theories, experience difficulties. We see the social nature of this environment as particularly important to the sort of learning we have in mind. It is one in which students talk with others, argue, persuade, are persuaded, and construct understanding.

The teacher plays a significant role in shaping this environment and also in participating in it. It becomes increasingly important for the teacher to support and to challenge, to shape a route and then reshape it with those who enter it. Paulo Freire has long articulated the difference in two models of education: in one, which he calls the "banking model," knowledge is seen as a sum of information to be deposited in the minds of students. Such education, according to Freire (1970), "attempts to maintain the *submersion* of consciousness" (68). To this Freire would oppose a "problem-posing" model, in which the object of knowledge is no longer the private property of the teacher but something that students and teachers think about and construct together in public dialogue. He emphasizes a new sharing of roles: "teacher-student with students-teachers" (67). The parental scaffolding described by observers of child development like Bruner, Vygotsky's accounts of the ways a teacher can extend a learner's existing competence into a "zone of proximal development," and Krashen's hypothesis about the importance of providing comprehensible input to second language learners also suggest the environment the teacher creates and the appropriate extension of the teacher's authority within it.

The environment that teachers shape for freshman writing becomes, in effect, the writing curriculum, whether it is shaped by the textbooks used or the readings assigned, by the writing tasks called for or the conversations that are allowed. We see effective writing curricula as having several particular characteristics:

- They are structured firmly enough to provide support for students' early efforts at intellectual inquiry and clearly define every activity's relationship to the overall topic and goal while providing students with many opportunities to work with a variety of different forms of language use (group discussions; dialogues; interviews; lectures; debates; films; reading in books, periodicals, and popular literature; and, of course, writing).

- They entail courses that provide students with coherent intellectual experiences and enable them to establish a coherent framework of knowledge, focusing on a particular topic that is at once challenging and considered to be of immediate importance. In such courses, the work is intense enough to engage the students' minds, capture their imaginations, and make them stretch beyond their current capacities.

- They are often interdisciplinary in nature, allowing the exploration of both disciplinary and interdisciplinary perspectives on knowledge, possibly even generating the sorts of reflections about knowledge that come as a consequence of learning a second language or form of discourse.

- They are multicultural, giving students who are frequently marginalized an opportunity to see their own cultural perspectives included in course material, allowing all students to engage with cultural perspectives that are different from their own, and addressing the question of how cultural perspective figures in what is taught and learned.

- Finally, they rest on the fundamental assumption that work in the classroom will be linked to work outside the classroom. The classroom is cast as a workshop linked to the thinking, learning, testing, discovery, observation, and gathering of information that goes on outside the classroom, while the world outside the classroom (the world of streets and parks, churches and synagogues, workplaces, dinner tables) becomes a complementary laboratory for the course.

In our teaching, we have come to see the value of these aspects of a curriculum gradually, through our own experiments, successes, and failures as well as through those of our colleagues, and through our increasing ability to let our students shape the work of the classroom

with us. At various stages of our own development of these understandings about the writing curriculum, it is the questions we have
asked, the constructs we have created about our enterprise, the goals
we have had for our students' learning, that have led us to devise
particular curricular responses as we shaped environments we believed would provide contexts for our students' discoveries and active
construction of knowledge.

The students of Chapters 2, 3, and 4 participated in an early
version of such a curriculum (typically with native speakers and
ESL students in parallel versions and sometimes integrating freshman writing with work in other areas of the core curriculum). We
were focusing on creating a firmly structured and coherent intellectual experience, one that would allow students to draw on their
own lives and on the different cultural contexts from which they
came as well as to use the disciplinary perspectives suggested by
their readings in their anthropology or psychology or history
courses. While course readings and writings varied, we were trying
to shape a curriculum that allowed students to consider their own
development and the things that had contributed to it. To provide
a view across cultures and a way of talking about different cultural
perspectives that would validate the experiences of all of our students, we began by asking them to write about their own early
memories and to read published accounts of such memories, for
example, Nisa's account from Marjorie Shostak's multivoiced work
about the !Kung woman's experience and about her own responses
to !Kung culture as a Westerner.

Over the course of the semester the classes of a typical course in
our curriculum would move through a sequence of informal and
formal writing assignments that connected personal experience to a
series of course readings such as Anne Frank's *The Diary of a Young
Girl,* Maya Angelou's *I Know Why the Caged Bird Sings,* and other
autobiographical accounts of adolescents growing up in a variety of
cultural and historical contexts. Students moved back and forth
between writing about their own experiences, listening to what classmates had written about their experiences, reading and writing about
the experiences represented in these texts, discussing all of this, and
returning to reexamine what had gone before in the light of each new
part. Moving from their own experiences to Nisa's to Anne Frank's,
students like Alison found that Anne Frank too tells about particular
events in her life, that something makes them significant. They began
to use evidence from Anne's diary to support hypotheses about her
development and values. Then, having used this evidence to interpret Anne Frank's life and having seen it in relation to a framework
that makes it meaningful, they began to conceive of a framework of

their own, to see what gives their own lives meaning, what made the particular events they told about seem significant to them. They began to take the kind of critical perspective on their own lives that Freire sees as a fundamental value of formal education.

Along the way, students did other readings that placed individual experience in a larger historical context. Students in Alison and Jean's class read some twentieth-century German history, for example, and reflected on the ways it influenced their reading and understanding. They read the communiqués written back to their superiors in Germany by Nazi commanders who were stationed in the Netherlands, and they compared the depersonalized language and the concern with numbers and completing a task in the communiqués to Anne's very personal responses to the news of each new round-up and deportation. Or, like students in Antonio's class, they researched the history of particular religious communities like the Hassidim and considered the conjunction of historical, cultural and religious experience that contributed to particular ways of looking at the world.

The development of language and thought in courses like these cannot be separated from the social/communicative context in which it occurs. The students in these classes talked with other students, read what they wrote, and drew on words and concepts that had been constructed in the common discussion of the classroom. Reading about the lives of others gave these students new perspectives on their own lives. Class discussions gave them new concepts, such as an evolving definition of maturity, that pushed them to new understandings of old events. Maturity is related to the ways of seeing oneself and the world that we have described as dialectical, and the sequences of readings and writings in these courses gave students the opportunity to broaden their perspective through engagement with others, in life and in texts, who gave voice to new ways of seeing and representing things.

In such courses, students also learn to use writing to record their processes of inquiry and to express the meanings they are discovering. At this point they can perceive writing as an active, personal, and constructive process. Antonio's description of his workplace in Chapter 2 was based on this kind of observation and interpretation. Again, successive opportunities (both formal and informal) to observe, read, and reflect on issues of work, family, and education help students to construct meanings for their own lives. They opened the way for Antonio to discover a theme he could use to create new understandings, returning in memory to his father's workplace and the reasons his father could not serve as his mentor, seeing the conflict between meanings offered by two routes of study in *The Chosen*.

A Critical Perspective on Our Own Curricular Efforts

Our understanding of why and how to enact curricula with the characteristics we have described has continued to evolve over time. At each stage of our work together, as we were finding answers to some of our questions we discovered new ones. In this we are like our students, who, if they are really trying out new ideas and acquiring new language, will keep creating new problems and making new "errors" as they leave the old behind. Some of the assumptions underlying the work we have described were problematic and led us to extend this work in ways we will describe in succeeding chapters. One of our assumptions, and we still believe a correct one, was that we could draw on our students' knowledge of their experience and their competence with language to establish a base for building new areas of knowledge and competence. A related assumption was that we could elicit that competence directly through the tasks we designed, allowing students to transfer what they knew from the larger world to the work of the college classroom. That second assumption needs to be examined more fully.

We have been describing curriculum as an environment for learning that can be shaped in ways that will be most conducive to that learning. The very nature of such an environment, however, is that it is not the outside world, no matter how much it draws on and connects to that world. Assignments that asked students to tell about something that happened in their earlier experience—an early memory, a family story, an account of their coming to the United States—were intended to draw specifically on our students' competence as narrators in ordinary conversations. But we now see that such competence could not be fully and immediately transferred to a classroom assignment in which the task of telling a story was not a natural one. In a conversation, Jean would not have told the story of her motorcycle accident unless it was relevant to what was being said at the time. When a long conversational turn is allocated to a narrative, the listener implicitly demands to know "So what?" "What's the point?" and lengthy, apparently pointless stories will most often be interrupted. Jean didn't lack communicative competence in naturalistic settings; she was fully involved in talking and laughing with her friends as she entered the classroom each day. But the classroom task, as carefully as it had been designed, remained artificial. It was not an underlying incompetence but her inability to see what was being demanded in this new environment that accounts for the flatness of her narrative. Her expectations for the classroom had been shaped by years of writing instruction that had focused on surface correctness. But that instruction also gave her little sense of what the real demands of formal writing might be. For her, this task must have echoed other school tasks. She knew the teacher was the real audience, and she had not generated the impulse to create the narrative herself as a participant in an ongoing conversation. So she just did what she was told, with little engagement. The adolescent storytellers whom William Labov (1972) studied *never* failed to make clear why a story was significant when it was self-generated—when they told a story that was meaningful to them and that they wanted to tell. But when asked by an interviewer to recount the story of a television program, they produced the same sort of flat, unevaluated narratives that Jean wrote.

In a way, the task was probably easier for Alison initially because she had fewer expectations of what this more formal environment would demand. Her schooling had given her little experience with writing, few opportunities to think about either the surface of a written text or what lay under it. She wrote her account of her mother's illness much as she would have told it to a friend, and so it was more natural for her to include just those details that would make a conversational telling coherent and meaningful. Ongoing classroom conversations, dialogue journals, and opportunities for reflective writing offered a bridge for her to the sort of dialectical thinking and writing we hoped to foster. But she was also engaged in that work, in those conversations, in a way that Jean was not, perhaps because Alison was thinking about her own life and her learning in ways that made them meaningful and relevant—they were not just school tasks.

Thinking again about the writing of these students and the classes in which it was elicited, we can now articulate a problem that underlay our continuing efforts to create a curriculum for composition that would help students discover and build on their existing competence. If new discourses were best mastered in the natural settings of the communities that used them, and if we wanted to help students build on their competence with their home discourses as they moved into the new discourse of the academic community, how could we link these two worlds in ways that would not be artificial?

We have had two responses to this dilemma, which we will explore in some detail in succeeding chapters. One is to make the classroom a place where more real conversations take place, conversations that are natural in that they work in the same ways as those that people have outside the classroom even though they may be about different subjects. In contrast to typical classroom discourse, one thing that marks such natural conversations is that they go on only as long as the participants share a common object of interest—as long as there's something they want to tell about or hear about or figure out together. Another is that while one person or another may take the lead at different times, all participants in the conversation feel equal responsibility to maintain its flow.

Of course, classroom conversations are not exactly like conversations in other settings, just as classroom learning is not exactly like the learning that takes place in the rest of peoples' lives. The sorts of informal, and sometimes formal, apprenticeships that people participate in as they move through the world allow for learning in naturalistic ways that are not possible to replicate in the classroom. Conversely, there are some things that schooling supports and allows that are not so easily attained in the outside world. The school setting, without the distractions of ordinary life, allows for focused attention on an object of study and some systematicity in the pursuit of that object. When students collaborate, they can collect many more examples of the behavior under investigation than one observer can note alone, and this richness of evidence allows for the discovery of commonalities and general principles and the development of a shared understanding. Bringing students together, especially in a multicultural classroom, offers an opportunity for multiple perspectives, for different ways of seeing, both from what students bring to it and what they read.

Our second response while trying to create classroom conversations that would be shared enterprises was to make the object of those conversations exactly the sort of study that schooling was good for—in fact, to study even the differences between the ways such conversations take place outside the classroom and inside it. Schooling helps us to develop ways of thinking that we can then turn back on the world, and using the classroom to develop methods for looking at the outside world is an important way of making classroom conversations real, because the objects of inquiry are real and the inquiry itself is also real. We can, for example, make a dilemma like the one Alison and Jean faced when they were asked to write a story or tell one in a classroom itself an object of study, so that students can inquire with us into the different demands of narrative in different contexts. We can make our different uses of language inside and outside the writing classroom an object of shared inquiry and conversation.

Having real conversations as well as studying how they are structured has now become a metaphor for us as we reflect on the authenticity of the work we structure for our students in the curricula we design and in our responses to that work.

Extending Our Curricular Framework

One of our own extended conversations about these issues took place with Shirley Brice Heath at a conference in 1985, a conference we had attended to talk about our own inquiry—our developing framework for seeing students' writing and our early curricular responses. Our notion of acculturation had been leading us to value not only the linguistic practices of the academic discourse community but also those our students brought with them—their narratives, for example. We had found in Heath's *Ways with Words* descriptions of communities that although they were in the Piedmont Carolinas, seemed much like those our students come from—South Boston, Dorchester, and Roxbury. In *Ways with Words* Heath had provided a wonderfully rich portrait of the language and literacy practices of different communities, showing the meaning and function of those practices within a culture. She had also shown how teachers and students in the schools of these communities engaged in genuine dialogue about their knowledge, discovering together how members of the community thought about and described their knowledge (for example, about planting and crops) and the ways in which comparable areas of knowledge were represented in the school terms of the textbook. That work reinforced our developing view of our students' expanding uses of different discourses as they entered the academic culture.

Heath, in turn, was interested in the ways in which we had been conceptualizing our work with our students and in what would emerge if adult students from urban backgrounds engaged, as the Piedmont fifth graders had, in a study of the linguistic practices of the university and of their own communities. So, still working to refine our own definitions and directions, we entered into a collaboration with her, continuing to collect and analyze the data of our students' work as they investigated, in a new system of research projects, the language practices of the world around them: their homes, their workplaces, their classes. It is these curricular efforts and what we learned from them that we describe in the next two chapters. These research courses made discourse itself the subject of investigation for freshman writers, enabling the students to discover their own and others' various forms of competence in the many settings they examined and to construct in the classroom new knowledge from outside the academy in areas in which *they* had expertise. In our reconceived classrooms, the nature of discourse in various contexts became a subject for common and collaborative investigation, reshaping the nature of our inquiry.

Chapter Six

Discovering Competence
Seeing Language in Contexts

Vivian's encounter with her composition student Sabena happened early in her college teaching, before we began the work we have been describing. But Sabena's comment, "It's too bad you didn't find out what we were thinking," highlights what became a major concern for all of us. In redefining our work as teachers of writing, we needed to explore our assumptions and to create a coherent theoretical framework for our practice as teachers. But in the process we also found ourselves developing a new relationship with our students, one in which they were not simply recipients of our curricula who at the end of the semester were allowed to offer a few comments on their experience of the course on a course evaluation form, but one in which their questions about their course work and responses to it were integral to the evolving work of the course.

Our premises for the curricula we've been developing are that they have to be based in inquiry but inquiry that is real, not artificial, and shared, not individual. On the one hand, we are responsible for constructing the courses we teach, and we have to know enough about the topic and about the methods of inquiry that are suited to it to offer appropriate structure and direction. On the other hand, it's important that courses revolve around inquiry into topics about which both teachers and students have real questions, so that students can bring or gain some authority and the data they collect and the interpretations they offer make a necessary contribution to a common construction of knowledge. The teacher can be a collaborating researcher with the students—helping them frame questions and design projects, suggesting ways to analyze data and readings that might answer specific questions generated by the research, engaging with them in discussions about these questions and whatever develops out of the work. This sort of a format casts the teacher as a co-searcher rather than a guide, a leader, or a lecturer, as one member of a collegial group all of whom share the responsibility for constructing whatever insights and understandings eventually derive from the work. In addition, we believe that the courses we devise must be structured in ways that allow what students *do* think about the work—about what they are learning and how they are learning it—to exert an authentic influence over the way that work proceeds.

Shirley Heath has also been involved in shaping new teaching/ learning relationships. In *Ways with Words* she describes her study, as an ethnographer of communication, of the discourse practices of Piedmont communities. But she also makes it clear that she comes to that research as a co-researcher with her own students—the teachers, business leaders, and mill personnel of the area. Pressed by concerns about desegregation and by reports of the low quality of public education, they formulate questions, framed by the course syllabus and by Heath's own areas of ongoing research in anthropological linguistics, that focus on a central concern: "What were the effects of preschool home and community environments on the learning of those language structures and uses which were needed in classrooms and job settings?" (2). Heath's field provides methods of inquiry that could help her students to answer these questions.

> They had an endless store of anecdotes about children learning to use language across and within groups of the region, and they asked why researchers did not describe children learning language as they grew up in their own community cultures. Their questions set the stage for me to encourage them to examine their own ways of using language with their children at home and to record language interactions as thoroughly and accurately as possible. (3)

The questions of Heath's students become her own questions as well and lay the foundation for the comprehensive ethnographic study that the first half of *Ways with Words* comprises. Over time, this joint inquiry shapes teaching practices, engaging young learners as ethnographers of community practices and thus helping them bridge the gap between the discourse patterns and uses of literacy in their rural Carolina homes and communities on the one hand, and the school on the other. Not only do teachers learn about the early language learning and home language practices of their young students, but, Heath concludes, the teachers in her study learn "to bring some of the ways Trackton and Roadville children shaped experience and expressed knowledge into classrooms" (386).

Heath's work has received a great deal of attention in the field of composition for the understanding it provides about the relationship of community language practices and school discourse. But it has also been singled out for the implications of its methods—the sharing of ethnographic research tools with students so that they can participate in such inquiry (see the May 1987 issue of *The Writing Instructor*). Our interest in her work grew out of our own context: the schema we were developing for understanding our students' development of new ways of thinking and using language, and the inquiry-based curriculum we were creating. It offered another way to foster the development of new ways of thinking and using language through authentic investigations by the students, and it suggested ways to extend the opportunities student research could provide for the sort of analytical and dialectical thinking that seemed to be particularly important aspects of adult cognition. Our interest in adopting this ethnographic approach also grew from our sense that with all we had come to know about our students and their writing, there was much that we still didn't know about what they brought to our classrooms and how they saw their own learning.

Our students come from diverse backgrounds and have had a wide range of experience. They are older than typical first-year students. And they generally come from non-standard English language backgrounds. Their patterns of language use are often much like those Heath described for the rural white community of Roadville and the rural black community of Trackton. These patterns differ greatly from those used in the schools, and many of our students have had little successful academic experience; they are unfamiliar with the norms and conventions of academic discourse and with the patterns of thinking that underlie its forms. But they bring a rich diversity of perspectives that have been shaped by their differences in class, race, culture, age, and gender, and that diversity enriches the work of our classrooms, making possible a shared examination of how knowledge is constructed in a multicultural society and of how language shapes and is shaped by this process. In our teaching we have wanted to counter the ways students like Antonio have come to see themselves as skills-deficient, as "bad" writers or learners, because basic-skills approaches have given them only broken bits of learning in the very small pieces they are seen as being able to digest. We wanted to create curricula that would give students the experience of engaging in serious intellectual inquiry while helping them to see their own existing competence as writers and learners from a new perspective.

In this process we have assumed that the key to full membership in an academic culture is a real understanding of the nature of scholarship and research, that such understanding can be gained most effectively by active participation in an authentic process of research, and that the acquisition of academic culture (like any culture) and the capacity to use its language are interdependent. It follows, then, that one of the most effective ways for "outsiders" to become full participants in an academic discourse community is to engage in genuine research about the nature of language. Through this kind of research, learners can discover the characteristics of that language, the reasons for these characteristics, and the ways in which that language is different from the language of the other communities with which they are most familiar (even the too-often fragmented and decontextualized school language that has marked their education).

Studying Language

Within this context we conceived, with Heath, of a new language-focused project that, like those undertaken with Piedmont learners, would teach students to use ethnographic methods. Our students would apply these methods to the study of language use within their families, home communities, and the academic community, and engage in research directed toward the subject of their own language use and that of those around them.

In focusing on the study of language, our initial aim was to provide the means through which students could:

- Discover for themselves the underlying rules that govern the appropriate uses of language in particular communicative situations.

- Develop a vocabulary for talking about language and an idea of how language functions structurally from real study and real need, as opposed to learning about it from a grammar book.

- Use their own formulations of the differences between their home language and their school language, spoken and written language, and informal and formal language to improve their skill at shifting to formal, written school language (both standard English usage and the larger organizational and stylistic patterns of academic discourse) when they needed to do so.

- Make conscious use of their wide repertoire of existing language strategies.

We assumed that this increased attention to language would fuel the kinds of writing and thinking development we had been trying to foster. But our goals went further. We wanted our students to gain knowledge about language—its forms and how it works—and to learn more about themselves as language users and as learners using language in formal learning contexts. We wanted our students to be able to see themselves as taking perspectives and developing stances through the language they used. We wanted to enable them to place themselves within the web of questions about language, culture, and society invoked by their entry into the college classroom and by the ongoing controversy in our field about the nature, value, and use of academic discourse. We wanted them to see writing in the university classroom, like any other use of language, as a natural act in which there is a direct correlation between honesty and quality.

In the rest of this chapter we describe some of the questions about language use that we have investigated with our students. Several fields of scholarly research provide a base for these investigations: linguistic analysis of the differences between speech and writing, speech act theory, and the ethnography of communication. We have now done the sorts of work we describe in these chapters in several different courses, with upper-level and graduate students as well as with freshmen. As might be expected, different questions arise with different groups of learners, who focus on different contexts. The outcomes of particular experiences have led us to some general understandings, and we look at some of these experiences in the chapters that follow.

There were two components to this phase of our development of a freshman curriculum. We were experimenting not only with courses based in language-focused research, but also with new ways of responding to this research. We began by designating two separate courses as language-focused, a basic writing section taught by Ellie and an introductory freshman studies seminar in historical and cultural studies taught by Suzy. Students in these sections carried out a series of investigations into patterns of language use in different contexts. Vivian acted as an outside researcher/correspondent, responding to letters in which students in these classes reported their research findings. (This parallels Shirley Brice Heath and Amanda Branscombe's collaboration [1985] in which Heath exchanged letters with students in Branscombe's ninth-grade class in rural Alabama about the things they were discovering as they used the ethnographic methods she had shared with them.) In subsequent semesters we restructured the freshman work into a combined six-credit freshman studies seminar/freshman composition course that Ellie and Suzy co-taught. We set up new letter exchanges—some between freshmen and seniors or graduate students, some between ESL and native speaker sections of freshman composition, some focusing on research findings and some on the experience of entering the university. We also extended the language-research model into the study of litera-ture and other aspects of literacy in courses at all levels.

Our preliminary investigations focused on three topics central to our general question about academic discourse and its acquisition: differences in spoken and written language, the nature of speech acts and writing acts, and the ways people use language in social and cultural contexts. We have used versions of each of these topics in different classes, where they take on different shapes and directions in relation to the actual data collected (we generally do the same investigations the students do and contribute our own data to the pool) and to the questions that emerge from the class's preliminary research. Studying such topics gives students a basis for further work in particular disciplines of the core curriculum (anthropology, soci-ology, linguistics) and for their ongoing understanding of the terms and concepts of disciplinary and interdisciplinary inquiry.

These topics, and the methods needed to investigate them, guide the inquiry, but the questions that emerge from the process are those of the students. In this context students' early pieces of writing become part of the inquiry. They are "data" to be studied and ana-lyzed, compared and examined for different stylistic features and strategies, rather than "good" or "bad" writing that will be evaluated by the teacher or responded to by a peer group. And their writing is cumulative—individual pieces of writing and observation build toward comprehensive understandings and are incorporated into longer, more developed texts. Students revise their perceptions, reorganize their arguments, and rewrite their reports in a process that is demanded by the larger enterprise, not by a fixed and discrete course requirement.

Inquiry into Spoken and Written Language

Students come into writing courses with their own assumptions about what good writing is and their own expectations about how the course might help them produce it. They tend to see written sen-tences as error free and well formed, as did the student who wrote, "Authors use no slang and correct grammar," and they may be par-ticularly concerned with being taught "the basics" of form and for-mat. They also tend to see speaking and writing as very different acts. Students who come into the classroom chattering with their friends may sit silently before a blank page, even when it is in a journal intended for their own ideas and responses. They expect writing to emerge fully formed from the tip of the pen, and when it doesn't they despair. They are not conscious of the ways in which, as speakers, they stop to think, back up, make repairs, revise, and start again. And they see the differences between speech and writing represented by orthography, punctuation, and paragraphing as more important than the similarities between speaking and writing as communicative acts.

Recent studies of spoken and written language have examined these issues. One strand, focusing on the "technology" of literacy—for example, the use of the alphabet for representing and encoding words—has found fundamental differences between speech and writing. The written text is seen as differing from the spoken not only in its means but in its consequences. Writing is said to allow the accurate representation of ideas and relationships between ideas so that writers and readers are no longer dependent on shared contexts for understanding (that is, the text is seen as *autonomous*), making possible more abstract thought. In this view, writing itself is a logical system with universal characteristics or "standards," and this leads to the assumption that getting its conventions right will make "good" writers. An opposing view sees writing as shaped by the contexts in which it is being used and varying in relation to the varied communities and acts of communication of which it is a part. Different communities develop their own assumptions about when and how writing will be used and read and what its forms should be. Writing is much like any other communicative act: successful written communication depends, as does spoken language, on the community's understandings about the nature of the conversation, on a shared notion of what makes a piece of writing worth reading, and on what gives it meaning. (In *Literacy in Theory and Practice,* Brian Street discusses many of the studies that have shaped these competing views.)

People in most communities, but particularly in academic communities, use writing to work out their ideas and to find logical arguments as well as to communicate with others. Students can be helped to move effectively between modes by studying the ways people in different contexts handle these different aspects of language use and the ways competing demands influence the different forms of speech and writing. One study of the effect of these competing discourse demands on speaking and writing processes is Wallace Chafe's "Integration and Involvement in Speech and Writing." Questions, then, of how communicative acts, both spoken and written, are structured, and of how shared meaning or context is evoked and created are important to our understanding of the work of any discourse community as it is carried out in one mode rather than the other, and even preliminary classroom investigations can provide important understandings for student writers entering a new community.

The study of spoken and written language is both accessible and linked to students' immediate goals as they enter a writing class. Our students begin their inquiry by looking first at their own speaking and writing as it is embedded in the larger work of the class. They interview one another and create written introductions, recount a familiar story told among their family or friends, or interview a non-class member about a particular topic. In each case, the initial narrative account is taped and transcribed, and a written version prepared. Once such data have been collected, typical activities include:

- Making observations based on the data (writing about the transcription process; writing about the process of turning a transcription into a finished written text; comparing oral and written versions of a story; looking at sets of transcribed stories for common features; looking at sets of written stories for common changes).

- Grouping and sorting the data (categorizing observations about language that emerge from the transcription of tapes or turning transcriptions into finished written texts; categorizing the differences in oral and written versions of the same story).

- Constructing larger understandings from the data (making general statements based on the data and pointing out evidence in the data to support them).

- Reporting on the findings.

Throughout their research, students reflect on the process in writing—what they are discovering, what new questions have arisen for them, and what they anticipate looking for next. In telling their stories or conducting their interviews, they are immediately conscious of the demands and constraints of these particular acts of oral communication and of the different ways they respond as individuals. Transcribing tapes (students usually transcribe one another's tapes so that they can attend to the actual text rather than to whether they have succeeded in executing their own meaning and intentions) heightens their awareness of the practical functions of written conventions— paragraphing, punctuation, and sentence boundaries:

> There is no use of punctuation in spoken material, but it is substituted by pauses and the use of such words as *umm* and *ah*.

They are struck by the surface confusion of transcribed speech:

> The language that was transcribed isn't as coherent to read as material done by authors.

And they discover an ongoing process of repair and revision:

> A lot of words are repeated and the person speaking has the tendency to change the structure of their sentences in the middle of the thought. By that I mean they start out a sentence and reconstruct what they started to say into something more understandable.

Creating a coherent written text from another student's narrative (whether the story is told to the class or elicited in an interview) leads students to make observations about larger structures and meanings:

> In order for me to make this spoken narrative into a satisfactory written essay, I picked the main point that the interviewee was getting across.

> I had to change the vocabulary in order for it to be in written form not in spoken.

> I read the transcription after I wrote it, and rewrote it the way I interpreted it, and consequently I condensed it.

A closer look at a transcription of one student's spoken text and his own written version of the same narrative, and at the observations made by his classmates, shows how the group constructs new understandings from these activities.

Shawn's oral story:

> My story is about . . . uh . . . when we were kids . . . real little . . . and . . . uh . . . we had a big yard and everything . . . and we had this tether ball okay . . . you know what a tether ball game is . . . it's just . . . its like a pole with a ball on a rope . . . and you swing it around the pole . . . you know . . . and you try to hit it . . . two guys . . . you hit the ball and it goes around back and forth . . . and you try to get it to wrap around the pole . . . so anyways . . . ya well anyways . . . it's a real dumb game . . . so you take the . . . the ball is held down with like a hook . . . you know . . . we used to take the ball off and swing the hook around, you know . . . cause it was . . . yeah . . . well . . . it was . . . you know . . . it would go around faster . . . you know . . . and um . . . ya . . . so anyways . . . my little brother . . . he was probably about . . . two or three . . . maybe older . . . I don't know . . . he was out there swinging the hook around you know . . . and . . . ah . . . all of a sudden it catches his face and it rips his . . . rips his lip open . . . you know . . . up to about here . . . you know . . . and me and my sister are way down the other end of the yard . . . we're, you know, playing catch with the ball you know *(laughter)* . . . that's supposed to be on the hook . . . right *(laughter)* . . . and um so you know my brother screamed and he's crying and we go . . . aww . . . he's just crying you know . . . don't worry about it . . . you know . . . so my father comes out of the house and he's like *(shriek)* and he goes nuts . . . and he starts panicking . . .

picks the kid up . . . starts running around the yard like . . . you know *(laughter)* . . . runs over to the neighbor's house who's been on vacation for two weeks . . . they're not there . . . he starts calling for them . . . you know . . . we're going like, Dad . . . they're not home . . . oh yeah . . . get in the car . . . he's piling us all in the car . . . you know . . . and we're trying to calm *him* down . . . you know . . . he's the one that's going crazy . . . and my brother . . . you know . . . he's crying . . . but . . . you know . . . he's not dying or anything . . . and . . . um . . . so my sister's taking care of him . . . and . . . you know . . . trying to take care of his face and everything . . . we were all in the car . . . you know . . . we go, is he gonna die . . . is he gonna die *(laughter)* . . . you know . . . and my father goes . . . oh no way . . . my mother works at the hospital there so . . . we took him . . . we took him to the doctor . . . and . . . and then you know he took care of him . . . and that's the story . . . and he lived *(laughter)*.

Shawn's written story:

"A Tether Ball Tragedy"

For those of you who don't know what a Tether Ball game is, I will provide a little explanation. A very primitive game, it uses a six-foot pole stuck in the ground with a four foot rope tied to the top, on the other end of the rope is a ball. To play the game, two people stand opposite each other with the pole in between. They then proceed to hit the ball, each in opposite directions, trying to wrap the ball around the pole. The first one to completely wrap the ball around the pole wins.

There used to be a Tether Ball game in our backyard. Not that it was any big deal, we just had one Sometimes we would play, but most of the time it would just hang there, motionless. One feature of our Tether Ball game that was unique, was that the ball was held on by a hook instead of being tied. All of us kids, being very young and curious, soon discovered that if you took the ball off, and just swung the hook around, it would go very fast. So fast that it would make this "woosh" sound as it flew around the pole. One day we were playing in the yard, me, my three sisters, and my brother Scot who was three years old at the time (four years younger than me). Anyways, Scot was swinging the hook around the pole when somehow the hook caught him in the mouth, ripping the corner up about an inch. Meanwhile my older sister and I were across the yard (playing catch with the ball that was supposed to be on the hook) when we heard him crying. We thought it was just an infantile tantrum and kept playing. Then, all of a sudden my father came running out of the house panic-stricken and shouting obscenities. He picked up Scot and started running toward the neighbor's house shouting for them, completely forgetting that they were on vacation, and had been for a week. After the rest of us (my three sisters and I) reminded him of that he piled all five of us in his little volkswagon, and proceeded to drive to the hospital where my mother worked, yelling at Lisa to tend to Scot's wounds the whole way. The rest of us were in the back seat asking questions like "Is he gonna die?" My father was too panic-stricken to do anything but drive and swear. Scot, not getting much comfort from anyone (with the possible exception of Lisa) was surprisingly calm.

When we got to the hospital, my mother, who was a nurse, acted very professionally and decided not to trust the resident surgeon but to send him to a plastic surgeon.

Needless to say, my mother had the Tether Ball game taken down immediately. More than that, she called the Massachusetts Consumer Dept., and complained about the way the ball hooked on the rope. To this day she will tell you that the reason why the balls are tied on Tether Ball games is because of her complaint.

As they analyzed the two forms of this story, Shawn and his classmates discovered a great deal about communication in speaking and writing. They found that speakers use a style appropriate to their audience and that with peers this style is usually informal. They observed Shawn's use of slang in speech, pointing to statements like "he goes nuts" and "going crazy." They also decided that speakers can rely on nonverbal, "paralinguistic" ways of communicating their thoughts, such as pointing to things around them ("It rips his lip open up to here"). They saw that speakers can check audience comprehension as they go along ("You know?"), and that the response of an audience affects the story (as their laughter affected Shawn's). They also noticed that Shawn had to think out what his story meant as he was telling it, and that he paused, or filled in with "uh" and "um" so that he could think of what he would say next. And they noticed that he used a lot of "ands" to connect his ideas as he moved from one to the next. In listening again to the tape, they realized that they had asked Shawn questions at the start of his story; as a speaker, Shawn didn't have to worry too much about whether he had given his listeners enough details because they could ask for more where they needed them.

When Shawn's classmates compared the written and taped versions of his story, they found that his written style, particularly after revision, was more formal, more appropriate for a wider audience. This time Shawn had put everything he wanted his readers to know into words. ("He didn't just say 'up to here.' He said that the corner of Scot's mouth was ripped 'up about an inch.'"). He was also very specific in his choice of words ("an infantile tantrum"). They noticed that his sentences were more complex, that writing had allowed him time to revise and to eliminate a lot of "ands," and that his writing had been "examined when completed for things like proper grammar." These students also commented on other opportunities available to Shawn as a writer but not as a speaker: that Shawn had begun his written version with a fuller introduction to his story, which gave his readers the information they would need about the game of tetherball (his listeners had had to ask for this); that he had told the story; and finally that he summed up its meaning. His classmates concluded that "written language allows the writer sufficient time to think and organize his/her thoughts." And they recognized that writers were more likely to "say exactly what [the story] means."

These students moved on to compare the texts of all their spoken and written stories, to decide on differences they thought were particularly significant, and to write group research reports in which they discussed these differences, drawing from all their data. In the process they discovered for themselves a great deal of what researchers have found out and what composition textbooks may (or may not) teach about writing.

- The students commented on the creation of shared knowledge:

  When we are speaking, we can let our thoughts be known without using words that we would need in writing. The audience can let the teller know if they understand, whereas in writing, the writer might not be there to elaborate if the reader doesn't understand. The writer must make everything clear to the reader.

- They observed the choices made by writers and speakers:

  When telling or writing the story I found that there were many different choices I could have made as to what the underlying theme would be. I could have made it dramatic and suspenseful or possibly sad, or it could have been used in context with a certain subject to bring about a point. In this particular case I decided to make it humorous. But the process involved in doing this was different from one version to another. In the oral version, after describing the mechanics of a Tether Ball game, I said: "So anyways, ya well so anyways, it's a real dumb game." In saying this I was subconsciously reacting to what I perceived to be the atmosphere of the class. Therefore I almost accidently set a mood for the rest of the story to be humorous. In the written version I made a conscious decision to write a humorous story, and then added sentences that would bring out the humor.

- They noted what was involved in maintaining a relationship with an audience:

  A storyteller will change their language depending on who their audience is, and a writer will try to be as broad as possible to insure the maximum audience. I doubt that if I told my parents my story that I would make it sound so dramatic, but when I am speaking to my peers about something that happened with my family, I use drama to keep them interested. In oral language you need to create a bond with your audience because it is a live situation. In written language the story can speak for itself. But it is important for writers to be aware of oral techniques so they know when their writing becomes too detached and impersonal and how to change it.

The results of this kind of study are startling to the students. They begin the semester with the idea that writing is just transcribed speech, that the criticisms of their writing instructors are founded on some special sort of requirement of composition classes that has nothing to do with real issues. They find that speech is structurally very different from writing, and that reading its transcription is exceptionally difficult. Suddenly, the need for punctuation, paragraphing, elaboration, explicitness of reference, and focus is clear. The processes of comparing transcribed speech and written essays and of rewriting transcripts gives the students an opportunity to discover and articulate for themselves the ways written texts differ from spoken utterances and the kinds of organizational, lexical, and syntactic work they need to do on their own writing as they prepare it for a reader. But it also leads them beyond a narrow conceptualization of speaking/writing differences and helps them to see both the continuity and the reason for the differences between these different modes of communication—to see the ways in which what they know and do as speakers provides the basis for what they need to know and do as writers.

Speech Acts and Writing Acts

In their study of spoken and written language, students begin to make observations about the relationship between language and social context:

> When I told my story to the class I said, "We were *like* sixteen." I would never say that in front of my parents because they have always corrected my grammar.

> The language used by people in speaking is very different from the language used by the authors I read.

> People use alot of slang and speak in different ways depending on their background or social groups.

They see that there are many subtle rules governing how people write or say things in particular situations. They have discovered that they unconsciously know many of the unspoken rules for contexts they are at least somewhat familiar with, such as telling a story to peers, even in the classroom. They know, too, that they shift styles as they move from one context to another—that they may repeatedly say *like* with friends but not use it with parents, or use slang in some contexts but not in others; that their school language when they are speaking, but particularly when they are writing, will tend to be more formal and they will choose vocabulary more appropriate to that formal setting (Shawn's father no longer "goes nuts" but is "panic-stricken," while tetherball becomes a "very primitive" rather than a "dumb" game); and that this more formal language is characteristic of the authors whose books they read. Through this sort of study, they have begun to experience the more formal ways of knowing and speaking that the academic world emphasizes. They now begin to speculate about questions like the effects of sex or age on the way people say things, and they begin to think about seeking answers in systematic study as well as in personal experience. They wonder:

- Are there observable differences in the ways men and women address one another?

- How many different kinds of speech are there? Does everyone use all of them?

- Do age, nationality, sex, professional position, family role, etc., influence the ways people speak to one another?

- How do people use language to express beliefs, feelings, values?

These are the questions our students have asked as they have turned from the study of spoken and written texts to the study of speech acts—how people use language to get things done in the world. J. L. Austin (1975) points out that we not only make statements with our utterances, we perform acts with them at the same time—we promise or apologize or bet. John Searle (1969) argues that *all* utterances are also acts, intended to *do* something as well as to *say* something. Speech act theory has shown the complex nature of the communicative act and of the things that need to be taken into account by speakers and writers. At the same time, the study of actual speech acts has shown the importance of communicative context and the sort of communicative competence that involves knowing (consciously or unconsciously) the many subtle rules that govern utterances in particular situations (for example, communicative competence in the classroom involves understanding that the teacher's polite request, "Would you like to sit down now?" is really a command). One way for students to become aware of the implications of saying something one way rather than another and to learn more about the sorts of rules that govern different discourse situations in writing as well as in speaking is to study specific speech acts.

Our students typically begin their inquiry by choosing a particular speech act—an apology, a greeting, an inquiry—and collecting data (in a notebook or on tape) on others' language use in different contexts—at home, at school, at the workplace, with friends or strangers. A student may discover that he makes a request differently of one parent than of the other ("Dad, you know how you said I could use your car sometimes? Do you think I could use it tonight?" versus "Mom, I'm taking the car now, O.K.?"). Or that a parent will use a request form to an adult but a command form to a child to get something done ("Would you mind doing the dishes?" versus "Do those dishes *now*!"). Students come to see that the people around them make these shifts in predictable ways according to the age of the speaker, the relationship of speaker and listener, their relative positions of authority, and so forth. We usually begin by brainstorming with the class to list the many "things you can do with language," and then have each member choose one such act (such as disciplining another person, making an apology, explaining, insulting, greeting, ending a conversation, requesting help, responding to insults, giving directions). As our students begin to observe and record the speech situations they find around them, they try to identify the kinds of variables that exert an influence on language use. A typical sequence might involve these activities:

- Identifying significant variables, that is, deciding on the sorts of things that it might be important to record about each particular instance of the speech acts students are observing. (Using these suggestions, the students develop worksheets on which they can jot down the date and time, setting, duration, and the characteristics of the participants for each event, make some notes about what actually happened, and add their comments.)

- Observing examples of these speech acts for a week and recording the observations.

- Discussing preliminary findings and refining the lists of variables to include categories that have emerged as important (age and/or sex of participants, relationship of participants) as observation continues.

- Recording observations for another week.

- Writing a report of findings (identifying the forms of behavior they have been observing and the procedures they have used; describing the general patterns of speech, gesture, timing, silence, expression, tone, they have found; discussing their findings in the light of anything they have read—we typically assign Peter Farb's *Word Play*—or learned in class; commenting on anything they feel their work has demonstrated about language use in social contexts and any questions that occurred to them as a result of their having done this project).

Alternatively, students may observe all of the speech situations they find themselves in over several days. Or they may keep track of their uses of writing over a period of time, identifying categories of use from their preliminary observations. Students often discover that they do many of the same things in writing that they do in speaking—performing actions in the world like apologizing, requesting information, or giving directions. But they also find that they use writing more freely—for their own thinking or imagining, for their learning, and in some cases, for pleasure.

Students who begin to observe speech or writing acts discover a great deal about what they are observing, about general features of language use, and about how initial observations can lead to more questions and hypotheses and shape further inquiry. They gain a sense of how empirical investigation might proceed: of how a framing question or hypothesis can lead to the collection of particular types of data, which in turn leads to further refinement of the hypothesis or theory. They also gain a new concern for definition. They see that in order to make sense of raw data, in order to organize this information and find out whether it can tell them anything, they first have to consider the real meaning of each term they want to use and define the categories they think appropriate for ordering their information. (What is important here is the group's own observation of salient features and its determination of definitions and categories, not the application of definitions from other research, although classroom debates lead with amazing frequency to issues that are currently being debated in the field and to students' requests for references to articles.)

Many of the students in these classes have been labeled "academically deficient" or "underprepared" in the university's placement process, yet they are raising academically significant questions about the defining characteristics of a speech situation. One group of students wanted to know whether a large lecture class in which the professor lectures and they listen (or dream) could be considered a true speech situation. Some of them felt that the fact that they were not required (or expected) to speak made this context inappropriate as a "speech situation." Others felt (and this was the final decision of the group) that the fact that they were expected (and required) to "attend" was the critical issue, and that a lecture (and, for that matter, a theatrical performance) was a true speech situation. One student presented a contrasting situation: he could be watching a TV ad that had sound, speech, and a message, but none of these would be affected if he got up and walked away; individual watchers don't seem important. The class agreed not to count as a true speech situation one in which there is no role at all for the listener to play.

This process of examination and definition leaves students fatigued but delighted as they come to new understandings about the process of learning and discovery: "You can do this with anything! You just keep poking and pulling and trying out stuff until you've got it! I never knew that's possible!" They begin to see that their own experience situates them in a world that can be explored and studied, and they are astonished by how much they can discover about their lives (and the lives of their classmates) by examining the records they are keeping of the speaking and writing situations in which they find themselves. They see that some people live more private lives than others and that working engages them in a range of social inter-actions. They are surprised by the number of exchanges they have with strangers (for which one group of students invented the category "polite limited"). The power of their own data amazes them. "I really *like* looking at the charts," one young man said. "It's like a puzzle: 'How many things can you find in this picture?' The more I look, the more I see—I even like keeping the records now."

Students who keep track of their writing acts discover how frequently they use writing for practical daily activities; to make shopping lists, leave phone messages, write down directions. They are surprised to find that even though they almost always speak to someone else, they frequently write for themselves, "freely with no regard for a reader." One group of students made a distinction between "writing acts," which, like most speech acts, were intended to have an effect on others, and "personal writing events." Others have been surprised to discover the extent of their concern with the reader's response in such seemingly neutral acts as transmitting phone messages—that they may choose their words more carefully or leave different amounts of information for particular family members. One student noted that after doing this study, her note to a professor asking to be excused for a late paper took her almost as much time to compose as she had been accustomed to devoting to a paper itself.

Students also find that they themselves manipulate the ways they greet people or present ideas or tell stories, depending on the audience and the situation. Many students have been particularly interested to discover differences in the ways men and women use language. They generally don't anticipate such differences, agreeing, as one student asserted, that these might have been present "in the olden days, maybe, but not anymore." But as they observe speech behavior, differences emerge in their data.

Maya collected data on greetings in three settings—in a bar, in the cafeteria, and in her classrooms—and these data led her to emphasize the effect of "environment" (context) in her own data ("In the bar people were much less formal with each other and tended to kid around more than in the restaurant or the classroom"). But when she followed up the questions that emerged from these observations with library research, she discovered an article by a sociolinguist that focused on a related speech act, the compliment, and highlighted differences in the ways men and women see this act. Her reading led her to think about her own data in new ways, and she returned to her observations, this time focusing on compliments and noticing that "in social situations compliments seem more directed at appearance or personality, and in more restricted places they seem to be more on ability, such as at work." She also discovered gender differences in her original data on greetings, a difference she hadn't seen before; she found, for example, that many greetings initiated by men in the bar contained personal remarks that were received by women as too familiar, as crude passes rather than compliments ("Guy #2: 'Nice Sweater.' Girl #2: no response. Girl walks away disgusted"), while women most often initiated conversations with a less personal "How are you?"

Students like Maya take from their own research a wealth of concepts, including insights into the role of social context in determining the use people make of their language. These students begin to gain a firmly rooted sense of how much context influences the ways people use language and of the extent to which interpretation relies on contextual knowledge. As they discuss their data and question each other, students see increasingly that they need still more detail to support their preliminary interpretations, more knowledge of whole contexts than their preliminary data have provided. And so they turn their attention to the extended study of particular settings, where they can see in detail how language works for social uses, in social contexts.

Students also extend an understanding they began to develop from their study of spoken and written language when they realize that they command a repertoire of styles, even for any one type of speech act, which they intuitively draw on when they are in different situations. This further validates their own communicative competence in using various styles. They stop seeing some of their language

as simply "bad," "lower-class," or without value; they see rather that
they use the words and forms that will have the effect they want in
a particular context. By studying language in relation to social and
cultural rules, they develop objectivity about different styles, recognizing that they know and use an impressive number of sociolinguistic rules, that their own language behavior is rule-governed in ways
dictated by many interacting factors, and that they know a great deal
about how to interpret and use these factors in a dizzying array of
social situations.

Ethnography of Communication

Through their study of speech acts and writing acts students begin to
discover that people use language to let other people know how to
get places, to show that they are sorry for their actions, to get other
people to do things for them—to assert themselves and act on the
world in a variety of ways. They also see that to get things done
successfully with language everyone must use conventions other
people accept, and they come to understand that these conventions
are determined by community.

In settings like families or workplaces, where people come
together over long periods of time and develop particular ways of
using language to interact with one another, speech communities are
formed. Heath's ethnographic study provides a detailed picture of the
way in which all aspects of a community's life and values are
extended and reinforced in its members' linguistic behavior. The
anthropologist Dell Hymes (1972) describes the ethnographic study
of communication as one that conceives of communication "as a
value and a determinant in society and in personal lives." He sees it
as asking: "What are the communicative events, and their components, in a community? What are the relationships among them?
What capacities and states do they have, in general, and in particular
cases? How do they work?" (25). When students move from the
observation of specific speech acts to more general, ethnographic
observations of the way language is used in a particular context, they
begin to look for patterns in the communicative events that take place
in that context and the values these patterns suggest.

Our students begin their inquiry into varieties of language use
within a community by doing ethnographies of particular settings:
their kitchens, classrooms, a table in the school cafeteria. In one
typical sequence, students study their workplaces and then analyze
the relationships among the various staff members in terms of their
verbal and written exchanges. Antonio's description of his workplace

(in Chapter 2), where he found an "ill interest to work," was written in response to an early assignment more generally aimed at developing students' observational skills. But we have found that students who come to this task with the kinds of observational skills and the knowledge of linguistic behavior and social variables that develop from the research activities described above can approach such description in a new way. For them it is not just a rhetorical task but an interpretive activity in which they can bring together their study of multiple aspects of human behavior while learning still more about language and their own behavior as language users.

Ethnographic activities in the workplace might include:

- Constructing a map of the workplace in terms of who does what tasks and who speaks to whom in what form of speech act (such as command, request, question, excuse, report, suggestion, complaint, praise).

- Considering the written texts produced in the workplace in the same terms.

- Considering other cultural patterns—the ways that space and time are used, the varieties and possible effects of dress (such as uniforms, suits, aprons, overalls) and tools.

- Organizing work into categories in terms of variables like difficulty, interest, status, and desirability.

- Writing reports that examine the ways in which particular forms of language use in work situations reflect power and prestige relations, and the balances of rights, obligations, pressures, and rewards within the system.

In this particular setting, students have found that there are complicated relations between job difficulty and status, and that it is possible to get a sense of the status of some of the more ambiguous job categories by examining the sorts of verbal exchanges the worker is likely to have and the sorts of interactions that might be considered positive or negative. For example, one student saw the difference in status at his job (at Burger King) reflected in the fact that to the manager the worst thing that could happen was for a customer to get angry about something and leave the restaurant in a huff, while to him the worst thing that could happen was for the manager to see him doing something that was against the rules and reprimand him.

To help them pay attention to the kinds of precise details that go into an ethnography, students in one class were asked to imagine that they were writing a play about the workplace and to describe the cast of characters and how they would be costumed. Jamie, who worked as a hotel housekeeper, listed a hierarchy of directors (male), costumed in three-piece suits; managers and managing assistants (female), costumed in suits and dress shoes; and housekeepers (female), costumed in uniforms, aprons, and white nursing shoes. In ranking the jobs by difficulty, she found that the difficulty of the work at the top of the hierarchy was related to having broad areas of responsibility ("The hotel director is responsible for the whole upkeep of the hotel and must answer to the corporation"), while at the bottom the housekeepers' work was most physically strenuous. Asked to explain why each job might be interesting or boring, she wrote that the jobs that require thinking and decision making were interesting, while her own job, the housekeeper's job, was at the bottom of the list, "the most boring in the sense that all she has to do is clean the same types of rooms all day long." However, as Jamie began to study the verbal interactions at this workplace, a more complex pattern appeared. She started noticing who gave orders, who had to take orders, and who had "no say in anything at all." This confirmed her picture of her own job as having the lowest status. But as she observed these interactions over a longer period she came to rank jobs from desirable to undesirable based on who had to answer directly to the most people. Suddenly the middle-level jobs (house-keeping director, housekeeping manager) became least desirable, because the people who performed them were caught in the middle, "constantly balancing out the needs of the housekeepers and the department," and "always upsetting somebody." In this new ranking, even the job of hotel director got a middle placement. ("It's desirable in the sense that s/he makes a lot of money and has a lot of freedom and choice about decisions. At the same time, however, s/he must still answer to someone," while the hotel manager "also has to answer to guests.") Eventually, Jamie ranked her own job as most desirable "because I am alone with only one responsibility, and I don't have to answer to anyone until my work is done."

Studies like Jamie's, carried out in one setting over a period of time, allow students to discover new patterns and to see even very familiar places from new perspectives. Through such work they gain a complex understanding of the ways in which language, social behavior, and social context are intertwined.

An Integrated Research Cycle

Albert corresponded with Vivian, who was acting as an outside researcher, while he engaged in research in Suzy's freshman studies seminar. In his first letter to Vivian, he describes his research and reports on his initial observations:

I have learned a great many things from the reading in this course. Alot of which I took for granted. I never realized how many facets there are to language. From the Book Word Play by Peter Farb I learned how people use language as a tool, and how language is formed. I find it amazing how a person can store so many different rules that they put into use without realizing it. I have learned alot about ethnography, which is one subject I was unfamiliar with. I find it very interesting and useful in alot of ways. Language and how it is used in different situations and context, really gave me a new meaning about it. I find myself observing, in a way, what I hear people say and what words I choose to speak.

For a weeks time I recorded the different situations that I found myself in when communicating. I've noticed that I speak in a different manner to my managers at work than I do the employees. The main thing I have observed are people have to communicate. Without language we would not be able to function. I've also noticed how people respond. A person gives their opinion or adds to what the other person says. Or if not interested in a conversation they make a dead end statement.

I noticed that men and women communicate in different ways toward themselves or each other. Women when they talk among themselves seem to have an untranslatable language. I hear my sister talk to her girl friend and they seem to talk around things. When men are talking to women or vice versa its usually formal talk. When I'm talking with the guys we usually use alot of slang. Women seem to pronounce things differently than guys. Guys talk a little more sharp and women seem to talk a little more passive. I see that changing now in the 80's where we are becoming more equal.

I found the taping and transcribing exercise fun. I haven't made a tape yet but have transcribed one. I noticed that after writing down what I heard, I found it to loose something. I read it over and it just wasn't the same. Writing cant take the place of natural speech as far as giving a sense of character to it.

My conclusion to all this is that language is a very complex subject. There are many answers that need answering of how and why. I think they will find them as long as the research goes on.

In her response to Albert's letter, Vivian comments on his account of his readings and observations. She acknowledges the research he has undertaken, and asks him to go back to his data, to observe more, and to elaborate upon and add further support for his conclusions, much as she would react to a fellow researcher. In addition, she begins to introduce metalinguistic terms and use a level of academic register that models language appropriate for such discussions and demonstrates the seriousness with which she is considering Albert's work.

The work you are involved with in your freshman studies seminar certainly sounds intriguing, especially since it involves what we all do when we use language. You refer to your reading and how it helped you better understand language and ethnography. Can you give me some examples from the reading that demonstrate how language and culture interact?

I am also intrigued by your own ethnographic study of language use. (Did you realize that you are now an ethnographer?) You referred to the way your language changes according to the speech situation you are in, but you don't give me examples of what you have observed. What characterizes the kind of language you use with your managers and your employees? Why do you think the language shifts to accommodate each of these situations? What happens to the language when the topic of conversation changes? For example, what happens when you are discussing a topic that is not work-related? Your observations about responding behavior are very perceptive. What you have noticed is what researchers call "discourse analysis." Can you provide me with examples of your observations?

You provide more specific detail about men's and women's speech, but I'm not sure how much data your conclusions are based upon. How much data did you collect as men and women spoke? This is important since we can't really draw sound conclusions if our data are limited. What were they talking about and where were they speaking? Did context and topic seem to influence the way they spoke? You refer to the changes in the 80's. How has the language that men and women use changed during this decade? By the way, do your conclusions about men's speech apply to you?

The transcription exercise sounds like it was very revealing. I would like to hear more about what you found that the transcription lost. Was the tape complete in and of itself? Why was the written version less satisfying? Does this tell you anything about the differences between speaking and writing?

I've posed a lot of questions for you and certainly don't expect you to deal with all of them. But try to keep in mind that when you draw conclusions about your data, I need to know what these conclusions are based upon. I am looking forward to hearing more about your research and discoveries.

In response, Albert composed a letter that not only attempts to deal with the questions Vivian raised but illustrates his growing understanding of language and his newly discovered sense of the relationship between language and meaning. After discussing what he's found interesting about language and culture in the books he has been reading (*Word Play* by Peter Farb, and *The Ethnographic Interview* by James Spradley), and what he's been learning from the research he has done, he continues with what he has noticed from his own observations, and what he is learning from his own "discourse analysis."

From my own ethnographic study I did with the people I know and work with, I noticed differences in usage. In work we use two way radios. One day I went to a fashion show with one of my managers whom is female. [On the car radio we heard a driver] talking to another driver about how he hurt his foot. He was talking in alot of slang and four letter words. Well, my manager got a kick out of it, but if he knew she was listening I'm sure he would have had another choice for words. When I am chatting with the guys in the shipping room we talk in a rough humerous way. We would not speak to any of the ladies like that because, I guess, our society puts such an emphasis on, being a gentleman, and just our social codes in general.

In our factory most of the women are either Italian or Spanish and they have their own way of speaking english. Immediatly when I enter into their conversations they change into a different tone of voice and how they speak. I need more observations as to describe exactly how they change. . . .

My data on the language between men and women aren't high enough for myself to draw conclusions. The reading I have done has helped. When I talk about the changes in the 80's, I'm referring to the roles of men and women. Things are more open now and women are more recognized, not that they never were. We are more equal now. Guys talk to women more about personal things as do women. Things are more open. Still society plays a big part as to how we communicate. It depends on your values, and the relationship you have with the person you are speaking to. So I guess most of my conclusions about men's speech applies to myself.

He concludes: "I wish I could say more but I haven't quite grasped the words for it yet."

Vivian and Albert's correspondence continued through another cycle, and Albert continued to grasp more of the words for the things he was discovering about language and social context. His letters and those of his classmates show their engagement in this inquiry process and how that engagement provided them with an experience in using writing to make meaning, to learn that they have learned, an experience that represents what Freire calls "a pedagogy of knowing." Students' attempts in these letters to make meaning of their observations and experiences represent a form of inquiry that is sadly lacking in most approaches to the teaching of writing, in which writing is often used to close down a subject rather than open it up. The letters show the ways students in these courses became colleagues in a discourse community that was investigating language, co-inquirers interested in one another's findings and knowledge. This shift in the relationship between teacher and students—from one that places the teacher in opposition to the students to one that casts teacher and students as peers involved in collaborative work—leads students to appreciate their own powers of discovery and intensifies their capacity to use teachers' suggestions and questions. And the empowerment that results from their own inquiry and their own awareness that they are learning is reinforced by the realization that their own language use is subject to investigation and has value. This empowerment in turn leads to a willingness to further explore, to take risks, to speculate, and to reflect critically.

Outcomes: Writers and Researchers

Activities like these have important consequences for the writing classroom:

- Since language itself is the object of study, students are allowed to discover for themselves the principles that underlie writing.

- Since the activities are sequenced and related, they support the development of a coherent framework for the interpretation of experience.

- Since perceptions and interpretations are revised as each piece of work is seen in the light of the work that follows it, students gain a deepening understanding of the value of revision in general.

Among students who are continually collecting data and reporting on what they find we have observed a growing willingness to write regularly because they now realize that writing can be a means of gaining control over what they are saying—of imposing logic, coherence, and order to their ideas—and of eliminating the inconsistencies and confusions that arise as work goes forward over time and new data are introduced.

The work also supports certain types of thinking that students must begin to do in order to make this use of writing feasible. They get used to stepping back from their own ideas so that they can reflect on them and assess them as a painter steps back from a canvas to get a better sense of the overall piece. They get used to considering texts, both spoken and written, in terms of intention, execution, and effect, in terms of both speaker/writer and listener/reader. They see themselves as having certain notions and intentions that may not be accurately reflected in the texts they produce, and at that point they can reach out to their peers and teachers for specific, practical instruction in the strategies they see themselves as needing. They begin to ask questions like "How do you show that the next phrase you're going to write is a sort of different opinion than the one you just said, that it's somebody else's point of view and you want to set it out and knock it down? Is there a word? An expression?" The conventional forms of academic discourse now appear in students' writing because they have particular functions that help the students do the jobs they've come to realize they want to do.

At the same time, students who have engaged in these projects come to have an understanding of what it means to do research that is quite different from the picture they get from the more common freshman research paper assignments. The first page of a widely used guide, *Writing Research Papers* (Weidenborner and Caruso, 1990), contains the following comment:

> As you think about writing a research paper, you may wonder how this assignment differs from other kinds of papers you have written. The fundamental difference is that most of the information that goes into a research paper comes from materials found in a library. Research papers do not grow out of your personal experiences to the same extent that other compositions do.

The guide takes students through the steps of the "research process": (1) "searching for a topic and for sources"; (2) "reading sources and reaching conclusions"; and (3) "writing the paper." Research is portrayed as different from the other writing and learning students do, as separate from students' personal experience of the world. It is a linear process with separate and distinct tasks, which reinforces the idea that writing is a matter of displaying what is already known rather than a means of coming to know. And it is envisioned as a solitary process in which students find their own topics and read about them alone in the library, apart from the classroom, from other students, and from the rest of their lives.

Students who have been doing the kinds of projects we have been describing come away with quite a different picture of the research process. They have moved through many sequenced and related activities, discovering questions of interest from their own observations and experiences and working within a coherent framework provided by the course and shared by other students, who have been gathering related data, pooling that data, and sharing questions about methodology. They have reflected on their own questions, problems, and discoveries throughout that process, and the structure of activities has led them to rethink their earlier discoveries and understandings, to view research, like all writing, as a recursive process. As we have found, "reading sources" and library research play complementary roles in this process, but such work follows from students' questions and their evolving body of data, so that the "sources" found in the library are read in relation to a developing framework of understanding. For her final research paper on language, Maya describes her process this way:

> In my preparation for writing this paper I have looked at three very different aspects of language and have tried to find out how they relate to the rules of language. I looked at greetings, compliments, and confrontations. After looking at those examples I found that there are two factors that affect the dialogues that I observed. They are gender and environment.
>
> I got my data for this paper in three ways. The first step was to collect greetings that I heard in a number of different places, chart them, and then draw conclusions about them. We then compared our data and compared what we found with Farb's [from *Word Play*]. The next step was to go to the library and find articles dealing with aspects of language we were interested in. Finally, I looked at my data again to see if I could find evidence that connected with what I read.

Maya moves back and forth, discussing her own data and what she got from her reading of Farb and the articles she found on language in social context. To her early hypothesis that context or "environment" is a key factor in determining the forms of the greetings she has recorded, she now adds a question about gender and sex roles, as her reading leads her to think about her own data in new ways. From this new perspective, Maya looks again at other course readings as well, asking new questions. Of Doris Lessing's story "The Old Chief Mshlanga," which turns on an exchange of greetings between a young white girl and an African chief, she asks, "If the young girl in Lessing's story was a boy, would he have behaved differently?" Of an exchange Farb recounts between a black Harvard psychologist and a white southern policeman, she asks: "If the conflict between Dr. Pouissant took place in Harlem would the doctor have been intimidated?" In the end, she reports,"it was astonishing to take seemingly unrelated language situations and find them all shaped by two common features like gender and environment."

Students also comment on the limitations of their observations, as Albert does in response to a question from Vivian: "My data on the language between men and women aren't high enough for myself to draw conclusions." But he too goes on to reflect on the reading he has done and how it has helped him to understand what he is finding. Students like Maya and Albert can comment from their own experiences on the problems they face as researchers, on the ways in which their assumptions influence their collection and interpretation of data, and on the ways in which the discussions they've had and the readings they've done have given them new perspectives on that data. The data have allowed them to approach their readings with firsthand knowledge and a critical perspective.

Students like these no longer need, in Bartholomae's terms, to "invent the university." Through their own participation and their own research, they have begun to discover what this community is about and that its discourse is both continuous with and different from that of the other communities they spend time in. They have begun participating actively in their new community as they use its practices, its methods of inquiry, to explore both what they know and what they want to know. In this process they also contribute to the invention of a *new* university, one that's been somewhat transformed by their presence and activity.

Chapter Seven

Extending Competence
The Language of Literature

Studies of speech acts and ethnographies of communication in settings such as the workplace focus, to a large degree, on the ways in which people use language to act on the world and place themselves in it. But as students begin to record the conversations that take place in these settings they find that people also use language for reflection, for exploring and passing on the meanings they find in the events of their lives, for framing those events and meanings so that they'll be remembered and retold—for telling stories. In fact, a large portion of the data gathered in conversations is narrative, and these narratives are often repeated, told at other gatherings, sometimes with different listeners and sometimes with different tellers. In the process, their meanings are probed and reshaped with each telling, until the original informal narrative account becomes a story, expressing something essential about the group's values.

"A Tether Ball Tragedy," for example, is told frequently in Shawn's family, though not with the exaggeration of "tragic" elements that made Shawn's telling of the story for the class so humorous. When Shawn collects the versions of the story told by other family members, asking them about the occasions on which they usually tell it and what they think the point of the story is, he finds that the members of his family use the story in different contexts to make particular points: his younger brother tells it to friends to show his courage; his mother tells it sometimes at her workplace, a hospital, to show how important it is to be "vigilant about accidents when children are around." But the story is told often within the family, and Shawn sees it as "bringing the family closer together simply by reciting the events" and "reminding us again of a traumatic time when we all pulled together." Shawn's story, then, expresses and reaffirms his family's values.

Shawn also finds that this story is most likely to be told on special occasions, when the family is gathered to celebrate holidays and birthdays. Telling the story becomes part of the ritual at such events, and the story itself is told in repeated and ritualized ways. Like the tellers of such stories in most communities, those who tell the story in Shawn's family draw on familiar patterns of storytelling that show that this account is a special event and deserves particular attention for the meanings it offers. Such patterns—the building of tension as Shawn's father races first to the yard, then to the neighbor's house, and finally to the hospital, the interplay between the father's panic and the young brother's calm—become repeated and formalized. It is through the repetition of patterns like these that, over time, more formal genres, whether oral ones like ballads or epic poems or the written ones that we now call poetry or fiction, are created within a culture. In most communities, then, the forms and uses of language that we associate with formal literature will be found in informal, personal contexts.

Although they are interwoven in our lives in natural discourse communities, these uses of language are typically separated in college classrooms, where courses are divided into writing expository prose (with a personal narrative or two thrown in at the beginning) and reading the literature written by famous authors (with the option of a separate course in creative writing). In his studies of the teaching of writing in British schools, James Britton (1982) found that students had little opportunity to connect the sort of reflective language so common in speaking with the writing they did in their classrooms. In response, he framed a new conceptualization of the nature and functions of writing that would see it as continuous with all other language use. Britton argues that throughout their lives people play two roles, roles in which language has different functions and therefore demands different modes of discourse. The *participant* tries to get things done in the world using *transactional discourse,* while the *spectator* evaluates or comments on actions or experiences using most often what Britton terms *poetic discourse*—language that provides formal expression of the meaning of events as well as pleasure in the telling. Both the transactional and poetic functions of language, Britton believes, begin with the speaker's attempt to express and characterize ideas in tentative, associative, emotional ways, in *expressive discourse*—the discourse of our private journals, of our exploratory conversations with ourselves and others.

The role of spectator allows speakers to think about the acts and events they've been involved in and to evaluate them in order to figure out what they mean from various perspectives.

> The process of creating our world is continuous in our waking hours and we interpret experience without being aware that we are doing so: we act, that is, upon assumptions without ever being aware that we have made them. But the process is intensified whenever we stand back and work over past experiences, whether in conversation, in writing, in acting, or in painting, or in any other way. In doing these things we discover meaning. (14)

Writing facilitates this process of thinking and making sense of the world and of communicating that sense to others. It gives writers an opportunity to transcend the immediacy and everydayness of experience, see that experience from new perspectives, and discover general patterns. In this way Alison comes to reconceive her responses to her mother's illness in terms of her own growing maturity. When Alison recounts the story of "when my mother got sick," she is not only conveying information to inform a reader about an event, she is reflecting on the meaning of the event to her as "one of the first and most frightening things I remember as a child." The language of reflection runs throughout her narrative as Alison thinks about the events and thinks about her thinking about the events: "I just thought," "What did I know," "I was very confused." Writing also makes it easier for Alison to compare her responses to two similar events later and to reflect on her own thinking about them: "I have matured and can look at things like this much clearer."

Implicit in storytelling, or in any use of the language of the spectator, is the understanding that any event has many possible interpretations, that stories bear retelling because each telling is a new event, allowing the possibility of new understandings and interpretations. Embedded in the account of any sequence of events is the possibility of others that could have or—from the teller's view—even *should* have happened. As we get older we become increasingly aware of the possibility of multiple realities: of alternatives to any one way of seeing a course of events, a set of responses, or a sequence of actions in the world around us. Shawn's brother's picture of his heroic courage and his mother's of her family's lack of vigilance can be extended into sagas quite different from the one about the tether-ball accident. The characteristics of adult cognition we discussed in Chapter 3 include the ability not only to think consistently and logically in relation to the concrete reality of the world before us, but also to construct alternative realities imaginatively, to hypothesize models (in Bruner's terms "possible worlds") and move through them in our minds metaphorically as well as logically. All of our poetic discourse—our stories and our literature—suggests such alternative realities and thus extends our range of experience and our capacity to think about that experience.

Some of the time people reflect alone on the events of their lives and on the possible stories these events tell. But much of our interaction with others involves narratives that work toward the development of shared meanings. William Labov's research shows that conversations are full of narrative accounts of events in which the teller tries to recreate the event and negotiate a shared sense of what the meaning or significance of the event might be, just as Alison's use of the term "matured" in her final account of her mother's illness comes out of the building of shared meanings through a semester of such conversation—of telling and reading and retelling many stories in a classroom community. Britton suggests that gossip, too, is an oral form of spectator language, affirming between speaker and listener shared attitudes to events that are often already known. Heath's accounts, in *Ways with Words,* of conversations on the front porches of Trackton or in the kitchens of Roadville show how such gossip and storytelling reinforce the norms and values of a community while creating a social connection among its members and building a shared pleasure in the shape or cleverness of the telling. As these informal exchanges are repeated and embedded in the community culture, they gradually take on more formal characteristics—those we associate with literature.

Britton uses the concept of the spectator to break down what he sees as a false separation of literature from the texts produced by ordinary speakers and writers. "Whenever we play the role of spectator of human affairs, I suggest we are in the position of literature" (49). Whoever creates it, literature is distinguished from other uses of language in that it comments in a relatively conscious way on human affairs. The student storytellers and writers whose texts we looked at earlier—Alison beginning her first account of her mother's illness with "One of the first and most frightening things I remember," Antonio beginning a description of his workplace by describing "the ill interest to work," Shawn figuring out how he can make his story humorous both in telling and in writing—are making choices about form, about whether the narrative will be in the first or third person, about whether it will begin in the middle of events or with an overview, and are thus involved in an essentially literary endeavor.

As children acquire the language and uses of language common to their families and communities, they acquire, embedded in all of those uses, but particularly in the spectator forms of language—

the gossip and stories of front porches or back rooms—the cultural meanings of their community. Studies of narrative in different communities show this relationship between narrative forms or styles and community values—that while we all command a range of styles of language use, these styles are determined in part by those of the discourse communities in which we interact. The Scollons' work on narrative and literacy among the Athabaskans shows how narrative discourse style is interwoven with other aspects of a culture: for example, Athabaskan narrative stresses audience interaction over content, building on a rich store of common associations that "interrupt" the strictly linear progression of the narrative while reinforcing the cultural importance of shared knowledge and experience. Heath finds that in Roadville and Trackton, too, the ways stories are told reflect both community discourse conventions and community values: for Roadville residents, stories must be factual accounts, elicited by someone else, of events in which the teller participated and must present a moral, a comment on individual behavior in reference to community standards; in Trackton, "true stories" are stories that although based on a real event, fictionalize that event, turning it into a fantasy in which the teller overcomes the real-world odds and emerges clever and victorious. Finally, Tannen's accounts of dinner-table narratives show in detail how narrative takes shape within a particular conversational interaction and how it is shaped by the cultural patterns of different groups within a literate society.

As our students study how language works in the world around them, then, the aspects of language that Britton calls "poetic discourse" emerge. And as a complement to the sorts of research activities described in Chapter 6, we have also, in different ways in different courses, extended students' study of language to focus on narrative in conversation and in literature, reconnecting parts of the curriculum that have typically been divided. By studying how they and those around them use reflective, poetic discourse, students can discover how we make meaning from our experiences, both individually and culturally, and begin to explore the part of the linguistic repertoire we draw on as readers and writers who are engaged in such reflection and meaning making. Such study supports the sorts of learning we have been describing in the following ways:

- It connects, again, what students know with what they learn in our classrooms—the stories they tell in their daily lives with the literature they will read and write—allowing them to discover the shapes and meanings and purposes of different tellings, to make explicit what they know about form, and to explore the forms of the literature and the complex expository texts they will read and write from that base.

- It increases their opportunity to see the continuum of spoken and written language, to see the ways in which writing may extend and facilitate their meaning making and the ways in which reading likewise involves their active involvement in reflection and meaning making.

- It deepens and enriches a multicultural curriculum, moving beyond current attempts to create such a curriculum through students' reading of literature drawn from different cultural traditions by bringing the literature being created daily in students' homes and communities into the classroom.

- It supports the students' development of both interpretive and figurative ways of thinking and using language.

Work that links the ethnographic study of storytelling in students' communities with the study of narrative literature makes connections that are important to the English curriculum and to the development of readers and writers at all levels. It helps students see themselves as tellers and interpreters of the world around them, as active readers of that world as well as active readers of texts. It allows them to become aware of how their own stories and ethnographic studies bring out the meanings of a particular cultural context that has commonalities as well as differences with other cultural contexts, representing aspects of a common human experience. Through such study a class actively gathers and creates both the materials and the interpretations that will provide a basis for much of the work across the college curriculum.

Stories in Context: Collecting Narratives

While students in Shawn's class completed the set of research exercises described in Chapter 6, in which they studied the differences between the spoken and the later written versions of a story they told to the class on the first day, they also worked on an intermingled set of assignments that asked them to look at these stories from other perspectives. Some of these assignments focused their attention on the context in which the story was typically told. Students were asked to describe the circumstances that tended to give rise to the story; to elicit other tellings by other participants; and to look at differences in the story components that were included or emphasized by different family members, in what the point of the story seemed to be, and in how that point was brought out—differences in point of view of the sort that Shawn discovered. Other activities focused their attention on the class stories as a set, asking students to find patterns in themes and in ways of telling, to group the stories and organize them for a short story collection, and to reflect on their own reading of other stories in the collection. Not surprisingly, in Shawn's first grouping of his classmates' stories he focused on their humor, speculating, "I wonder if people tend to remember the good times more than the bad. Or maybe they weren't so funny when this happened, but as time goes by the bad parts become less relevant and the more important aspect of feeling that they are a significant part of the group takes over." He concludes:

> People want to feel that they belong to something, that they are a "significant" part of a group. By telling these stories over and over again, everybody can have their own "heritage" and reinforce a feeling of who they are and where they came from.

We extended this ethnographic research into other parts of the English curriculum, beginning first with an upper-level course on language and literature that Ellie was teaching. The things we discovered from the research done by students in that course helped us see our work with freshmen in new ways. We would like to look at the discoveries, made by two of these students, that helped us see more clearly how students can find "their own heritage" and bring that heritage into the classroom in ways that foster important understandings about language and literature in a multicultural society.

Kathleen and Ruth began their research by exploring the ways stories are told in their own families and communities. Like the freshman courses, the language and literature course opened with stories students told to their classmates, followed by several data gathering assignments and related readings (Heath, the Scollons, Labov, Tannen). One part of the assignment required the collection of ethnographic data about the use of narrative in conversation among family and friends. It was framed as follows:

> An ethnography is a description of a culture, an effort to understand the vision of the world held by a member of that culture and the ways in which all aspects of the culture—its marriage patterns, its art, its stories—both derive from and contribute to that vision. The ethnographer of language focuses on the role of language in the culture, not simply on what is said or written, but on when, why, how, to whom it is said or written, and even on what does not have to be put into language but is assumed as common knowledge among the members of a group.
>
>   For an ethnographic study of narrative in your family or community, you will record not only actual narratives told by members

of the group, but also (1) when a story was told (a description of the setting, both the larger context and the immediate situation, including who was present); (2) why the story was told (to illustrate a point in a discussion, to entertain a child, in response to a request; there are also more complex and less obvious reasons for telling stories, which will emerge from your later interpretation of your data); (3) how the story was told (matter-of-factly with little change in voice or gesture from the rest of what was said, with a pause to indicate the start of something different, or with dramatic shifts in tone of voice or gestures—like a "storyteller").

For the purpose of collecting this data we will define narrative as any recounting of something that has happened (or is presented as having happened, whether or not it is historically true). The recounting may be in the past tense, "I went to the store," or in the present, "So I go into the store, see, and she says. . . ."

Students collected data in three ways: by carrying a notebook and making field notes of any narration they heard; by taping the conversation at a gathering, such as a family dinner, transcribing the narrative portions, and noting the contextual details; and by eliciting and taping the telling of familiar stories by family members or friends to gatherings of the rest of the group. As they began to study their data, striking patterns of form, style, and purpose began to emerge in each context.

The studies done by Kathleen and Ruth show a great deal about how a group's discourse practices help to shape and transmit family and cultural heritage.

Kathleen's Research:
Formal Discourse and Cultural Tradition

Kathleen collected a set of family stories about life in the old country (Ireland), in which her grandfather was the central, almost legendary figure. Stories in Kathleen's family were told by a few traditional tellers—her mother and aunts—to listeners—herself and her cousins—who always played the role of audience. Sitting at the dinner table one night, Kathleen's mother told this story:

> They used to go around house-to-house begging. There were these old guys who wound up in the workhouse. Not tinkers, you know. Ordinary people. They wound up in the workhouse—this guy probably came from—the nearest I can think of is the county home in Killarney. Or he slept on the side of the road.
>
> This old man—he was a beggar, anyway. He was sitting east the gate. And he came to the house, begging. And he was a very old man—maybe he was about seventy—he was bent over. . . .

And he asked Grandpa for food. He was barefoot. And Grandpa felt sorry for him because he was barefoot. And he gave him an old pair of shoes of his. But they had holes in them and everything. Grandpa had his Sunday shoes, and other work shoes. But these shoes were special shoes that he had made for the farm. They had like oilcloth—leather, like water didn't soak through and they kept out the cold. They were specially made. He had them made in Sneem by Mr. Golden. And they had hobnails.

The shoes he was replacing he gave to this old beggar, but then he was sorry for giving him the old shoes, so he decided to give him the new shoes, he felt so much sympathy for this poor old guy. He gave him his new shoes.

The old guy prayed and blessed him, he was so pleased. He couldn't believe that he got a pair of new shoes. He prayed that God would bless him and that he may live a long time. And he went off, blessing him and thanking him.

Kathleen wrote her own version of the story for a class collection:

Grandpa and the New Shoes

In old Ireland, shoes, especially new shoes, were a possession not taken for granted. Shoes were a blessing and a source of pride, like home itself.

But back when my grandfather was a young man, both shoes and the security of home were hard to come by. Landlordism held the reins of power, and many common farm folk lost their land and their homes because they couldn't pay their rich landlords. These homeless people became roadside beggars where their ancestors had lived for years; their once proud cottages became silent shells where cattle wandered in and out.

Grandpa managed to hold onto the Sheehan land, and had saved enough money to have a new pair of work shoes made. He walked over the mountain behind the farm, into the village cobbler, and picked up the prized pair of shoes to bring home. He showed them to all at the house that evening, delighted.

A very old, scruffy beggar came to the door. His clothes were torn—no match for the gales and the rain of Ireland—and he had bare feet. Grandpa let him in and Grandma poured hot tea for him, and the children watched curiously. Grandpa went and fetched his old pair of work shoes, which were not good for the farmwork anymore because they were ragged and had holes in them. He decided to give them to the old beggar as he was leaving the gate.

The old man was overcome with joy, and his eyes sparkled happily as he tied the laces slowly, savoring the feel of shoes on his feet as he stood up.

As he watched the sheer delight the old beggar had in the worn shoes with the holes in them, something stirred Grandpa. He turned back to the house, took out the parcel with his brand new shoes in it, and returned to the beggar, who was walking down the dirt road. He gave his new shoes to the old man, and kept his torn, worn-out ones.

The children asked him about it, and he just said he felt glorious about giving them to the beggar.

NB. The beggar blessed him and wished him a long life. Grandpa lived to be more than seventy.

In her analysis of these two versions of the story, Kathleen discovered many of the features of spoken and written language we discussed in Chapter 6. But because she was comparing a story told within the family with one written for the class, she also discovered a lot about her family's shared culture, or what she calls "assumed common knowledge." For example, she contrasts the statement in her written version that "landlordism held the reins of power, and many common farm folk lost their land and their homes because they couldn't pay their rich landlords" with her mother's informal account to the family, where all that's needed is a quick abstract: "Not tinkers, you know. Ordinary people." But what's shared in the family goes beyond such background knowledge to include particular uses of language. Kathleen goes on:

> Now any other audience would have trouble understanding the spatial relationship here. . . . "East the gate" does not mean east of the gate; it means east at the gate. Also, why is "east" included at all? It is there because it is formulaic in Irish discourse to refer to places in terms of North, West, South, and East; even if it's just rooms of a house. Therefore, formulaic language is always included and is a large part of the ethnicity and color of the informal narratives, whereas it must be omitted from the formal telling, because of the semantic cultural background needed to understand it.

Here Kathleen is drawing upon her insider knowledge as a member of a group to explicate the language patterns that appear in her family's stories. She uncovers the shared cultural bases that determine the linguistic choices a teller from her family will make in a particular situation. Kathleen is an expert on the material she presents to the class, and her discussion is full of observations of stylistic detail that draw upon that knowledge.

Kathleen decides that differences between spoken and written language are less important than those between the teller and the audience and whether this relationship is a familiar one among people who share cultural knowledge or an unfamiliar "formal" one, where the teller may not know, specifically, what the audience knows.

> There always seems to be a theoretical "audience" everybody treats the same way when they think of "formal written" narrative. But when you consider the forms of discourse as they're told, you learn that *how, why, when,* and *to whom* matter as much as *what.*

Kathleen went on to discover more about the cultural knowledge shared within her family. She collected twenty stories—stories that are known by all family members and retold frequently. The stories are passed on from one generation to the next, and it is the older family members, like Kathleen's mother, who hold the rights to tell these traditional stories at family gatherings. All the stories take place in Ireland, and virtually all recount the grandfather's exploits. Many highlight aspects of life in the old country (for example, for social contact her grandfather would have to row twenty miles across a bay to a *ceili*). But they also show his virtue and strength of character. All the stories are fairly formal in that they adhere to traditional forms and are told, complete, by one teller. Kathleen and her siblings and cousins are the audience for these stories, learning traditional cultural values and meanings that they will pass on as they, in turn, tell them to a new generation. These traditional stories form the background against which present life is lived.

Ruth's Research:
Collaborative Storytelling and Shared Meaning

Ruth began her research by keeping a notebook of daily observations of conversational narrative and found that her family too had a familiar and repeated set of stories. But in her family, unlike Kathleen's, these stories focused on events in which she and her siblings and parents had participated, and they participated likewise in the telling. When Ruth taped a family dinner conversation during which a series of familiar family stories were told, she found that her family's stories, known to all present, were constructed in common by the interjections of several family members into the main teller's version. Ruth sees this collaborative development of shared meaning in the story of the cat named Lollipop.

Mom: Tell the story about when he killed that cat.

Dad: Tell the story.

Laura [Ruth's sister]: When we were little we had a dog . . .

Dad: Jeff had a dog.

Laura: Jeff had a dog, and the dog . . .

Dad: And Mrs. Tillingast had a cat.

Mom: An old black cat—we *hated* it—it used to *always mess* in our back hall. *(Laughter)*

Dad: So one day Jeff came over with his dog . . . and the dog got to chasing the cat . . .

Mom: And the cat died of a heart attack. *(Uproarious laughter)*

Dad: Yeah.

Laura: *(Laughing so hard that it's difficult for her to tell the story)* It was so sad though. Me and Jeff were sitting there out in the woods, you know, we must have been vicious kids or something like that, but we—we just loved seeing this dog attack the cat—it would attack it—it would try to run up the—run up the tree—but by the—right at the tree, and then it couldn't—it didn't have enough time to get up so the dog would *drag* it down again— *(Laughter)*—try to run up the tree again—and the dog would *drag* it down again—and before you know it, you know Jeff and I are poking the cat with a stick—you know—'cause it was—she was—dead—*(Uproarious laughter)*— and we didn't know what to do. Mrs. Tillingast comes up to us a few days later—she—"Have you seen Lollipop?"—*(Laughs so hard she cries)*—and Jeff says "No!"—It's in the woods with its eyes open.

Dad: You went back to look at it?

Laura: *(Still laughing)* Yeah.

Dad: The eyes were still open?

Laura: We didn't even have the decency to bury it—we just let it kind of decompose there . . .

Mom: I think Mrs. Tillingast *did* bury it after she found it.

Dad: She did?

Ruth: She found it?

Laura: That's sad . . . oh—my God—you didn't tell us? You were afraid to tell us?

Ruth says of this story:

> The Lollipop Story . . . is told by Laura, but begins with an abstract from my mother which encapsulates the story—"he killed that cat." The story then proceeds into an orientation aided by my mother and father, who, in the Roadville tradition, make sure the story is structured and factual. My Father corrects Laura's "we had a dog" to "Jeff had a dog," and completes the list of characters by adding Mrs. Tillingast and her cat. My mother then interjects a description and an explicit external evaluation of the cat. She comes right out and tells us that "we hated it" and why. This provides meaning for the story. Laura then continues her narrative, only to be interrupted by another abstractive statement from my mother—"And the cat died of a heart attack." Amidst uproarious laughter which she was a part of, Laura provides a piece of external evaluation when she says, "It was so sad though. . . ." This statement from the present reveals

mixed emotions from Laura, which are not explicit in the narrative, but embedded in the evaluation surrounding it.

Ruth continues her discussion of the telling of the story, finally pointing out the tension between the family's reception of this story as a familiar humorous tale about an annoying cat that met its just desserts, and her sister Laura's guilt over allowing the dog to chase and kill the cat and over not burying the cat afterwards.

Seeing each story in the series in the larger context of the family's communication, Ruth discovers that while she had expected the stories to be told primarily for entertainment, they in fact provided "assurance that we all make the same mistakes," an assurance reinforced by how the stories are sequenced in conversation. Her mother follows Laura's story with another story about a cat who died, this one in a kennel where it was placed at the mother's suggestion.

> The Butterscotch story immediately followed Lollipop, and served two purposes. First, my mother felt guilty about her suggestion to put the cat in the kennel, which she believed killed it. Our laughter and my father's comment, "It's a little far fetched," perhaps eliminated my mother's perception that the cat was mad at her. Secondly, as a response to the Lollipop story, it told Laura that she was not the only person who perceived herself as being cruel to an animal.

Ruth concludes:

> In my family, sharing stories in an environment of acceptance and humor is a way of dealing with mistakes, guilt or disturbing issues. . . . The emergence of patterns in the telling and response to stories amazed me. In examining these patterns, I have concluded that my family has deep rooted feelings of love and caring for one another, which has allowed these patterns to emerge.

The events of Ruth's family life are retold and reexamined collaboratively. As in Kathleen's family, these stories assert a common sense of values and meanings—a shared understanding. But unlike the practice in Kathleen's family, the meanings are renegotiated with each telling, not only within the stories themselves but through their placement in a larger sequence. Shared meaning is constructed more than it is passed on.

Studies like Kathleen's and Ruth's were carried out, in this particular class, by thirty-three other students who collected data in their homes, their workplaces, their churches, at daycare centers, restaurants, hospitals, community sports programs, and Al-Anon meetings. The patterns they discovered, the features that emerged, affirm both commonality and diversity in the ways that we tell stories to make sense of our lives, to create shared knowledge and affirm shared values, to dissent from those values, to structure and give meaning to our experience. The narrative styles of Kathleen's family, whose stories come from the old country and whose values and rights are passed on from older to younger generations, and Ruth's, where children are likely to tell the stories and where meanings are examined and renegotiated collaboratively with each telling, with all the differences of language and form that these different patterns imply, are but two models of many that emerge from such research. For students who work together on making sense of their data, on analyzing the texts they have collected and considering the contexts in which they have collected them, a picture of the rich resources of language and the rich variety of human forms and cultures emerges, as well as an expanded sense of their own possibilities as readers and writers. As Kathleen put it: "Analyzing my own family stories helped me to see a clear line of progression from my family's simpler communication to deep literature."

Tellers and Listeners: Writers and Readers

As students discover the ways in which "literature" comes to be created in their own families and communities, they see their own active role, even as listeners, in shaping its forms and its meanings. This understanding leads to another, that just as speaking cannot be separated from listening, writing cannot be separated from reading. Readers, like writers, are actively involved in creating meaning from texts, just as they create meaning from all of life's experiences. Reading, like writing, is an inventive, constructive activity.

Ruth's research makes it particularly clear that in ordinary conversations the boundaries between teller and listener are often quite fluid and turns pass back and forth as each participant builds on what has gone before. Like the listeners at Ruth's family dinner table, the reader too is active, making connections with and building on the words on the page, as Frank Smith's (1988) research into the reading process shows us. Recent reader-based theories of literature, in contrast to earlier text-based theories, also build on an understanding of the reader's active role. Students' research allows them to see that the communicative act of reading written texts, like listening to spoken ones, depends on the continuous building of shared knowledge between reader and writer, that the reading and writing people do in the real world is almost always related to contexts they know or have expectations about, as are the stories they tell and hear. Each literacy event involves a transaction between reader and writer, just as each conversational exchange involves a transaction between speaker and listener. Active conversation, with its turn taking and questioning and its use of "you know," makes this transaction explicit.

Some communities make the reading/writing event itself collaborative, part of a larger conversation. Heath found in Trackton, for example, that letters and newspapers were most likely to be read out loud, with a group of listeners discussing them and speculating on their meaning and, if necessary, composing a response. Readers in Roadville embedded the reading they valued most—reading from the Bible—in talk as well as in Bible study groups, using lessons from such readings as codas for their accounts of their own life experiences. Increasingly, as more is understood about how learners acquire new discourse, the academic community too is starting to treat reading and writing not as solitary acts but as collaborative ones in just these ways. The research done by Kathleen and Ruth highlights two other issues that have affected the teaching of writing. One is that writing has been seen as wholly different from spoken language, existing outside the particular contexts of and requiring different strategies from those we use in conversation. As a consequence, the forms of written discourse, whether expository models or genres of literature, are seen as absolutes, not as arising out of particular acts of communication in particular settings. Kathleen's research shows that the forms of a narrative are determined by context, that the formal aspects of the story her mother tells, like the one Kathleen writes, are not inherent in the writing and the telling but emerge from the reinventing of a tradition in ways appropriate to the occasion for which they are told or written.

Part of what Kathleen discovers—the different ways a teller might tell a story for different audiences and respond to a need for "common assumed knowledge"—is linked to a second issue, one that has surfaced in current literacy debates with E. D. Hirsch's (1987) assertion that students lack the "cultural literacy" they need to read complex texts and that the way to give them this cultural literacy is to have them memorize lists of facts and definitions that are part of what Hirsch would define as the "common culture." Hirsch's common culture is extremely restricted, leaving out much of the cultural experience of people in the United States, and his picture of how a culture is acquired is equally limited. Both Kathleen and Ruth have explored how shared knowledge is created and maintained as a social act within a community, whether this is done in talk or in writing, and the research they have done makes it clear, once again, that in order for readers and writers, like all language users, to share the common culture of a community, they must be active participants in that community, sharing in its enterprises and its systems of understanding.

The data sharing and interpretation that our students have been engaged in as part of their ethnographic research builds new frameworks that carry over into all of their reading and writing. Freshmen who have done research into speech acts construct knowledge that allows them not only to understand relevant portions of Farb's *Word Play,* but to begin to make sense of journal articles on sociolinguistics. And students who have been collecting and studying narratives in their families and communities are prepared to approach literature in new ways, with new understandings.

In their introduction to *Ways of Reading,* David Bartholomae and Anthony Petrosky give an example of the sort of reading they hope to encourage in their students, a combination of reading, thinking, and writing they call "strong reading." They select the passage from Richard Rodriguez's book *Hunger of Memory* in which he talks about his reading of a book by Richard Hoggart, *The Uses of Literacy,* focusing on the description of the scholarship boy and how this concept allowed Rodriguez to "frame the meaning of my academic success."

> Hoggart provided a frame, a way for Rodriguez to think and talk about his own history as a student. As he goes on in his essay, Rodriguez not only uses this frame to talk about his experience, but he resists it, argues with it. He casts his experience in Hoggart's terms but then makes those terms work for him by seeing both what they can and cannot do. (3)

"Strong reading," in these terms, asks the reader to engage in conversation with the text, to bring to it their own arguments even as they work to understand its terms. We, too, hope to support our students in doing such reading, and we find that students who have been carrying out the sort of research into language and community we have been describing are ready to engage with their reading in this way. Some of this strong, active reading grows out of the questions students have been asking and the answers they have been finding, and some may derive directly from the feelings of personal competence, engagement, and responsibility that result from their having done that work.

Students who have studied greetings, for example, have a new basis for understanding why Farb describes an encounter between a black psychologist and a southern policeman who insists on addressing him as "boy" as a clash between the rules of two speech communities. And they understand the ways in which power relationships are encoded in the exchange of greetings between a young girl and a chief, the incident at the center of Doris Lessing's short story "The Old Chief Mshlanga." But they are also prepared to disagree with the interpretations of these events that come out of only one frame of reference, as Larry (one of Shawn's and Maya's classmates) questions the limitations of the linguistic framework that has shaped the work of the course. Writing of the Farb and Lessing incidents, Larry argues that looking at language alone is not enough.

> Both Caucasians in the aforementioned incidents were armed with lethal weapons and had the backing of their respective governments. These particular conversations had their basis in the country's time period, in the moral and social attitudes of the time. They have more sociological and ethical value and present many other issues besides a simple exercise in word play. The bigger social and moral issues leave the language game only a small part in this play.

Larry's class went on to read Toni Morrison's *Sula,* which echos other features of the language they had been studying in their own communities. The style shifting that Sula does when she comes back to the town of Medallion, bringing new ways of seeing life there and using new words like "aesthetic" and "rapport," is striking to students like Larry, who have studied their own shifts in style, the changes in their own language as they move among their homes and workplaces and college classrooms. As Larry discovers, new words bring more than a linguistic difference; they are linked to new knowledge and new ways of understanding.

Larry himself is a clever storyteller whose stories are most often humorous. In his initial contribution to the class collection he describes a weekend of "dust and drudgery" cleaning out his parents' basement and thinking he wouldn't survive, when the Grim Reaper appeared, said "Fudge it. I can't take the dust," and left sneezing. Over the semester, as Larry studies the stories other students contribute, he sees the different ways in which his classmates deal not only with life's small defeats, but with its larger ones. He finds many that focus on tragedies, on the sorts of things he "chooses to forget, not to write about," and he sees that in his own writing he passes difficult subjects off lightly rather than probing them in any depth.

In his final paper, however, an analysis of *Sula,* Larry uses the framework he has created through the work of the semester to support his own strong and penetrating reading of the novel, placing himself within it and contributing to the imaginative world created there by extending the story beyond the novel's present frame. Larry continues the story of Sula with a letter to her, written by her one-time lover Jude long after she has rejected him and he has left town. Larry imagines that Jude is attending a small black college near Detroit, and as he recasts the events of the novel from Jude's new perspective, he shows the ways in which language affects people's interpretation of experience.

> A college education has helped me to understand how you could bed me, then discard me like the robin shit that first appeared when you returned to Medallion. So many new words I've learned. One that helps explain your behavior is the word "environment" from Psych 101.

But he also imagines other knowledge and other experiences that give shape to the world as Jude might see it.

> Your family started you on the road of desperation and when you left Medallion and traveled across America and saw the despair of our people, that finished you. It's finished me too. Marcus Garvey wants us to return to Africa and W. E. B. Dubois preaches equality via a socialist state, but it's not going to happen.
>
> You came back to Medallion and brought that knowledge and that pain of Black America giving up, giving out and dying. I didn't realize how happy I was isolated in my own little microcosm, opinionated with white 18th century homespun values. Now I've seen some of the world and it weighs heavy on my mind. Knowledge is not the key to freedom. Education just lets you know how desperate things are.

The storytelling represented in Larry's first work of the course is continuous with the language of literature in a way that allows him to inhabit what he reads imaginatively and to recreate and extend its meanings, shaping a coherent world of his reading and writing. In this final piece of writing Larry explores in depth the pain a young black man like Jude (like Larry) might begin to name with his college education.

At the same time, throughout the course Larry has been active as a teller and a listener, as a writer and a reader, reflecting on what other students' stories can tell him about his own and on what his own understandings can show him about the world created in the literature he reads or the theory presented in a sociolinguistic study like *Word Play*. He has entered as a full participant into the acts of reflection and meaning making that go on in this community, into its conversations. In evaluating the explanatory power of Farb's theory of language as a game for understanding particular encounters and events and comparing his classmates' writing with his own, he enters as well a conversation about evaluation and assessment, one that cannot stop with the submission of a paper but must continue in ways that we explore in the next chapter.

Exploring the values and traditions shaped by the poetic discourse of different communities like Kathleen's and Ruth's, bringing
the perspectives of race, ethnicity, gender, or class to bear on the ways
we know and the things we know as Larry does, are important parts
of the work of the college curriculum in a multicultural society, and
we will return to those issues in Chapter 9.

Chapter Eight

Assessing Competence
Extending the Conversation

Thus far we have been arguing, first, for a model of writing instruction that recognizes the linguistic, communicative, and intellectual competence our students bring to our classrooms, and second, for the creation of curricula that will help students and teachers recognize and build on that competence as students move back and forth among the different communities, including the academic community, in which they are participants. We have argued that the most effective curricula are based in authentic inquiry—in research that links the classroom and the world and examines, for both contexts, the ways of thinking and communicating that predominate and the values embedded in those ways. At the same time, we have argued that such curricula must create new relationships between teachers and students and engage them in genuine conversations, as co-searchers and researchers, about the things they discover and about the process in which they are involved.

The classroom environments we shape are situated in a larger institutional context, however, and it is that context that may pose the greatest problems and conflicts for us as we attempt to resee our students' writing, redefine our role as teachers, and reinvent the curriculum. Where there's a conflict between the model of learning that we are presenting here and institutional perspectives, it most often centers on issues of assessment. The competence that is being assessed must also be considered in an institutional context. While writing competence in an insurance company may be defined by the ability to write error-free memos about actuarial tables, the sort of writing needed in college and university classrooms is, as we have seen, much more fluid and complex. Issues of competence in this setting must focus on the nature of an academic discourse community, on how people function effectively in a community that is focused on learning and inquiry as opposed to straight transmission of information. And assessing the competence of student writers in such a community is interwoven with assessing the courses themselves and our teaching of them. Assessment is a feature of the communicative context in which the conversation we have with our students takes place. It must therefore be a part of that conversation, not apart from it.

Assessment begins for teachers, of course, in their own classrooms in the ways in which they respond to and evaluate student writing, and most often, responding practices are determined by the ways teachers interpret external demands, not by what they know about the acquisition of written discourse.

Conversing and Corresponding

The theoretical underpinnings of our work and the curricular model we propose leave little room for responding to students' texts in narrow or traditional teacher-to-student ways. We know that learners acquire new languages, new discourses, new ways of thinking, and new modes of communication through meaningful participation in the ways of a new community. We know that teachers in and out of classrooms can facilitate this process by providing comprehensible input, by building on what the students know and extending it. And we know how to read students' texts to discover their competence and their potential, to see (as we argued in Chapters 3 and 4) what the surface tells us about their systematic acquisition of a new discourse. But we also know to look below the surface to seek evidence of changes in how students are thinking and approaching problems, to look for those changes as they occur over time and in response to a variety of work, and to value the evolving evaluative frameworks students are developing to make sense of what they are learning.

We know how limited in meaning and in understanding most "teacherly" responses, however well intended, really are, how little they contribute to the sorts of authentic communication that foster this acquisition. In her study of teachers' responses to their students' writing, Nancy Sommers (1982) found that they most often "take students' attention away from their own purposes in writing a particular text and focus that attention on the teachers' purpose in commenting" (149); that teachers often give contradictory messages to students, telling them to find meanings and develop ideas at the same time they correct errors and create final, edited sentences ("Check your commas and semicolons and think more about what you are thinking about" [151]); and that "most comments are not text-specific and could be interchanged, rubber-stamped, from text to text" (152).

Likewise, in her research on teachers' responses to the texts of ESL students (1985), Vivian found that these teachers misread students texts, were arbitrary and inconsistent in their reactions, provided abstract and vague prescriptives, responded to all texts as fixed and final products, and attended primarily to surface-level features rather than to larger discourse concerns. They rarely offered specific strategies that would help students resee their texts.

Of course, what we know about language acquisition argues that responding in these ways is worse than useless in supporting our students' writing development, that acquisition of new discourses in speaking and in writing is supported when the learners are engaged in meaningful communication with other members of the discourse community. As our students have discovered from their own research, being a member of a community involves engaging in its conversations. But the authentic conversations of an academic community are very different from the exchanges between teacher and student that typically take place in students' papers.

In *Lives on the Boundary,* Mike Rose describes what was involved for him as he began his own college studies and writes of the teachers who invited him in.

> My teachers modeled critical inquiry and linguistic precision and grace, and they provided various cognitive maps for philosophy and history and literature. They encouraged me to make connections and to enter into conversations—present and past—to see what talking a particular kind of talk would enable me to do with a thorny philosophical problem or a difficult literary text. . . . They liked books and ideas, and they liked to talk about them in ways that fostered growth rather than established dominance. They lived their knowledge. And maybe because of that their knowledge grew in me in ways that led back out to the world. I was developing a set of tools with which to shape a life. (58)

The conversations Rose remembers best are spoken ones that took place "in backyards and on doorsteps and in offices as well as in the classroom." But many of our academic conversations are carried out in writing. To help students enter into these conversations as writers requires a change not only in how we create occasions for student writing—in curricula built around the sort of discovery and collaborative research described in Chapters 6 and 7—but also in how honestly functional we allow that writing to be. In conversations, whether spoken or written, the speaker speaks or the writer writes *to* the listener or reader to inform or persuade or convince but also to hear (even if only in the writer's mind) what the other might think about what's being said and how the other might respond, to build a dialogue and a basis for shared understanding. We know, however, that most composition courses are built around writing *for* the teacher, not *to* the teacher or *to* other real audiences (no matter what assignments might say about imagining an audience), and as Arthur Applebee (1989) found, almost all of this writing is used only for evaluation.

Edith, a graduate student in a course on the teaching of writing, explored this problem in her own journal.

> It occurs to me that I am writing all this either "to" or "for" the teacher. When I am writing "to" her (as in a letter), it is easier than "for" her (as in an essay). Some weird psychological mechanism separates the *For* (grab the safety net) from *To* (pull out all the stops). But writing should always be writing *To* since it requires taking the plunge, taking risks.

Edith captures here a critical distinction between the kinds of constraints that affect us when we write *to* a reader who we assume is genuinely interested in what we have to say and when we write *for* a reader who has certain predetermined expectations and evaluates the text accordingly. School-based writing typically establishes "writing for" conditions for students, requiring them not only to write about prescribed topics in prescribed formats but to write in order to demonstrate certain skills, the mastery of which is determined by one reader, the teacher. And for teachers as well, most school writing is not writing *to* the student but writing *for* correction, improvement, and evaluation. But since written exchanges like this are not genuine conversations, they cannot contribute much to the acquisition of written discourse.

What are natural conversations—the sort that do provide the kind of meaningful and comprehensible input that fosters acquisition—really like? The data gathered by our own students, particularly Ruth's study of her family's dinner-table conversation, highlight a number of important features. First, a conversational event is a collaborative production. Within that event, participants take turns, some longer, some shorter, but the length is determined cooperatively by the participants, in part by how much the contribution of a particular moment contributes to a larger (though not specifically defined) goal. Different groups will have different expectations about appropriate lengths of turns (linked to culture, class, gender, or age, as we saw in the contrasts between Kathleen's and Ruth's family storytelling patterns) and make different allow-

ances for interruptions and overlaps, but in most successful conversations these expectations and allowances, when not shared, will
be negotiated. As with Shawn's telling of the tetherball story, participants also monitor the flow of the conversation: the speaker
checks in with listeners ("you know?") and reacts to their responses; the listeners ask questions and give feedback. Participants
also share information and move toward the construction of a
shared frame of reference and a common understanding, as Alison's
classmates do with the concept of maturity. For all of these aspects
of the conversation, there will be shared responsibility between or
among the participants or else the conversation simply won't be
maintained. A useful chapter on examining conversational data is
included in Michael Stubbs's *Discourse Analysis.*

The written conversations we have with our students should
have all of these features. Vivian's correspondence with the student
researchers whose work we described in Chapter 6 highlights the
difference between having genuine written conversations and
"responding" as it is usually practiced. As someone who was also
doing research into language practices, Vivian established a common
base of interest with the things the students might already know. She
probed the students' discoveries, asked for more information, and
connected what they were finding with her own research and with
what was known in the field in a written conversation not unlike one
she might have with a colleague. In the process, throughout the
correspondence, Vivian modeled, in authentic ways, the discourse
patterns of the academic community.

In her responses to students' letters, Vivian did a number of other
things that we might do in response to the texts our students write *to*
us. She asked questions and provided related information, as in her
exchange with Albert. She offered restatements of what had been
said, just as a listener might respond: "Oh, I think I know what you
mean." She pulled together the many parts of the conversation that
other interested parties hadn't had a chance to hear, sometimes
aggregating data when she wrote to a whole class rather than individuals, as she did in the following excerpt, where she begins by
listing related findings on a number of topics, such as paragraphing.

Most of you recognize the importance of paragraphing:

- Paragraphs direct the reader's understanding. (Paul)
- Paragraphing allows you to divide ideas into precise and com-
  plete thoughts. (Evangeline)
- Paragraphing affects the way stories are told and read. (Richard,
  Isabel)

- Paragraphing separates different thoughts to keep the reader from being confused. (Mark)
- Paragraphs tell something step by step, in order, so that when someone reads your story, he/she will be able to understand it. (Susan)
- Paragraphs let the reader get a better understanding of your thoughts. (Michael)
- Paragraphs take readers from one idea to another. (Ella)
- Paragraphs establish the sequence of events; they introduce new characters, convey new thoughts and actions. (Heather)
- Paragraphs are for separating ideas and topics. (Thomas)

As you can see from these statements, you have a very good notion of the purpose of paragraphing. I was especially impressed by how many of you realized that paragraphing helps us meet the reader's needs.

After providing similar lists of what students had discovered about the beginnings and endings of written works, about the nonverbal elements in spoken communication, about accuracy and elaboration in written communication, Vivian turns to what students have said about the writer's relationship with the reader, pulling together their comments but extending them as well.

Finally, I would like to mention that you referred to an important factor that affects all language use, both written and oral. This factor is the relationship the speaker/writer has with the listener/reader. Richard and Valerie pointed out that it is easier to tell stories to friends, and Mark indicated that the nervousness experienced while telling the story was the result of not knowing the people who were listening. This informs us about an important dimension of language use and further explains the differences between spoken and written texts. We usually tell stories to people we know, and their relationship to us allows us to be less formal, less organized, and less detailed; these listeners may in fact know something about the story or the people involved even before we begin to tell the story. Thomas and Valerie, in fact, point out that when we speak, we use phrases like "you know" because we assume everyone understands what we are saying. But the more and more distanced we are from our listeners/readers, the more information we need to provide. That is why when we write, we need to be clear, accurate and precise. That is why we have to try to take the point of view of the reader into account and try to imagine what that reader needs in order to understand what we are trying to express.

The letter concludes with a confirmation of the framework of the conversation and a validation of the students' participation in it, connecting what they have discovered with what Vivian and other "language researchers" have learned.

> It is obvious that you have already learned a great deal about the differences between oral storytelling and written texts. As a language researcher, I have read about and studied these differences, and you should know that you have come to many of the same conclusions that have been published in scholarly journals. That's quite an accomplishment!
>
> I look forward to hearing about your next project, for I am learning a great deal from all of you.

These written conversations were much like spoken ones in many ways, and their first goal was to build understanding and bring students into the conversations of the academic community simply by having the conversations themselves. But another way to bring students into this community is to talk not only about the things they are learning and discovering, but also about how they are progressing as learners and how they can become more effective participants; commenting on that progress becomes a second goal of most of our exchanges. These twin goals provide the framework for the conversation and set its subject matter. And the second goal, like the first, is met in part through the event itself, not through direct attention to it. In these letter exchanges, because students were communicating with a reader who was outside their classroom contexts, a reader with whom they could communicate only in writing, they were forced to articulate their thoughts clearly to someone who, unlike their teachers, had not been present throughout the process of translating these thoughts into writing. They needed to be explicit, define terms precisely, and present supporting data in order to draw conclusions. They were not explicitly directed to do these things. But the fact that this group of students was involved in observing and studying language no doubt made them particularly sensitive to their own written language. They became concerned about presenting their experiences as learners accurately and came to worry about finding the right expressions and appropriate terms. As Albert remarked in his letter, "I haven't quite grasped the words for it yet."

This very recognition, that "grasping" words is essential to the process of articulating thought, influenced the students' attempts to explain and discuss their ideas. They began to use the terms that Vivian had used (which they were learning about in Suzy's and Ellie's courses), adopting the kind of language that Albert began to use, terms like "my own ethnographic work" and "discourse analysis." They were, in fact, trying out the very realizations about written language they were discovering in their research. As they recognized, for example, that the reader is not present in a written narrative as the listener is in an oral storytelling situation, they had an opportunity to test out their hypotheses about how to anticipate the reader's needs, and they were able to find out from their correspondent's responses when these hypotheses did and did not work. Thus, their development as writers proceeded in much the same way that language develops: through trial and error, through hypothesis testing, through risk taking. They had opportunities to make meaning and receive confirmation about their attempts within a genuinely communicative context.

We discovered, however, that the correspondence also supported students' development as readers (the counterpart of the listener in a spoken conversation). The fact that Vivian read these students as authors and researchers in their own right and responded in a way that reflected this attitude modeled the kind of reading we expected of them. But beyond this, they read their course materials and tried to make sense of them in light of the investigative work reported in their letters, and they read the letters in light of the course readings. Their own letters, along with their other writing for the class, allowed dialogue with these materials, opportunities to explain these texts not only to their reader but to themselves.

Finally, the correspondence modeled ways in which a framework of shared knowledge must be created in a written exchange as in a spoken conversation. By making reference to what these students already said or to the knowledge they had already shared, Vivian was helping them see that their ability to comprehend and interpret her letters was based on her understanding of their prior knowledge. Their letters to her then began to take into account their predictions about her needs as a reader and the interactions that were likely to occur between this reader and their texts. And in many instances their experiences as engaged readers influenced what they came to provide her as a reader. For example, they started to establish contexts for their responses, beginning their replies to her with phrases like "About your questions about . . ." or "You asked me to. . . ." They would then go on to discuss the insights that Vivian's questions, proddings, and suggestions were intended to provoke, again revealing their appreciation for what their reader was anticipating.

After Vivian's initial correspondence with the students in Suzy's and Ellie's classes, we went on to build other letter exchanges into our teaching, to create other opportunities for authentic written communication between groups of writers in various classes. There were correspondences between freshman ESL and native speakers, between graduate students in composition or in the bilingual education/ESL program and freshman writers, and between ESL

students and students in a multicultural course in the teacher certi-
fication program. One such exchange took place between students in
Ellie's advanced class on theories of literacy and students in
her freshman writing class. The exchange was intended, in part, to
give students a chance to hold an extended conversation in writing.
When students analyzed these letters and reflected on what they
had learned from engaging in this genuine act of communication,
they found changes over the semester in the writing of both participants. The advanced students were particularly surprised to find
that changes had taken place in their own writing. They had antici-
pated that freshman writers would learn new ways of expressing
their ideas. But they found that the correspondence had involved a
process of negotiation, with each partner responding to the thoughts,
words, and meanings of the other, so that learning went on in both
directions.

One feature that changed, especially for the freshmen, was the
explicit analysis of meanings, an important aspect of thinking in
academic contexts. Emily, a student in the literacy class, describes
this feature, an aspect of her own writing, as it begins to appear in
the writing of her freshman partner, Cathy.

> In relaying my experiences to her about transferring to UMass, I
> write self-evaluative comments in the midst of my text, and this is
> my "natural" style. I do not simply describe my experience but
> analyze it as I go and draw on past analysis. Then . . . I try to engage
> her in this analytical thinking about her thoughts concerning re-
> turning to school.

Emily finds that in her letters Cathy begins to analyze her experiences more and to use phrases Emily had used in earlier letters.

> Two shared phrases are about having "grown up" from being out of
> school and being "ready" to learn. At first when I read this I thought
> she must be uncomfortable for some reason and repeating back to
> me my ideas rather than her own. But at a closer look I saw that she
> had really applied the phrase about "growing up" to her own
> context/experience.

Another feature that changed through this correspondence was style
or level of discourse. Emily tended to use an academic discourse style,
but she found that

> Cathy's writing has a very honest direct quality. . . . I prefer to use
> the more distanced, detached language of written style . . . keeping
> the reader more at a distance by using a third person construction.
> As a result of this investigation, I can see my tendency to do this,
> and I value [her] openness.

Emily comes, in the end, to see the process that she is engaged in as one of "negotiating meanings" and building a relationship that is sensitive to the concerns of both conversational partners.

> Thus I see more clearly how to approach our exchanges with more sensitivity to her reluctance to share her ideas and with more appreciation for the efforts she makes. I don't mean to sound judgmental. In fact, I am surprised, having been a tutor for three semesters, that I myself was not more sensitive to these dynamics earlier.

For Emily, who has been helping first-year writers with their "writing problems," this kind of genuine conversational negotiation with those students has been missing. In analyzing this correspondence, she sees how the elaboration of ideas and meanings and the extension of language develop naturally through communication.

We have used what we learned from such correspondences to reformulate the nature of our participation as teachers in written exchanges with our students. In these exchanges we now try to become better at doing the very things our students were becoming better at: to respond as writers and as readers and to engage in creating shared understandings.

As writers, we try to respond to our students' writing as we would to any conversational partner whose thinking we want to come to understand, assuming that they can participate fully in such a conversation and that our task as writers is to help create the basis for mutual understanding. As readers, we assume that students' texts are meaningful and that it is our task to find that meaning. Just as we have been trained to do with the writing of published authors, we search for connections, seek clues, try to make sense of what we see and to discover the writer's intentions, purposes, and strategies. We write about what we experience in students' texts as readers, contributing our speculations and questions to a conversation with the writer. And we work to create a shared frame of reference, to discover what the student writer intended in a piece of writing and what she saw as our intentions and purposes in suggesting a particular activity, to reach a consensus about where any particular piece of writing fits in this conversation, whose subject is often writing itself and how to keep a real conversation on the topic moving along. We often use dialogue journals, responding to the substance of students' entries with our own queries and concerns. We write lengthy letters as well as marginal comments in response to extended pieces of student writing. Finally, we try to extend the negotiatory stance we described in Chapter 4, keeping in mind the ways that, as Emily discovered, we too are changed by becoming partners in this conversation.

Making Assessment Part of the Conversation

While we have been moving from the practice of responding to student texts to corresponding with student writers, we have been trying out different ways to include the evaluation of their writing in the conversation. We have seen that many of the features of natural conversation are carried over into correspondence and can be used in our responses to student writing. But if we really welcome our students' full participation in this discourse community, these features should also be carried into our evaluation of the work they produce and our assessment of their competence as college writers.

Because this conversation has as one of its goals extending our students' competence as writers within this community, that goal too must be an explicit part of the conversation. One step toward incorporating an evaluation process into the conversation, then, has been to elicit from students their own sense of this goal, how they might approach it, and what might have led them to see it as they do. Again, accounts of the sort we saw in Chapter 2 of their own past experiences with learning new discourses and of their experiences as readers and writers contribute to our common understanding of their processes and experiences as they undertake particular tasks in the context of our courses. Just as students have a great deal of knowledge about language that has never been made explicit, they know a lot about writing and about themselves as writers. Eliciting this information helps us find out where students are following rigid rules and misguided advice and where they are using practices that, with modification, can eventually become effective. And encouraging students to make their own knowledge explicit helps make that knowledge available to be used consciously. So we include the writing itself as a topic of conversation, whether a single piece of writing or a collection of related pieces. And we always consider any individual text in the context of the extended conversation, in a portfolio of writing that includes both sides of the conversation to date.

Suzy, for example, typically asks students to identify their own objectives for their work in writing. During the week before a specific piece of writing is due to be turned in for comment, she asks students to respond to these questions:

- What would you like me to bear in mind as I read your paper?
- What are some things that will help me read it?
- Is there anything in the assignment that has given you trouble?
- How have you attempted to deal with the difficulty?
- If you solved the problem, how (briefly) did you do it? If you didn't, how did you get around it?

- Are there ways in which I can be helpful to you now, before you are finished working on it, things we could go over in class?

- Is there anything else you'd like me to bear in mind as I read your paper?

We also include students in the process of evaluation by asking questions that set forth our assumptions about what constitutes writing progress and placing their responses at the center of our conversations. The questions reflect our own efforts to see the students' writing more clearly in the ways we described in Chapters 3 and 4. Students might be asked:

- To describe the process they go through in writing an essay (Do you jot ideas down freely at first and then come back to choose particular points to expand on? Do you write more than one draft? Do you stop to read over what you have written to see if you have said things as clearly and as fully as possible? Do you change things around within a draft, moving a sentence or paragraph from one place to another? Do you change words, eliminate words or sentences that don't fit, add words when they are needed to make things clearer?).

- To consider the relationship between their writing and their thinking (Are you writing longer papers? Do you try to think about what things mean and explain them? Do you push yourself to think more about the subject, even after you have written your first ideas? Do you actually learn something as you write?).

- To consider the structure of finished essays (Do your finished essays focus on one main topic? Do they move logically from one point to another? Do you include both specific details and a larger generalization or characterization to which those details point or which can be drawn from those details? Do you decide, in the end, on the most effective order in which to discuss particular details?).

- To consider the perspective of a reader (How do you let the reader know what you are writing about? Do you include enough information so that any moderately informed reader who picked up your paper could make sense of it? Do you use paragraphs to lead your reader through the groups of your ideas? Do you leave the reader with a final point, drawn from the rest of your discussion, which shares whatever insight or meaning you have discovered in writing the essay?).

- To see themselves as readers (What do you do as you read? Do you ever read aloud? Do you use writing to help you make sense of the reading? What kinds of writing? Do you use a dictionary? How often?).

- To see themselves as editors (Do you proofread your paper before handing it in? Do you read aloud to catch the differences between the ways you have written and said the same thing? Do you keep a list of the words you frequently misspell and try to catch them? Do you use a dictionary or spellchecker when you have one available? Do you reread papers that have been returned to you and look at explanations? Do you ask a question when you have received a comment or explanation that you don't understand?).

- To see themselves as learners (What have you learned about writing or about yourself as a writer that you didn't know or see as clearly when the semester started? When you learned something new, what helped you to learn it? What would you like to do or have more of? What do you want most to work on next in your writing?).

Such questions provide an opening to more extended exchanges. Alison worried that she had trouble "coming up with ideas," but Ellie could provide assurance, affirming the work she had been doing: "I don't think that 'coming up with ideas' is as big a problem in your writing as you think it is. You have done some good thinking about [the Anne Frank paper] since your first draft, and the fact that Anne benefitted from her new life as well as suffered from it is an important insight. This paper shows me that you *are* starting to probe below the surface of your first, simple ideas." In response to Alison's concerns about "mistakes," Ellie suggested that Alison mark the "mistakes" she found and the features she wondered about on a paper so that Ellie could see "what you already know and can monitor on your own" and "what you still really need to learn about."

The language research activities we have described brought students new insights and new concerns when thinking about their own writing. After his research into spoken and written language, Larry commented that he had been particularly interested in what had emerged about "the thought process during speaking and writing," and that he had been noticing the ways in which a public spokesperson like "George Schultz, after the Reykjavik summit talks, spoke ever so slowly and thought carefully about what he said." Larry then described the ways he approached his own writing and stated his concern that on the one hand he was, in his own terms, "too loquacious and wordy" in his writing, but also his fear that as he worked on his writing he would have to give up his oral style. One example of this style was ending even serious, analytical papers with "toasts" like "Here's to you, kid." In response to one question he commented: "I end my papers when I tire of writing. My final points at times aren't drawn from the discussion. They tend to be humorous and offbeat. I've been told about this habit. I don't have endings with any depth to them." At the same time, he wanted to work more "on grammar and punctuation and those skills which will help me pass the Writing Proficiency Exam."

Ellie responded to Larry's concerns, first reviewing the writing he had done during the semester (observation notes, reflections, and early drafts of papers as well as longer essays and reports), describing what she saw in the endings of the papers included there, and then offering the following comment:

> I know that you don't want to give up your style, and you don't really have to in the long run. As you become more skilled as a writer you will find ways of embedding the same sort of life that your oral language has into your writing, and you will find alternatives to such lifeless beginnings as "the topic I am going to write about." But the two sides—formal written language and liveliness—can't come together unless you begin to practice the side you don't have experience with, unless you practice, in a serious way, giving full and careful and detailed explanations of how things work, which come to real conclusions rather than toasts. Doing this kind of thinking and writing will not cause you to lose your own voice as long as *you* really do the thinking and explaining instead of just using other people's words as shortcuts for working out your own ideas. And as you work to be more precise in your presentation of your ideas, you will find that you will have gained a more fine-tuned understanding of how to use punctuation effectively as well.

Conversations like these create a meeting place between our students' concerns as writers and our concerns as their teachers. Larry had generalized an earlier comment by Ellie or a classmate about the way a paper ended, and that comment, as well as his observations about spoken and written language in the world around him, had focused his concerns about his own style. The written dialogue allowed Larry and Ellie to explore these concerns without the pressure of reaching early agreement that a face-to-face conversation might present. Larry went on to try out modes of writing that would allow him to keep the important aspects of his oral style while working to push his thinking and present it more carefully. Responding to his reading of *Sula* through a letter in Jude's voice was, as we saw in Chapter 7, one successful strategy.

Very often, as in Alison's and Larry's cases, the concerns of teacher and student are the same, though they represent different perspectives. But they can also appear to be quite different. Like many students, Larry came to his freshman writing class wanting to work on surface features like punctuation, because he saw those features as most important for a future test of his writing proficiency. Ellie's response, as well his own research in this course, may have resituated those concerns for him within a larger enterprise. But the problem of conflicting agenda, of sharply differing expectations about how to meet long-term goals, is bound to emerge in courses that operate without the authority of the standard textbook.

Assessing Both Sides of the Conversation

Students do have expectations about the work they will do in our classrooms, and they engage in an ongoing silent outside-of-class assessment of that work. End-of-semester course evaluations offer too little information, too late; their primary purpose is usually an institutional one and, for public purposes, students usually want to praise the teachers they like. Only the occasional side comment like Sabena's to Vivian (see Chapter 5) is likely to raise larger questions about a course's direction, purpose, and pedagogy. But students do have those questions, particularly about the sort of curricula we have been describing. And it's important that we hear their side of the conversation about our courses and about the work they are doing for them.

When we began structuring courses around the sorts of activities we described in Chapter 6, we wanted to learn as much as possible about our students' responses to that work. Lucy, a student in Vivian's graduate course on theories of writing, was also preparing to teach in our composition program. For her internship, she worked with Ellie's section of freshman writing (the class that included Shawn, Maya, and Larry) and at the same time carried out ethnographic research in that classroom. Lucy's discoveries proved most important to our growing understanding of the process we're engaged in with our students.

While observing and participating in the class, tutoring students, and gradually assuming responsibility for co-teaching, Lucy also conducted a series of interviews with students and teacher throughout the semester. Lucy's data included student comments that highlight several possible areas of conflict in this curriculum, beginning with a larger, philosophical one. As Lucy put it, the view most students have that "the teacher's role is one of passing on important knowledge and imposing discipline, is in conflict with the view that the source of both knowledge and discipline resides within." Other differences in expectation follow. One, for these students, had to do with the principle of building on what students already know and bring to the classroom, on "discovering competence":

> I've learned what she's making us learn, but I kind of feel like I've already known it, like she says, I've already known it, I just didn't realize it.

A second was in building the course, at first, around the students' own research:

> The fact that it was our own work all the time made people not take it as seriously. You tend not to give yourself much credit with coming up with original ideas.

A third was in the way assignments were structured, with observation notes and small daily in-class and out-of-class reflections building into larger papers:

> We do these little assignments, but it's not like you take it home and grammatically you say, "I'm gonna write this paragraph." It's just something you write, you answer—so it's not like it's helping my writing. It's more helping my ideas flow, but not giving me any answers as to how to correct my writing. We haven't really written any *paper* assignments for a time. I hoped to improve my writing skills, but it's really not been doing that, just kind of helping my ideas flow.

Students wanted to work on specific skills that would help them pass the writing proficiency exam as they perceived it:

> I'm not sure I'm learning anything that's important for it. What you're doing now is not what they will test me on. I was more expecting working on subject, predicate, and every other thing. Time is just rolling by.

And there were concerns about how the work of this course was meeting a larger agenda:

> For an English 101 course, it seems we should be learning our basics—like term papers. Learn how to footnote, find a book in the library, 'cause that's a *big thing*, organize a term paper.

Finally, although the course was structured around ongoing research, students could not connect this with "research" as they knew it, the model fostered by the research guides students have seen.

> The steps to research? Get the reading down, I'll read those and take up significant points. I always do an outline, and the first thing I do is get a thesis to support with the research.

Such comments make it clear that students enter the freshman writing conversation with their own frame of reference about the forms that conversation should take and the way it should be carried on. Ellie's students wanted to focus on what they saw as "the basics" of writing—on grammar, on research papers—within a familiar structure that held the teacher and the book as absolute authorities. Ellie, too, wanted to work on "the basics" of writing, but for her, as she said in the interviews with Lucy, this meant having students do writing that "involves some thought of theirs, some real understanding, that shows they're able to make connections and express something about those connections in their own words"; helping students "get to trust themselves as thinkers more so they also get to trust their own ways of expressing themselves"; and "structur[ing] things so that people have to go along with the inquiry process, so they can't rush to some sort of closure, say 'This is *just* . . . this is what she wants' and race to the library and do a research paper and that's it."

A conversation that begins with conflicting expectations and perspectives requires a great deal of negotiation of the sort that Emily described in her correspondence with Cathy if it is to be maintained. Classroom discussions, conferences, written exchanges, evaluations, must work toward the negotiation of shared meaning in a shared enterprise. Otherwise, the conversation breaks down and both parties become judges, not partners. In this case, the negotiation eventually worked and the conversation continued. On one side, the students did come to appreciate the work of the class, at the end voicing sentiments that were the opposite of their earlier ones:

> The way this class is set up and the way she presents it, you're only given a few things and she's making you work for the rest, so you have to think a lot more and everything—it's like you create knowledge, you know what I mean.

> Using our own work gives everyone a feel we did something on our own. It's not just a bunch of knowledge drummed into our heads by somebody else.

> I saw that the course was much more helpful than I had thought as far as the daily exercises and assignments. It *was* about putting together a paper.

And they saw differences in their own writing:

> In the beginning half of this semester I thought the class was really strange. I didn't really see where we were leading up to. I had taken a freshman English class at a junior college; we had a paper assigned that was due every Friday, you know, like an argument paper. It was pretty cut and dry. English has always been easy for me. In this

junior college course I had all A's in English and never had a problem.

But here I know my writing changed. It became more specific and I started putting more time into it, going over it and really thinking about it instead of just writing off the top of my head. Now I see how many little pieces can add up to a whole paper whereas before I always wrote a paper at a single sitting. I think it makes it a lot clearer when I get the bits and pieces and try to connect them.

And students came to see that their work as writers was supported by the focus of the research tasks as well:

I never thought that oral vs. written was so important but now it's very significant for me. When I write I am much more conscious of the reader to make sure he or she understands what I am saying. I would take nothing for granted.

On the other side, Ellie came to understand more clearly the ways in which the sorts of work she asks of students, like "*really* thinking about anything, is going to make them insecure," and she tried not only "to increase their tolerance level" but to make the process of the class and the support systems (like working in small groups) a more explicit part of the conversation.

Tutors or interns or researchers can play an important role as facilitators of these conversations, as Lucy did in this one. Her questions led both students and teacher to monitor the conversation in explicit ways, to articulate their own expectations, and to try to learn more about those of the other participants. We often invite our advanced students and graduate students to include our classrooms in their research. And sometimes students in our freshman classes turn to the classroom community for their own inquiry—for example, when Vivian's ESL students investigated the extent to which gender bias could be identified in their classrooms.

Much of what we would say about the assessment conversation as it takes place within courses can be summed up in a comment made by one of Vivian's ESL students, in a similar classroom study carried out by Ann, a graduate student and tutor. When Ann asked a student what made Vivian's class different from her other classes, Martha responded: "She is more approachable. She includes herself in our situation and is our friend too. She gives confidence. And she corrects you delicately." Ann pointed out how Vivian, as "a friend," makes classroom conversations continuous with conversations in the rest of students' lives; "is approachable" in being available to extend the classroom conversations outside of class; "includes herself in our situation" both as a writer who shares her own rough drafts and writing difficulties with her students and as an individual who has had life experiences similar to those of her students; and "gives confidence" by reading aloud and having students read, at the start of class, passages from one another's work that are particularly poignant or powerful (not samples of problems that need to be corrected), valuing each student as an author worth reading. Finally, she "corrects delicately," helping students clarify their own ideas and putting into practice what she learned from her own study (1985) on responding to students' writing, that the teacher needs

> to establish a collaborative relationship with students, drawing attention to problems, offering alternatives, and suggesting possibilities, so that student and teacher can exchange information about what the writer is trying to communicate and the effect that this communication has upon the reader. (97)

Like the students in Ellie's and Suzy's courses who as a result of their experiences with reading, writing, and researching came to appreciate the purpose of this work, the students in Vivian's courses too, ESL students whose expectations were that they would be practicing grammar and writing, came to value their writing-to-learn experiences. As one student put it, "Before my attitude towards writing was just finishing the homework and earning some credit. But now . . . I am not just finishing my homework, but learning as well."

We have been describing some of the ways that we have found to create this collaborative relationship, to carry on the conversation between student and teacher. And we would argue, in the end, that it's a conversation that has to go on throughout the course about the course. Student and teacher need to talk and write to each other in authentic ways about what they are learning and how they are learning it, about what their goals are and their strategies for reaching those goals, about how they see their progress toward those goals, about their roles and responsibilities in this process. They need to include themselves in each other's situations. And they need periodically to look back over the conversation, at the portfolio of writing that has made up the conversation by both partners, including student writing and teacher responses, to see how it has progressed, how goals have evolved, and to negotiate the continuing dialogue and new directions.

Student and teacher also need to negotiate how they will respond to the outside constraints on their conversation— constraints placed by curricular sequences, by external assessment measures, and particularly by the grading system. We believe that grading interrupts rather than supports the learning process for most writers, a "mark" treating as complete at one particular time or with one particular performance a process that is in reality fluid, continuous, and recursive. But we realize that the ability to come to closure on a piece of work is also important. Deciding when a piece of writing is finished and when it is ready to be read from the perspective of other readers in an institution is an important part of the negotiatory stance and the communicative process we describe. In some of our courses—for instance, the freshman studies seminars taught by Suzy and Ellie— we have not assigned grades to most of the individual papers but encouraged students to return to their earlier writings by incorporating them in later ones, doing formal assessment in the form of grades only when that process is complete. In recent years, Suzy has drawn students into the evaluation process by having them tell her when they give her a piece of written work to read whether they want a grade on it. At the end of the course they are asked to select four or five of the semester's individual papers to be considered along with the last, integrative one for their final review, and they are invited to revise those pieces and include the earlier versions along with the revisions in the portfolio.

We have been making portfolios rather than individual texts the subject of our formal assessments and grading conversations, even at midsemester, so that our comments and grades reflect the evidence a portfolio provides of overall competence, not discrete performances. We try to negotiate the criteria for assessment and grading with a class as a whole, bringing together what we know about institutional norms and expectations with what we know about students' goals and progress. And we take these conversations out of the classroom and carry them into the rest of the institution and beyond.

Bringing the Conversation into a Larger Arena

In our institution, a significant part of the conversation about writing assessment goes on in relation to the writing proficiency exam, which students must take by the time they are juniors. We have seen that the exam looms threateningly in the minds of our students, even as they (wrongly) anticipate that it will focus particularly on the forms and surfaces of their writing. But the exam, and the alternative portfolio assessment that we encourage our students to prepare for, also provides an opportunity for many faculty, students, and administrators to talk about what true writing proficiency is and how it can best be demonstrated or assessed.

The criteria for proficiency in writing at UMass/Boston identify proficiency at the junior level as the ability to:

1. Focus on a question or problem and explore it logically and systematically.

2. Support assertions with evidence.

3. Indicate explicitly how the various elements in the essay are related.

4. Assess (and address appropriately) the audience's character and needs.

5. Use forms of discourse that are appropriate to the situation.

6. Integrate one's own ideas with those of others (taken from readings).

7. Examine explicitly the relationships that exist between general concepts and specific details that are being discussed in the essay.

8. Assume a personal authority for the writing that is being produced: write with an identifiable, personally defined purpose, and in an individual, personal voice.

9. Use effectively the syntactic and mechanical conventions of written discourse.

We don't disagree with these criteria for junior-level writing proficiency, nor do most of our colleagues in the field of composition. Suzy, who was involved in the design of the exam for many years, was also responsible for a study of the exam that was carried out a few years ago. About thirty composition experts around the country were asked to describe their criteria for writing proficiency, to respond to a particular example of the UMass/Boston exam as an effective means of eliciting a demonstration of such proficiency, and to assess a set of student exam essays in terms of whether they met their own criteria. There was little disagreement among the experts in the field about criteria; most felt that the exam was an adequate assessment tool; and on only one student essay was there significant disagreement among the experts, and between the experts and the UMass/Boston faculty readers, about the student's level of proficiency.

These criteria are those of our academic discourse community—both within the institution (where their meaning is negotiated as faculty across disciplines gather to write exams and to read students' essays) and, to a great degree, in the field of composition (where they are discussed and negotiated at our conferences and in our journals). They are part of the context in which our conversations with our students take place. The criteria suggest that the work we are doing with our students is not different in kind from that the institution will assess. Suzy has argued that the criteria measure three forms of engagement, which in fact are fostered through all the work we have been describing:

- Engagement with the question (through which students can find their own ways into the writing they are asked to do on such occasions).

- Engagement with the texts (whereby students can generate their own questions about the texts, situate them in time and place, and begin to connect them with their own knowledge and purposes).

- Engagement with the reader (through which students consider their readers' needs, writing in ways that reflect those considerations about how to involve their readers in their discussions of the texts).

This translation of the decontextualized criteria of writing proficiency into forms of engagement points to goals that we can share with students in our conversations with them and to ways in which they can personalize the frameworks of knowledge and responsibility they are working with us to construct.

Suzy has used them, in fact, to guide her own process of responding to revisions of papers written by students in an experimental course, which she developed as an alternative method by which students can produce portfolios and demonstrate writing proficiency. These responses were always in the form of letters addressing a particular stage in the repeated revision of papers for the course, each letter containing a series of comments, suggestions, and reactions to what the student had written. This was an opportunity to use the letter-writing approach, which was originally developed with freshman writers, to respond to the writings of advanced students who were anxious about their writing and under considerable pressure to satisfy the institution's proficiency requirement. A few examples of the kinds of comments Suzy made in these letters follow. Each refers to something in the student's paper that has a matching number.

- Concerning engagement with the question:

    (1) I get the impression that you really didn't understand what I was asking you to do in this assignment, and hence, this sentence seems unclear. Your principles and values aren't *in* the newspaper story that you're analyzing, are they? You are discussing how your principles and values create a response in you and suggest a solution to the problem. See the difference? I think you need to rewrite the whole sentence so that

it is clear that you are focusing on how *your* principles suggest solutions to the problem you have noticed in the news story.

- Concerning engagement with the text:

  (5) Actually, although it complicates your problem (for which I apologize), and your sentence here is very nice, if you go back and reread the article you'll see that the author didn't *hypothesize* the point you are referring to, he *showed* it. It's a *finding,* based on a study of Japanese people who are living in the U.S. and eating American foods. Note that he says *they found that* the incidence (that's the number of cases) of these kinds of cancers was the same for those Japanese people as it was for non-Japanese Americans. Since the relationship between *hypothesizing* and *finding* in scientific work is rather crucial, I think it's important enough for you to rework that sentence.

- Concerning engagement with the reader:

  This is looking good, but there are still a few problems that we might be able to clear up now, once and for all. (1) Where you discuss the way in which a person's sense of reality is "constructed," it's pretty abstract. If you could give some concrete examples of such constructions, of the parts out of which the construction is built, and explain how it is done, it'd give some clarity to the discussion. I also think that your essay would take on more life. This abstract discussion doesn't have the usual excitement I've come to expect in your papers. I admit that the article I asked you to analyze is pretty dry stuff, but illustrations can make *your* paper a bit more lively.

The premise of Suzy's course is that it provides a context in which the teacher can work with the student in the development of a collection of writings that will demonstrate the student's proficiency as a critical reader and writer to outside readers. It has importance for our considerations of how teaching and assessment can be brought into accord because, in this situation, the teacher is allowed to work cooperatively with the students, helping them to realize their abilities fully in the portfolios, and is not forced to compromise her role. At no point is the teacher required to transform herself from helper into judge. It takes the assessment process back to its etymological roots in the Latin verb *adsideo,* which means to sit, stand, or be at someone's side as an attendant, aid, or protector.

To be effective in our roles as writing teachers, however, we must do more than recast criteria and develop special experimental courses. We must become true partners in our institutional conversations, bringing to them all that we know about language and writing development so that the criteria that are posed are continually questioned and renegotiated in response to the changing needs and goals of a whole community—of all of its participants. Such a conversation has taken place at UMass/Boston. Over the course of several years we have worked with faculty to help them become aware of their instructional goals, their purposes for assigning written work, their means of reading and assessing student work, and the roles that engagement, context, and classroom dynamics play in promoting learning. Through these exchanges, in committee meetings, in faculty seminars, even in informal hallway conversations, faculty have begun to question how appropriate a timed, single-sample essay is for determining writing proficiency, and they are now working more consistently to ensure that students are doing a variety of types of writing in their courses and developing portfolios they can submit to demonstrate writing proficiency.

Conversations like this can begin to change a community and its practices, so that it moves from assumptions about absolute criteria to the recognition that even our understanding of what constitutes proficient writing rests on particular sets of beliefs and values that have to be reexamined and renegotiated to include all members of the community. In the process, new space is made in which a range of different student voices come to be heard and appreciated, contributing to and informing the conversation about what effective writing in this community might look like.

Chapter Nine

Enriching Competence
Constructing Multicultural Frameworks of Knowledge and Understanding

In "The Old Chief Mshlanga," Doris Lessing describes an encounter that takes place between an old African chief and a young white girl. The encounter involves a simple exchange of greetings:

> "Morning, Nkosikaas," he said, using the customary greeting for any time of the day.
> "Good, morning," I said. "Where are you going?" My voice was a little truculent.

The girl's tone of voice is truculent because the chief has in fact greeted her. He and his companions have continued to advance toward her along the path, although it was considered "cheek" for an African not to stand off the path the moment he caught sight of a white. This exchange involves more than the rules of a "language game" (as Larry argued in the essay we excerpted in Chapter 7), which plays only a small part compared with the "bigger social and moral issues" raised when a young girl walks with dogs that she has been taught to set on "the natives" and the African chief is expected to step aside. Nevertheless, in this moment the young girl and the old chief reach a small point of recognition and understanding. They do not really engage in a conversation, and they certainly do not tell each other the stories that might bring them into a shared frame of understanding about the world. But with their exchange of greetings comes a moment of contact in which their differences in age, race, gender, and status are bridged and a larger human connection is established. After a few more words, the narrator reports "We all smiled," and the young girl begins a quest for understanding that leads her to recognize for the first time the social and moral issues Larry alludes to. There is a moment of connection despite the deep rift between their two worlds, the lack of knowledge that can mark the experience of those who live physically adjacent yet culturally separate lives, particularly when that rift is maintained by unequal power relationships supported by law.

Similarly, the students in our classrooms may live in adjacent buildings, on adjacent blocks, or in adjacent towns, but too often they are deeply cut off from one another's lives. The work we have been describing can provide rich openings to understanding those lives, to seeing that a group's ways of telling stories, having conversations, making sense of their lives, share elements common to human meaning making. We can learn about those elements and use them to gain new perspectives about ourselves, integrating them into the larger framework through which we make sense of the world.

Throughout this book we have described our concern with building frameworks that can provide coherent underpinnings for our students' work of discovery and from which they can argue, construct new understandings, make sense of the positions of others, and offer interpretations of their own. It's one thing to have uncovered some of the discourse patterns that typify how a topic might be introduced in an informal conversation. It's quite another to move beyond an effective opening and say something substantial about it. In the same way, while it's important to know enough to be able to construct an account or argument that will provide entry into the conversation (this time the academic one), it's quite a different enterprise to acquire the personal connection to that knowledge that allows you to place yourself in it and to act effectively in the world. For freshman writers, the work of building and using specific frameworks of knowledge must occur simultaneously with the study and practice of the ways of academic discourse, and with the work of reflecting on self and community.

Part of the work of the freshman and sophomore years is building such frameworks for further learning in American history or chemistry or, as Larry has imagined for Jude in Toni Morrison's *Sula*, Psych 101. These new frameworks may help our students see aspects of their lives and of the world around them in new ways, just as the term "environment" helps Larry/Jude make sense of Sula's actions. But if our students are to feel any efficacy from their expanding knowledge, to feel they have gained anything through their education beyond an understanding of "how desperate things are," they need to see that their own developing competence as knowers and language users rests in who they are and how they situate themselves in the world—how they converse with those around them in their speaking and in their reading and writing. They also need to see how they can enter new conversations in ways that might affect the directions those conversations will take in the future. In this chapter we argue that the frameworks our students use to interpret and evaluate their new discoveries and experiences should be multicultural.

Culture and Curriculum

Two issues have dominated recent discussions about curriculum, and both are immediately relevant to our enterprise. One is about the value of (and nature of) a multicultural curriculum that expands the canon of Western tradition (as in British and white American literature) to include people from different classes, races, cultures, and genders and actually tries to understand how the world might look from their perspectives. The other is whether the students who enter our college classrooms have in fact become "dumber," not because they are inherently less intelligent but because they lack the kinds of knowledge that earlier generations of college students are assumed to have possessed. The two concerns are linked in the minds of some, who see expanding the canon to include multicultural perspectives as "watering down" the curriculum, so that current generations of students will not have the opportunity to study the same things earlier generations studied (and thus to quote Shakespeare in their letters as E. D. Hirsch's father did, as so he tells us in *Cultural Literacy: What Every American Needs to Know*). The consequence for college students, according to this view, is not to open minds but to close them. This is the position taken by Allan Bloom in *The Closing of the American Mind,* where he argues that our democratic principles applied to education have resulted in a curricular openness that has weakened the curriculum, particularly for the "good" undergraduates, those at the "good" schools where he has been teaching, and has closed their minds to a long and rich cultural tradition. He mourns the loss of the old view of education.

> Class, race, religion, national origin or culture all disappear or become dim when bathed in the light of natural rights, which give men common interests and make them truly brothers. The immigrant had to put behind him the claims of the Old World in favor of a new and easily acquired education. (27)

In its place he finds a new "education of openness . . . [that] pays no attention to natural rights [and] does not demand fundamental agreement or the abandonment of old or new beliefs in favor of the natural ones." Bloom finds in the current education of young Americans only "a smattering of facts learned about other nations or cultures and a few social science formulas. None of this means much, partly because little attention has been paid to what is required in order to truly convey the spirit of other places and other times to young people" (34). And he decries the "demagogic intention" he finds behind most requirements that students take a course in non-Western culture. Bloom's position has taken hold on campuses, where concentrated opposition to required courses organized around diverse and multicultural or non-Western cultural perspectives has emerged.

But these debates seem to miss the central point, largely because they remain focused on what gets put into or left out of the curriculum. Most of the adherents on both sides of the argument still see the fight in terms of which texts they will assign to—and usually interpret for—students. And the language used by Bloom points to a related limitation in his view of the student-teacher relationship: "little attention has been paid to what is required in order *to truly convey the spirit of other places and other times to young people.*" Bloom sees *the teacher* as conveying the spirit of other places and other times *to the students.* In his view, the teacher is the active knower, the students are passive receptacles of the knowledge being conveyed to them. We have been arguing that both of these views— that a curriculum is a list of readings and that learning is the absorption of knowledge by a student from a teacher—are essentially flawed.

For Bloom (and even for some proponents of multicultural education) any curriculum is constructed around a set of texts and is *about* those texts. The students and teachers appraise, discuss, critique, compare, and contrast the texts but always remain safely apart from them. We think this approach is more likely to reinforce a feeling of discontinuity than to create a sense of shared experience and connectedness. An alternate approach to creating a multicultural curriculum emerges from the kind of work we have described, which is grounded in a view of curriculum as an environment, a system of structured intellectual and investigative endeavors that enables students to construct knowledge and in doing so to discover their own competence. In a course that provides a multicultural environment, students and teachers can place themselves inside not outside what is being studied.

So what does it mean, then, to work from within multicultural resources and perspectives? Creating a multicultural curriculum means more than just adding to the old canon of white male authors a few books from the newer canons of works by women, Native Americans, African Americans, Asian Americans, Hispanic Americans, and so forth. It focuses attention not just on cultural artifacts but on cultural knowledge, on how this knowledge is situated in a society, its meaning and value, and how it is generated and used within a culture and within a group. It engages students in a process through which they discover their own traditions and personal meanings and make connections between these and traditions in the larger community. Instead of denying the immigrant's culture and experience, or that of the African American or Native American, it uses that experience to do just what Bloom says it cannot, "to truly convey the spirit of other places and other times." It supports the discovery of the underlying competence *of* all the participants in our larger common culture *by* all the participants.

For the most part, it has been our feeling that the education our students bring to our university classrooms has been too closed rather than too open. Schools have left out much of the language and most of the stories that help students from nonmainstream backgrounds shape and define and interpret their experiences. In her essay "Poets in the Kitchen," Paule Marshall tells how important it was for her to discover the work of black writers. Though she'd read "everything from Jane Austen to Zane Grey," she had never read anything by minority writers until she came across the work of Paul Laurence Dunbar in a public library.

> I turned to a poem at random. "Little brown baby wif spa'klin eyes / Come to yo' pappy an' set on his knee." Although I had a little difficulty at first with the words in dialect, the poem spoke to me as nothing I had read before of the closeness, the special relationship I had had with my father. (139)

Marshall says that no grade school literature teacher of hers had ever mentioned Dunbar or James Weldon Johnson or Langston Hughes, that she didn't know that Zora Neale Hurston existed. Nothing had confirmed her experience, nothing helped her to discover her own history or literature, to integrate her knowledge of life with her school learning.

The experiences of others echo Marshall's and often reflect greater distance between the cultures of home and school. In *Storyteller,* Leslie Silko writes of her Aunt Susie, educated at the Carlisle Indian School, who returned to teach on the reservation.

> She had come to believe very much in books
> and in schooling.
> She was of a generation,

the last generation here at Laguna,
that passed down an entire culture
by word of mouth
an entire history
an entire vision of the world
which depended on memory
and retelling by subsequent generations.

She must have realized
that the atmosphere and conditions
which had maintained this oral tradition in Laguna culture
had been irrevocably altered by the European intrusion—
principally by the practice of taking the children
away from Laguna to Indian schools,
taking the children away from the tellers who had
in all past generations
told the children
an entire culture, an entire identity of the people.
(6)

Aunt Susie, whose eyesight was failing, wrote down what she could and told the children the rest. Silko says it is "all of us remembering what we have heard together— / that creates the whole story / the long story of the people." And though she remembers only a small part, she will tell what she remembers.

For Marshall and Silko, as for the many other writers whose language and stories have been left out of the literature they read in schools, finding the ways to express the personal and cultural self that is represented in these words and stories—speaking and writing the literature that gives shape to their meanings—becomes a way to create their own possible worlds, to name themselves and shape their own stories. For our students, to read the too-often silenced words— the poems and stories that speak to them as Dunbar's spoke to Marshall—and thereby to retrieve their own words and give voice to their own silences, is an essential part of their lives as writers. So one thing a multicultural curriculum should do is include words and stories that speak to their lives, if not precisely from their own cultural tradition then from many others that leave room for their own in a way that one dominant tradition does not.

While Marshall's and Silko's experiences are similar in some respects, they are different as well. Marshall as a school child was cut off, in any formal tradition of literature, from her cultural and personal experiences. Silko, who was not sent off to the Carlisle Indian School that aimed to eradicate Native American ways, was embedded in such traditions as they were passed on by her aunt. Marshall's task, then, is one of recovery and rediscovery, while

Silko's is one of remembering and recreation: "I remember only a small part / But this is what I remember." A multicultural curriculum should create spaces that allow students to do both things—to discover missing traditions and to remember and bring into their current learning the ones they know.

Marshall's discovery of Dunbar's poem was a chance one. At the time, she had no way to frame her experience of the poem except in personal terms—it reminded her of her relationship with her father. It is the language more than the particular event it describes that awakened her sense that this poem came from a culture that was hers. Silko knows, as she hears and reads Aunt Susie's stories, that they represent a continuing heritage she herself is a part of. A multicultural curriculum should offer a context in which students are allowed to examine the full range of their experiences with cultural identity, and with both sameness and difference.

The tradition Marshall discovered is an ongoing one that will continue to be shaped and reshaped in the African American community in the kitchens of women like her mother, who speak as poets while they fry the potatoes. The tradition Silko will pass on is one that has changed, forcibly interrupted by the dominant culture through efforts to remove children from the reservations and from their traditional ways. It must be reinvented in ways that connect the past to the present by creating, as even traditional tellers did, "a new story with an integrity of its own, an offspring, part of the continuing which storytelling must be" (227). Our students come from different cultural traditions, but they also have different relationships to the evolution of those traditions as the traditions themselves change in relation to a larger American or world culture. A multicultural curriculum should be built around themes that help students to explore these relationships, to consider difference, change, and the relationship between particular cultural traditions and a common culture, and to place themselves in relation to both.

In addition, we would argue, such a curriculum should grow out of the work we have been describing, providing a structure in which students can become co-researchers with their teachers about multicultural knowledge in the ways that they've been co-researchers about language in social contexts. In this way the knowledge both students and teachers bring to the course can be shared and examined, transforming all participants. There is no reason to conclude that this sort of curriculum makes less rigorous intellectual demands on students and teachers. The ability to read and write critically, to engage seriously with authors, to construct logical arguments, and to write with power and coherence is no less likely to emerge from a course that draws students into the perspectives of multiple cultures than from a course in which students read and analyze texts drawn only from American and English culture. On the contrary, students seem to be more open to reading critically, engaging personally, and writing meaningfully about some of the most traditional components of the traditional canon—Homer, Shakespeare, Molière—when these writers' works are included in courses exploring compelling themes and problems with a variety of cultural and historical perspectives than when they are arrayed in a list of great books and thinkers.

The very notion of a multicultural curriculum suggests to us something that is not fixed but is continually renegotiated with new participants in a classroom community and new concerns in a changing world. From our own cultural experiences—from the cultures of our ethnic groups, our families, our education, our present lives and relationships, as well as from the different communities that have been created in our many different classes—the three of us bring to the classroom ways of seeing that shape our approaches to all we do. The perspectives we share on the teaching of writing have been redefined and renegotiated continually during the ten years we have worked together. As we have tried to create for ourselves a common culture across our different and shifting institutional roles and perspectives, we have been engaged in a process much like the one we would have our students undertake. And often we must frame the argument in our own voices to create the larger understandings that encompass but recognize our particular ones. For the rest of this chapter we describe, in our separate voices, how each of us has begun to frame an approach to a multicultural curriculum. The approaches we present are not exclusive of one another: implied in each is a recognition of the work of the others and an understanding and negotiation of common principles.

Ellie: Discovering Cultural Selves in a Multicultural World

A poem by Paul Laurence Dunbar speaks to Paule Marshall "as nothing I had ever read before" of the private world she shares with her father. Her earlier reading, although it built for her a wider world, did not speak to that self in the same way, and it's the connection to the self that she returns to when she reflects on the things that have helped her become a writer.

The developing writers in our classrooms need a curriculum that is multicultural because they need to be able to see the self *and* the world—and to find ways of placing that self in relation to the world, as Dunbar's poem does for Marshall. The writer's authority comes from being able to trust the voice of the self in the very moment of describing the world. Without that authority our students' voices are too likely to remain only the "invented" academic voices of outsiders.

Now, it seems that some of this discovery must have come about through the very sorts of curricula we've been describing. Antonio finds his conflict with his Cape Verdean father echoed in the experience of a boy from a Hassidic community in *The Chosen*. Alison, growing up in a Catholic community in Boston, defines the changes in herself in terms of the developing maturity of a German Jewish girl hiding in an attic in The Netherlands in World War II. Winnie and Bertha and Vito draw on their own early memories from different countries as they read about those of Nisa or Maya Angelou. Larry carries his own voice to his reading of the experience of another black man in *Sula*. Shawn tells a family story to the class and ends up discovering that in his own family, where the parents bring different backgrounds of culture and race, such stories create a new family "heritage." Ruth and Kathleen discover their families' different cultural ways. Over the years we have been trying to create occasions in which all our students, named and unnamed, can bring into our classrooms the stories of their own cultures and the language of their own communities, to connect their worlds with those of their classmates and with those of different writers from diverse backgrounds. Hasn't this whole book been about creating a multicultural curriculum?

But the book has also been about seeing and reseeing—our students' writing, our teaching, and finally even the curriculum we've been trying to create. As I resee the work we've done, I also see what we haven't done or, rather, are only starting to do. While we've built a base for the work of connecting self and other, we haven't always made the nature or the importance of this work as explicit in our curricula as it should be. We have drawn in the experiences of our multicultural students, but we also need to teach them (and ourselves) in more explicit ways how to build a framework of knowledge about cultures that are not their own. We need to teach students who don't perceive themselves as having strongly rooted cultural experiences that they can still find in their own lives a basis for understanding other cultural perspectives.

One attempt to create a curriculum that would help students learn how to understand a different cultural experience was a freshman studies seminar/freshman composition course Suzy and I co-taught that focused on South Africa. The course had two themes: "language and identity," and "language and power." Suzy and I began by asking ourselves what we knew, what we wanted to know, and what resources we might bring to bear on the study of this topic. We considered our ongoing research interest in language and the sources and limits of our own general knowledge about South Africa. We imagined the process we would go through in expanding our own knowledge, and we made this process explicit in the curriculum: we would go through a "research" process and reflect on it with our students. In addition to requiring some research into the language in their own lives (described in Chapter 6), we asked students to work with us to gather data about South Africa from newspapers, television accounts, journals, interviews, and literature like Doris Lessing's "The Old Chief Mshlanga," Athol Fugard's *Master Harold and the Boys,* and Winnie Mandela's autobiography. We talked about the new names and terms we came across in news accounts, about the picture of news coverage of a country that emerged from charting different accounts in different newspapers over time, and about what we were learning from the literature that detailed the experiences of life in that setting, both past and present. We moved back and forth between writing about personal topics like "What things are important to you?" and analyses of information about South Africa, trying to link personal knowledge and our growing understanding of something outside our experience. We began to see the world around us in a new way. A student noticed (as I had not) an "End Apartheid" poster on a teenager's wall on *The Bill Cosby Show;* another noticed a car bumper sticker in Boston calling for an end to apartheid and even knew that it was in the colors of the ANC flag. A world of events and experiences that had seemed far from our own suddenly came close.

One student, Nancy, had made it clear in her journal entry on the first day of class that her own experience in the world would be important to her as a learner (although in the typically brief text of a basic writer she did not elaborate). She asserted:

> The three things are important to myself are the following, one that I am hispanic which has a great deal to me. To be able to influence by another language and traditions. Second, to be able to share myself with other people. I have always found it rewarding to be able to be a friend to come to me and for help or just to fool around. Third, I am a friendly person, which helps me to know alot of people. I could never know enough people. These three thing I am proud to say is part of me. I do not know if I will ever know my complete identity. I only know that I recognize these three and could stand by them.

Midway through the course, in a lengthy five-page review, Nancy summarized some of the things she had learned from her study.

There are many things I have learned in this course. Principally the situation in South Africa. I did not know what the word "apartheid" meant any more than I knew that it existed. I came to understand the power of language, how it can make you submit and debate arguments. I have learned how to write a research paper. This involved how to choose a subject, gather data about it.

During the course, a few things about the work raised questions in my mind. Why is South Africa our topic? What is the history of apartheid in South Africa? Why don't the whites in South Africa change when they know they are wrong? How are we making a difference in knowing what we know? These are some of the questions that I was left with. I am almost sure there were more but I cannot remember.

At the beginning of the semester, my greatest problem was to get my thoughts on a piece of paper. The constant assignments have made it easier to write and indeed to express myself. In addition, the ability to better express myself stems from the fact that I have been discriminated against in my life. This has resulted in my being able to relate in personal matters to racial discrimination, which is an important part of apartheid.

I have progressed in the following ways. I have become a better writer. I am also more aware of the problem of apartheid. I was exposed to South African black literature and I have developed an interest in it. I think my listening and conversational skills have developed because of the many interesting class discussions. . . .

My highest priority is to further develop my writing skills. I would like to learn about verbal manipulation and other writing techniques. I would like also to participate to a much better extent in class discussions. It is important to me to learn more about people who are exploited. For example, I would be very interested to find out more about the situation about Central America.

Nancy's response makes clear how engaged she had become by the issues raised in this course, how they fueled all of her uses of language, including her "listening and conversational skills," how she learned to do research and gather data in the context of this study, and how her exposure to new literature led her to develop new interests. She now appreciates the power of language in a new way, and she wants to use that power in her own writing. She has real questions about South Africa that will carry her beyond the end of the formal unit of study. She sees how her study of South Africa can provide a model for studying other contexts, for learning about "other people who are exploited," and particularly that her own life as a Hispanic American has its roots in a political context she can learn more about. And the changes in her writing reflect her growing authority as she makes these very connections.

So it would appear that this particular course met many of our goals. Yet I would argue now that the two lines of focus, on the self and on the world, were still only parallel in the curriculum. Nancy was looking at something outside herself, at an experience that was very different from her own, and she made the sorts of connections we hoped for between her personal experience and the framework of knowledge about South Africa we were building. But except for the review essay, the writing we had called for had treated these strands separately, with little that explicitly helped students to place themselves, as writers, in what they were learning. (This makes Nancy's own accomplishment all the more impressive.)

I have come to see this problem more clearly, even as we've been writing this book. Recently Vivian handed me some writing by one of her students that exemplified the understandings that can arise when a course builds explicit connections between self and world like those we described in Chapter 6. The course readings were by writers who have had different cultural experiences in the United States, and the theme was "The American Dream: Myth and Reality," a theme not unlike "Language and Power in South Africa" and a new area of inquiry for many of the recent immigrants in Vivian's class. But Vivian was explicit in creating a sequence of reading and writing assignments that actively encouraged students to make the sorts of connections Nancy made—to use concepts and ways of looking at experience that at first seemed to be outside their experience, to look more closely at what's near and again at what's far. The class had been discussing the concept of "marginalization." In this selection from a journal, Thao moves from observations of differences in the ways men and women participate in conversation in her own home, to applying that term to her own experience, to seeing how the experience of her home connects with other events in the world.

> Let join in my family's dinner once, you would find yourself interested in concluding something. At the beginning a person who opens the conversation is always one of us, my mother, my two sisters or me. Something happened in our workplace, in our classes or at home was carried out to discuss or argue. We who first open the conversation, give the subject, later become listeners unintentionally. On the other hand, my father tends to dominate rather than simply participate in conversation. He interrupts us more often than we do. And truly saying, he is always a winner of our debates. In conversation, he is perceived as authoritative, while our speech sounds tentative.

Thao then comments, "Applying a new concept from our class; marginalization in my family, I felt so sad with my finding. I asked myself when my mother unintentionally became marginalized and why none of us realized that." A few days later she observes her workplace, the school media lab:

> At the beginning of each semester, there are a lot of students who stop and ask for the classroom. So it's not strange that in the evening, one young man showing a syllabus with his teacher's name and phone number on it, asked for help. My friends used phone book and schedule book to find out his class: room 88. After he left we led our talk to a new subject that came from the name of his book: "Alcoholic users and alcoholism." A few minutes later, one lady stopped by and asked for the class of "alcoholism teacher" and they replied to her "sorry. We don't know." I asked them, "Why didn't you tell her, you knew that its the same room?" They answered me: "the class has already begun for two weeks but she still doesn't know where her class is. What a girl!" Again I asked, how about a young man? They couldn't say anything else except "I don't know."

Of course, Thao finds a pattern in these conversations that also appears in the larger society.

> Going home I talked to myself that it was only one small thing happened in our lifetime. A man doesn't want to help a woman to find out her classroom. A teacher allows only his male students to speak out their opinions. It's so upsetting that women's advocates just raise their voice after Mike Tyson was convicted. They were so scared to do anything as William Smith and Clarence Thomas gained their acquittal on rape or sexual harassment charges. Irrefutably, men have power and dominate our society.

In reading Thao's journal entries I came to understand the ways in which Vivian had structured the course to foster these kinds of connections throughout each aspect of their writing.

So the writer's work of connecting self and the world can be supported by a curriculum that encourages such connections. What happens, though, when the students (and teachers) who would build on their own experiences as a way to approach those of others all come from seemingly mainstream cultural backgrounds and have not in obvious ways experienced cultural difference? At our urban university, the non-ESL writing courses at the freshman level do include students with a wide range of cultural experiences, but the courses of others who are grappling with the issue of a multicultural curriculum are not filled with such convenient diversity, at least not obviously so. And in our upper-level courses in particular majors, like the course on language and literature, we are often challenged to create a multicultural environment in what appears to be a unicultural classroom. Of course, what we read and how we read it matters here. But I want to argue that to approach multicultural understanding, all of us must explore the base of our own cultures, and that even in an apparently homogeneous community students bring to it different cultural ways. Most of the students in the language and literature class were white, for most English was a first language, and few had had any significant experience with other cultures yet many wanted to teach in schools with much greater diversity. The very curriculum we have described worked to build an understanding of quite different ways of using language, of creating "literature," of finding meaning and interpreting the world among students who had seemed quite similar. Discovering diversity, even within an apparently common culture, can provide a base for building new multicultural perspectives. In fact, few students in the United States are very far away from different cultural roots.

Kathleen is quite explicit about the role that stories about her grandfather play in her family's cultural traditions: "to inspire the young and to reassert the traditions of pride and strength in the family." But she finds a generational difference in response to these stories:

> The third generation, my cousins and myself, are deliberately being reminded, over and over, of where we came from and how much it took to get where we are. Surprisingly, however, once we realize how lucky we are to be where we are, where we are (America) is conveyed as being not as good as where we were before. . . . We are inspired, and we continue to love the stories, but for us, the "American" generation, this inspiration is not applicable to our own lives—here, today. We can't imagine telling our friends and neighbors that we saw a black dog fly into the sky and have them back us up on that. Our way of life depends on our understanding the culture we live in, which is different in almost every respect from the old way of life.

For Kathleen, knowing her family stories helps her understand the framework within which experience is interpreted and evaluated by her mother's generation. But for her, the canon of grandfather stories must be reinterpreted against a new background—life in America.

As writers all of our students must place themselves in relation to the private voices of the self and the family and re-place themselves in a different and larger world. Building curricula that integrate both pieces of this work is, I would argue, essential for supporting the work of each individual writer as well as for building a multicultural community.

Suzy: From Cultural to Multicultural Studies

It is one of my deepest convictions that education can foster a process whereby the individual comes increasingly to see connections between self and others, and to develop a sense of reciprocal responsibility to those who are, though distant in a variety of ways, becoming part of an expanding definition of self and like-self. With age and education, there can be a growing sense that one is attached—by filaments of awareness, responsibility, and caring—to an everwidening world of others, so that there may be mutual influence exercised by thoughts and perceptions, decisions and actions. This is a process that begins in childhood. As our contacts with others increase and with them our ability to imagine other ways of life, other places, other times, we come to see ourselves amid widening circles of allegiance: at first the self and like-self may be confined to family and intimate friends. Later this identification commonly includes groups or institutions—the block, the school, the town, the hometown team, our nation, the people who share our religious beliefs, and possibly members of our race, gender, ethnic group, or economic class. As a function of certain types of experience—and I see education as a particularly powerful example—the ripples of awareness and connectedness can continue to expand outward in several domains. They can include an increasingly greater diversity of human beings: those living in diverse cultures at great distances in space and time; those who speak different languages, dress differently, have different limitations and abilities; possibly even members of other species, may come to be included in this web of relationships of which we feel ourselves a part.

As a teacher, I have sought to use my courses as contexts in which this sort of process will be fostered and to develop curricula through which students are enabled to discover their own intellectual and verbal competence. We had designed the thematically focused, research-based freshman studies seminars to focus on topics in the historical and cultural studies area of the core curriculum. In addition to inquiry about language, the courses in that program have examined concepts like justice, friendship, adolescence, religious commitment, conflict resolution, and the functions of humor and comedy in human societies or focused on particular cultural experiences—the village as a way of life, the Latin American experience, the culture of Native Americans. It was our hope that such themes would draw the students into engagements with attitudes, assumptions, and conventions at a distance from their own, and thereby provide opportunities for them to experience those forms of otherness and discover that despite striking differences in perspective, in ways of doing things and using language, they had many things in common with people living in different cultures and times. We also hoped that they would examine their own attitudes, conventions, and assumptions in the light of the unfamiliar and see how these, too, were rooted in a particular historical and cultural perspective.

I see a multicultural course as plunging students and instructor into a series of different cultures, immersing us in their diverse visions, making us listen to their diverse voices, demanding that we stretch ourselves to accommodate the otherness we are encountering. The themes should be things that lie at the heart of our own cultures—that on the one hand are held to matter terribly and on the other are treated in different ways by different cultures. Ultimately, the goal is not to give students a deep knowledge of the theme (this is not a matter of knowing something that is fixed). It is to help them discover complexity where there appeared to be simplicity, to see how the lenses and filters of culture influence our perceptions.

The freshman studies seminars were "multicultural" by normal standards, since they allowed for an exploration of different perspectives, practices, ways of using language, while keeping the theme or topic as the primary focus. But my own notions about the value and character of multicultural courses shifted when, because of a chance error in the registration process, the ESL-designated section of the course was eliminated and ESL students were enrolled in the section I was scheduled to teach for native speakers. For this mixed group of students, I designed a new course, one that would more directly draw on their multicultural experiences. The new theme was to be "concepts of courage and commitment," to be explored from the perspectives of a variety of cultures, some ancient, some contemporary. The texts included mythical images of traditional warrior forms of courage from Bronze-Age Greece (Homer's *Iliad*) and biblical Israel (David and Goliath) through medieval England (Malory's *Morte d'Arthur*) to precolonial Igbo society (Chinua Achebe's *Things Fall Apart*), as well as examinations of real nineteenth- and twentieth-century lives, including the abolitionist and feminist Elizabeth Chandler, South Africans Steven Biko and Winnie Mandela, Martin Luther King, Jr., Albert Schweitzer, and finally, Helen Keller's teacher, Annie Sullivan.

Other freshman studies seminars had examined the cultural determinants of knowledge, used texts drawn from a wide range of cultures, and provided a safe environment for a multiracial, multiethnic group of students to examine their feelings about cultural differences. But this multilingual, multicultural class became a place where the differences in the students' backgrounds were a valuable part of the course. I believe that the course would have been considerably less effective, missing an important part of its multiculturalism, if all of the students had come from similar backgrounds.

The new course on cross-cultural images of culture and commitment was, I believe, a true multicultural course. It explored the differences in how cultures view the emotional and social meanings of courage and its relationship to commitment, providing students with the chance to examine the different ways in which cultures interpret experience and define values, and—something I have come to see as the second necessary layer of multiculturalism—class members themselves were drawn into these different interpretations from a very *diverse* set of backgrounds. The fact that the class was mixed, ESL and native speaker, made it more likely that each text, and the culture it was drawing us into, would be discussed from a diversity of perspectives, requiring us all to stretch ourselves to meet the perspectives of the texts *and* the perspectives of the other interpreters of the texts. Together, students and teacher found that we had to use our imaginations to get beyond our own understandings and assumptions, and accept those that may at first have seemed alien. We came to discover things about our own attitudes that surprised us.

For me, then, a truly multicultural course requires three components: (1) a multicultural class of students, (2) a personally compelling theme that touches on deep-seated values across cultures, and (3) the use of materials in this exploration that immerse the class in a diversity of culturally influenced visions. The development of multicultural curricula that truly do help students develop the kinds of competence regularly assessed by the institution requires careful planning and a willingness to draw students into the worlds in which the texts are rooted, asking them to seek out information about their cultural, historical, and geographical contexts. An important aspect of the work we did in the courage and commitment course involved these kinds of explorations of the worlds of the texts. Working with maps, we familiarized ourselves with the geographic areas where they were created; we did library work in order to learn about historical and sociopolitical conditions; we considered those aspects of the original languages and textual forms that were accessible to people who did not know the languages. We wrote words and names in Hebrew, pronounced names and expressions in Igbo, listened to a reading of the opening passages of the *Iliad* in Homeric Greek, learned how to "scan" a line of poetry for its metrical pattern, and collectively developed "time maps" of the world in order to discover what was

going on in all of the places from which the students and their families came in the years the Greeks were laying siege to Troy, when
David was playing music to the distraught Saul in his tent, when
Launcelot was wandering through the forests of Britain looking for
action, when the foundations of British colonialism were being established by the missionary advance guard in Southeastern Nigeria.

In the microcosm of this classroom, it also became important for
students to be able to "tell their own stories," to establish with
honesty their understandings (and confusions) about courage and
commitment, and to locate themselves with respect to the investigations into different cultures, uses of language, and ways of seeing and
knowing the world. Such opportunities keep students from feeling
lost in a wash of new and foreign concepts, terms, and attitudes and
lessen their tendency to feel as if their own ways of knowing are
not valued. In fact, giving the students numerous opportunities to
situate themselves honestly with respect to the course material
increases the likelihood that they will not close themselves off to it
and reduces the need for them to create pretenses in their written
work. Thus, in such a multicultural course it is useful to interlace,
among the conventional assignments that require analyses of literature and cultures, assignments that ask the students to explain, in
their own voices, who *they* are and where *they* stand with respect to
the texts, the cultures, the work they are doing. The writing students
do in response to these assignments ("What do you know about the
Bible?" "How do you feel about writing?" "What is your personal
definition of 'courage'?" "Please tell a story about a person who
represents 'courage' for you." "What do you think the following quote
means?") establishes the students' writing character. It creates opportunities for them to examine the language of the texts closely and to
assess their own thinking and articulate their own ideas and knowledge, and it allows for continued honesty in the analyses that come
later.

For example, Hung, a Vietnamese student, was well prepared but
silent in the classroom and in his early written work had always
carefully stayed close to the assignment. He had regularly gone to the
library and gotten background on things before writing but had
revealed nothing about his own relationship to the material we were
discussing. After the course had been going for about a month, before
we began reading the biblical story of David's encounter with Goliath, Hung handed in this response to the question: "What do you
know about the Bible?"

What do I know about Bible? Since my foot step on the stage of life
I was confuse on every thing, and a bunch of question came to my

head, Such as Why do I have to involved in a Society? Why do I have to be continuos battle in order to Survive in life? What's right? What's wrong? I'm totally confuse. I'm decided to Searching for the answer in religion, but It doesn't Satisfied my thirsty, my ambitious. then I turn to tradition. Also I found nothing there eighter. there fore I decided to Searching for the answer by myself. I decided not trust in anything what is tradition, custom, what people this is right, that is wrong, but rather to use my own mind, to find out what is right and wrong. finally I think I could not Sactifact your question, I have to say that I don't know anything about bible.

Hung's way of saying that he doesn't know anything about the Bible is actually an elegant demonstration of what he does know about its contents and place in American society. His comments reveal that he knows about the Bible's function as sacred authority and the source of traditional values and received truths concerning moral behavior. In addition, however, he has used this brief piece of writing as an opportunity to give a moving account of his own willingness to take the risk that some people see as calling for the greatest courage a human being can muster—the rejection of received truths and the insistence on thinking for himself.

At first, the students were reluctant to approach material whose origins were distant from them in time and place. They expressed considerable trepidation about reading and understanding an epic about the ancient Greeks. But by the time the class had worked on the culture of the Mycenaeans, learned about the excavations at Hissarlik, and worked closely with the imagery of Homer's language, they seemed comfortable making judgments about the courage and commitment of the various characters. Here are selected passages from a paper written by Choi, another Vietnamese student, on the heroism he found in the *Iliad:*

> What makes Hector interesting as a hero is his courage to dangerous situation even though he knows that he's going to die and is full of fear in his heart. Before he fights Achilles, the greatest warrior in the World, he keeps running away from him. But he realizes that he should fight. then he stops and faces Achilles when he knows that he will die under this great warrior's spear. "Great Hector of the flashing helmet spoke first, 'My lord Achilles, I have been chased by you three times round the great city of Priam without daring to stop and let you come near. But now I am going to run away no longer, I have made up my mind to fight you man to man and kill you or be killed ...'" (P403) I think fighting someone with fear needs more courage than without fear, and that's where the real meaning of "courage" lies.
> [...] Comparing Hector and Achilles, Hector is calm while Achilles is mad and cruel. Before they fight Hector asks Achilles to

return his body to Trojans if he's killed. But Achilles refuses in a cruel manner. (P404) Achilles is very eager to kill Hector. When Hector's dying, he begs him not to give his body to dogs, Achilles refuses again. (P406) Achilles is heartless. On the other hand Hector is kind. He says that if he kills Achilles he's going to only take his armour and return the body to the Acheans (P404). The difference between Achilles and Hector reflexes Hector more as a hero and a human being.

In addition to learning how to set up a comparison and contrast of two key characters, how to build a sound argument and cite references in support of his assertions—not to mention mastering the spelling of Greek names—Choi is also learning how to write about the essential truths he finds in the literature.

While the primary emphasis in such a course is on the variety of ways in which a socially valued and culturally determined quality like courage can be construed and on the fact that the students' own assumptions and values are rooted in their cultures, a powerful effect is the recognition that within diversity there is also a certain kind of universality. Toward the end of the semester Tatsu wrote a twenty-five-page paper on the different forms of courage that are exhibited by the characters in the African novel *Things Fall Apart.* In this paper Tatsu made connections between the many things that were discussed in the course and his own experience, and brought these connected elements to bear not only on his way of understanding and writing about the novel, but also on his understanding of human experience.

> While Okonkwo resists against the whites for Okonkwo himself, Obierika confronts against the whites for Okonkwo, for the Ibo people and for "justice and truth," although he is greatly afraid of them. Actually, "for the Okonkwo" and "for the Ibo people" may not be proper. He does it for nobody. Or he does it for everybody (both the whites and the Ibo people) including himself. He does it just as a human being. What he does is just pursue "truth and justice." And this is universal commitment for human beings. But this is the most important and the most difficult commitment to carry out.
>
> When we pursue "truth and justice," we frequently have to deny the society we live [in], and have to deny ourselves since we are not perfect. People are the most afraid of denying themselves: their past and future, their ideology, their religion, and so on. So we just deny only others in order to protect ourselves. We try to sneak away from "truth and justice." We are all such egoistic people. However, if each person pursues "truth and justice," and if each person recognizes

and reveals his/her weakness as if Obierika does, all war will end
up and universal peace will come into the world. And Okonkwo's
misery will never happen again.

In conclusion, what we need is not Okonkwo's courage rooted
in fear. Nwoye's commitment and courage are not really neccessary,
too, because religion does not pursue "truth and justice," sometimes.
And historically, religion used to be the reason of war. Therefore,
what we really need is Obierika's commitment and courage: the
commitment and the courage for universal "truth and justice." If all
human being have Obierika's, things will never fall apart.

The main discovery that a multicultural course offers students is
that people living in different cultures experience the world quite
differently. Yet in the midst of all this difference, they can also
discover that a human core persists. The writing they did in the
"courage and commitment" course expressed their growing sense that
they share certain essential things with people who lived in Bronze-
Age Greece, in biblical times, in precolonial Africa. They put into their
own papers their feelings about the parts of themselves they found
and understood in all the people they encountered in these texts. With
remarkable candor, they revealed in these writings that they had been
touched, excited, angered, moved to tears, by the words and feelings
of people living in far distant times and places.

Vivian: From the Margins to the Center

For years I had created composition courses that explored a particular area of content, based on the conviction that language was best
acquired in the context of using it to make sense of rich and complex
subject matter. As I planned these courses, I had repeatedly returned
to considering content that would deal more explicitly with the
situations of my particular students, students who had shared with
me the difficulties they had experienced as a result of their minority
status, their inability to use English as well as their native speaker
counterparts, their sense that they were invisible both at UMass/Bos-
ton and within the larger society. My thinking about this was
informed by the same conviction that shaped my decisions about
other thematically based courses I had created: if students' language
and writing are promoted as a result of their engagement with issues
they view as intriguing, illuminating, and authentic, then a course
that places their realities at the center rather than on the margins
would be all the more dramatic in its impact. Yet I continued to shy
away from the idea of such a curriculum, afraid of what might

happen if we overtly addressed these issues, afraid that this material was far too disturbing, too risky. In retrospect, I realize that this fear stemmed not just from how I thought my students would react to this material but from a concern with how I might be drawn into the center of a course that focused on issues inextricably connected to my life.

The more, however, my students' experiences as outsiders seemed to affect their lives, the more I was drawn to reconsider taking the risk. At the same time, incidents of racism and discrimination at UMass/Boston were on the rise, and the UMass/Boston community was beginning to explore how it could address this problem through its policies and through curricular changes. With these efforts came the institutionalization of a diversity requirement and attempts to create courses that would explicitly acknowledge the "differences" our students brought with them. The combination of these factors gave me the courage to deal directly with the realities that were too often left unrecognized and unrepresented, the voices that had too often been silenced, and the stories that had too often been left untold.

The freshman composition course that evolved was one in which students explored the myth and reality of the American Dream, a dream that almost all of them had embraced uncritically, despite the everyday tensions that seemed to chafe against it. They examined the extent to which the promises of America applied to their realities and raised questions about incidents and events that revealed "broken promises." They tried to come to terms with the factors that had marginalized them, thus allowing them to see that their situations were not just the result of some personal difficulty or problem but were interwoven with larger and far more complex conditions. And given these realizations, they began to understand the ways in which they could transcend their voicelessness, their invisibility, so that rather than being appropriated by the institutions they came in contact with, they could transform them in the same way that all participants in a culture contribute to and shape that culture.

In the context of this course, students read, examined closely, and wrote about key documents and court decisions. They read newspaper accounts and analyzed reports in the media related to immigration experiences and issues. They read pieces by authors (Maxine Hong Kingston and Richard Rodriguez, for example) that uncover issues of identity, loss of a first language, assimilation, and the relationship between language, culture, and authority. One student, Fukiko, created a dialogue with herself in the context of writing her first paper on language, culture, and identity.

A: Why do you suffer with English?

A1: I have freedom of choice. I mean I could go back to Japan anytime, also I can stay in this country.

A: OK, you should go back to Japan. Your English is no good.

A1: I know, but I want to try how much to improve my English. Now I go to school and study English every day.

A: No, No I don't think so. You married with American over ten years. You had lots of chance to practice English untill then.

A1: But we never speak English with each other. I was not planning to live in this country, so I didn't need to learn English. I thought. but my husband died so I have to think my own life and I have to bring up our son by myself. Maybe I will go back to Japan after I finish school.

A: Listen! You are not young. You should decid quickly. Don't waste time for learning English.

A1: But I have my child. I'm single mother. Its seems more comfortable to live in this country than Japan. I don't know.

A: Are you OK? you will struggle with English whole your life in this country.

While the paper in which this dialogue appeared was problematic from the standpoint of the assignment, it told movingly of the tensions and struggles Fukiko was experiencing and became the basis for her subsequent revision.

Students read revealing interviews in Studs Terkel's *American Dreams: Lost and Found* and conducted interviews of their own. They read poetry by Langston Hughes, selected work by Martin Luther King, Jr., and autobiographical pieces by Ann Moody and Audre Lourde, and considered the civil rights movement in light of the promises of the American Dream. As the notion of the American Dream was (re)considered, questioned, and (re)constructed, they looked at the way racism had manifested itself with respect to the ethnic groups represented by the students in the classroom, reading and writing about the work of authors from these groups. Students kept observational notebooks in which they recorded events that reflected the ways in which people are marginalized in different settings—the home, the educational institution, and the workplace. In these notebooks students described their observations and re-corded their responses to these observations, making connections between the course work and the variety of cultures they inhabit, as Thao did in her field notes on her family's dinner-table conversation. Students also participated in a semester-long correspondence with a class of graduate students, most of whom were teachers in urban schools who had enrolled in a course on the importance of multicul-turalism in education. At some point during this correspondence, the two groups of students met in order to interview one another, and the data collected during these interviews were included in their subsequent papers. Through all of this work, which immersed students in a rich and deep study of these issues, I invited students' reactions, analyses and interpretations, and the connections they made between their work and their own experiences and assumptions.

Organic to this work was a sequence of reading, writing, and firsthand research that built on itself, so that as the semester progressed, students referred back to previous work, both the texts they were assigned to read and those they themselves had written, in order to demonstrate the knowledge they brought with them as well as their growing expertise. This did not produce neat and predictable essays that could be plotted against some standardized continuum. Instead, this kind of work generated compelling and memorable pieces that reflected the questions and issues students were grappling with, their active engagement with the material, and their use of the material to think about the world around them. They became authors alongside the authors they read, thus reclaiming authority for themselves. In short, their work represented their own dialectical interplay with the course content, which clearly spoke to complex issues and questions of central concern to them and allowed them to speak back. As the material exerted an impact on them, they contributed to and transformed it in some fundamental way.

A powerful illustration of the ways in which this dialectical transformation took place was the class poem that we generated after reading Nellie Wong's "When I Was Growing Up," a poem that movingly tells of Wong's desire as a girl "to be white," to be American. Both the students and I could immediately identify with Wong's recollections, and all of us wrote at least one verse reflecting individual responses the poem had triggered. Mine, which revealed some of the conflicts in my own history, including the moment when my name changed from Aviva to Vivian, is the next to the last verse.

> When I was growing up,
> I dreamed to become a millionaire.
> I wanted to come to a place
> Where is called Gold Mountain and
> Melting Pot.
> People could mingle together, hand
> By hand, swarm by swarm.
> Let us go to pick gold on the street. . . .
>
> When I was growing up
> My own language,
> I don't know how to write.
> My aunt told me, my skin color

Will color all my English.
Perhaps, she has seen who I am
In insulting eyes of my friends parents. . . .

When I was growing up,
I saw western movies.
I saw the white gentlemen behave
Dignified, humorous, and brave.
The white women are pretty and well-treated.
The scenes were so beautiful that
I wanted to be a part of them. . . .

When I was growing up,
I was so proud of having dark hair.
Small eyes. Yellow and short.
When I came to America,
I couldn't be proud of
My dark hair, yellow skin, and small eyes
Anymore.
It seems white skin was best in this country.
How sad!
I wonder why we can't be proud
Of our own country and figure.

When I was growing up,
I had to play with dolls and not with cars.
With dolls that were white with blue eyes
And beautiful dresses. I never had a black one.
I did not know why!
Dancing and singing around girls.

When I was growing up,
During my kindergarten,
I painted a picture
That was a boy; but the color I put in
His face was yellow, and the nun erased it. . . .

When I was growing up,
I found myself in this strange land,
With a small portion of yellow people
Living in a little town.

When I was growing up,
All I saw was white in the walls, lights,
Schools, Presidents, media,
And even the clouds. . . .

When I was growing up,
My parents' language, their accents,

Their quaint ways
Shamed me.
I craved sameness.
I longed to belong.
I changed names.
Was that so wrong?
Now I embrace
My life on the margin.
Now I trace
My roots, my beginnings.
Now I can face
Aviva.

I don't want to be white.
Did I disappoint you?
I feel comfortable being a palette's painting
Where everybody has their stains,
A crop with different grains.
A bearable rainbow through the rain
An accidental landscape
Where the shades have a freeway.
I crave the dawn,
The marriage between the night and the day,
And the childbirth of the dawn.
The sunrise red
The Indian's race.
Did I disappoint you?
Did I give you enough reason?
I'm sorry, but I want to be what I am.
The union of all human beings.

As is obvious even in this excerpt, the poem is full of powerful images that reflect the ways in which we were coming to terms with both our childhood expectations and our realizations about these expectations. Some of these images commented on Nellie Wong's experiences, others referred to pieces we read earlier in the semester, still others allowed students to transcend Wong's worldview.

Other texts students composed were essays that revealed their ability to write about the readings and use them to make meaning for themselves. These texts were as variable as the students' individual voices and perspectives, each representing their original ways of (re)composing these issues. In one text, Thao, influenced no doubt by the number of readings that used the images of color and paintings to refer to the experience of acculturation, began by creating a metaphor that reflected the role that color played in her framework of understanding:

Coming to campus everyday, have you ever paid attention to the blocks of colored stone on the driveway near the bus stop? And shopping over weekend, have you ever concerned about color of clothes? In my country, no one ever think of coloring a rock and you could rarely find any multicolored, gaudy clothes in the stores. But in this country, colors are extraordinary, so important and so troublesome as well. Colors themselves have their own meaning. And no matter on a piece of cloth, on a painting, or in the society, while colors blend in themselves, they fight to each other so strongly. That is what Sasaki once ironically said: "America was creating a masterpiece and did not want their color." Yes, "America is great because it is composed of almost every race in the world," as Nakasian said. So a masterpiece that Americans made was wonderful because it combines any colors. But since there were people "dirty," "humble and mean," a masterpiece got stained and its color was disliked.

After beginning in this way, she introduced verses from the class poem we had written:

> Colors of this masterpiece! Obviously, we all know that
> "It seems white skin was best in this country,"
> and
> "When I was growing up
> All I saw was white in the walls, lights
> Schools, Presidents, media,
> And even the clouds . . ."
> (When I was growing up—My class's poem)

She went on to discuss research findings that students had read and written about, shifted again to another verse from the class poem, referred to some of the autobiographical pieces that had been assigned, quoted a verse from Nellie Wong's poem, and then discussed the other readings before returning to the metaphor of color in her final section. This open-ended and recursive movement reflected her impressive ability to shuttle back and forth not only between different texts but between different types of texts. And the connections she was able to make between such disparate pieces, the ways in which she was able to integrate research findings with poetry, for example, resulted in a piece not just *about* multiculturalism, but one that in its very voice, tone, and content *was* multicultural.

Yet another illustration of the kinds of texts students created as they were addressing these critical issues is this one, written later in the semester by Fukiko, which begins powerfully by confronting the reader with a set of troubling questions:

Who is marginalized in the United States? It is ethnic group and women. Who has pushed them away to the margin? It is people who have power. Who has power in the United States? Usually these people are white, rich males and they never know how it feels to be marginalized so that they don't care about marginalized people. It seems that ethnic groups have been marginalized since their child-hood schooling. According to Sonia Nieto in *Affirming Diversity,* she reported, "Teachers tend to pay more attention to their white students than to their students of color." Several of the authors we have read this semester deal with the issue of marginalization in education. I want to discuss how ethnic children are marginalized by teachers at their schools in the U.S.

Fukiko went on to a full discussion of the extent to which Nieto's report is corroborated by some of the accounts of schooling experi-ences that the class had been assigned to read, after which she turned to the ways in which this issue is related to her own experiences:

> From what I have observed in my class at U.Mass, When I am in E.S.L class, I am so comfortable because E.S.L teachers know the students' diversity or they try to understand about students' diver-sity. On the other hand, I feel that I am isolated from the majority of students, When I am in the non-E.S.L class. However, I realize often minority students are alienated by themselves in their class and don't communicate in the class with teachers. Usually they don't speak out, and sit in the corner of the classroom. Nieto points out, "Relationships between teachers and students also bear out these findings." Many teachers do not discriminate against ethnic students on purpose. Most teachers want to be a good teacher for every student. But many teachers are unthinking about students' diversity. This reminds me of Takaki's excerpt. He said, "My teach-ers and text books didn't explain our diversity."

Note the relationships Fukiko saw between the research findings reported in the readings and her own world of experiences. Note, too, that she was not just drawing on her experiences to support what other "experts" had found, but was also foregrounding her own findings and using one of these "experts" to reinforce her own claims. She went on to conclude her paper this way:

> I think teachers should teach more on our diversity than any sub-ject. We must think and educate for generations "what America is." Do we have specific ideas to eradicate marginalization for people of color? Yes, we have one. It is to educate teachers in muticulturalism. Multiculturalism in education is the key that will open the magical doors to equal society.

In the course of writing this paper Fukiko offers a solution to the disturbing and complex problems the class has been grappling with, the very solution that faculty across the curriculum at UMass/Boston and other institutions are trying to enact in their own teaching.

Toward the end of the semester, Fukiko returned to the issue of language and identity as she reacted to the texts of two authors who describe growing up with mothers who were perceived as limited and incapable because of the ways they spoke English. After tracing her own troubling experiences with the English language, explaining how easily she could identify with these women, Fukiko concluded:

> Both Amy Tan's and Manjarrez's mothers are so strong as compared with me. Because I always escaped all troble in my life. May be I should confront all troble by myself in this country. As long as I live in this country I have to deal with identity, language and culture every day. If so, I should enjoy two identities, two languages, and two cultures. May be I might be one lucky persons because I could live with two worlds.

Fukiko has moved dramatically from her initial position, revealed by the dialogue in her earlier paper (see page 185). She has stopped questioning whether she ought to return to Japan because of her "struggle with English" and has begun to see her "two identities, two languages, and two cultures" as "lucky." She has transcended what she had viewed earlier as her limitations and now values what both a first and a second language, both her own and another perspective, make possible, choosing to embrace multiculturalism as a way of life. Although Fukiko's initial texts were so problematic that I questioned whether she should have been admitted to the course, the strength of her later writing demonstrates what can happen when students are invited into the center of work, when they are recognized as knowers, when their perspectives are not only acknowledged but viewed as essential to our own. It speaks not only to the ways in which educational institutions can foster the language and critical thinking of students but also to the ways in which these students, with their multicultures and their multivoices, can contribute to and transform the very institutions they inhabit and thereby enrich the lives of all of us who work there.

Afterword

We began this book with the story of Suzy's encounter with the starlings in the catwalk. Her story helped us to frame the ways in which we have come to see the work we do with our students—the sorts of support we try to create, the ways in which we try to make it possible for them to do what they know how to do. Given that the work we have described depends on seeing teaching and learning as reciprocal processes that we share with our students, we think it is illuminating to return to the parable of the starlings and reinterpret it so that the birds are now seen as *us,* the teachers who are struggling to understand the work we have to do, often within constraints both institutional and self-imposed, flapping our wings madly against impenetrable though invisible barriers, fluttering in frustration because whatever we try seems to fall short of our aims, retreating before beginning the next foray. We too have sometimes gotten ourselves into places, perhaps somewhat elevated, that were not what we thought they were, that we misinterpreted. And we too have struggled through such situations, often unable to discover our ability to fly, acting as we thought teachers ought to act. Like our students, who are trying to acquire other ways with language, we too have felt "lost," as if our words no longer "stand for things."

By recasting *ourselves as the learners* in our parable, we can return to our earlier discussion and find that the same features we described as necessary for our students are those that have allowed us in our collaboration with each other to learn about and recreate our own teaching. In fact, the very language we have used to describe our learners' processes of development and needs speaks to the process that we ourselves have undergone and continue to undergo. For our own learning process, we had to be able to set aside the "stuff" we often found ourselves carrying (the "stuff" of our earlier models of teaching and learning, the "stuff" handed to us by our own institution) in order to create the supports and structures that would allow us to find a way in—to engage in ideas, issues, and problems and to communicate our thinking to one another without becoming disheartened by failure. We had to have the patience to allow our development to evolve responsively and organically, and the courage and imagination to work out new routes through which we could draw ourselves into learning and inquiry about our teaching, "holding" each other firmly without stifling our capacities, and offering each other the means to learn actively, to explore problems and questions as they arose, and most important, to discover in these enterprises our own competence as observers, thinkers, critics, creators.

As is true for our students, we have learned through an authentic immersion in the work of the community we are part of—speaking, listening, reading, and writing with each other about the issues that matter, that burn at our hearts; listening to one another, having our own words read, being held accountable for the ideas they express; being responded to with honesty and care. We, too, have taken risks to try new ways of representing ideas, of communicating, involving ourselves in discussions we hadn't entered before. We, too, have moved away from the norms and conventions we had embraced, that felt comfortable to us, away from our previous way of thinking about the world of teaching, learning, and constructing meaning from it, in order to cross a boundary and raise new kinds of questions, formulate new understandings, discover new ways of knowing.

Our process of learning has revealed that as long as we remained outside or on the fringe of the community in which we and our students worked—trapped in the catwalk—we would share the plight of the starlings: we would remain unable to interpret for our students and for ourselves in any meaningful way what we were trying to do. Our own efforts would continue to be directed in inappropriate ways for what we needed to accomplish, and we would grasp little of what was obvious and significant in our students' attempts. We would miss the point of what our students were reading, hearing, and writing and again smack up against the impassable walls that kept us from succeeding.

Our collaboration has gone far to free us from these walls, allowing us to learn under the same conditions we have tried to enact for our students, allowing us to see that it is our very learning and our reflecting on that learning as our thinking evolves that makes teaching possible. We have invited one another to be exploratory in our approaches, taking comfort in the knowledge that if we confront an obstacle, there are other passages that we can point to or construct with one another. We have taken risks and tested out hypotheses, trying out tentative solutions and discovering new problems. We have taken on authentic, engaging work that has pushed us beyond what we first saw as limitations and suggested to one another new routes for further exploration. We have taken on the responsibility of finding ways of guiding one another into intellectual work that affords or heightens for us those pleasures we know to be the potential outcome of our joint intellectual enterprise. And we have created what we knew was essential to all learning, a place of safety in which this engagement, reflection, inquiry could take place.

Reimagining the starlings as ourselves, we can see the critical role we played in one another's thinking, reshaping and reframing the understandings that informed earlier stages of our pedagogy, making sense of our efforts and those of our students, and gaining insights through the process of reflection. But as the work described in this book makes obvious, this collaboration extended beyond the three of us and embraced the community we established with our students. It is through such a community that we could enter into a relationship of care with our students, a relationship that would help us redefine and reconstruct our role as teachers, that would require students and teachers to play reciprocal roles. Our students have guided us throughout. Through their attempts to learn, they have suggested other possibilities and have drawn us into their inquiry and thinking at the same time they engaged us in our own inquiry into learning and teaching. By listening, speaking, reading, and writing with them, we have become learners together, co-searchers, exploring the issues and concerns we share in common. By engaging them in attempts to investigate and closely examine concepts, issues, ideas, and problems, we have constructed "real knowledge" and found new ways to think about our world. As students moved away from their old patterns of seeing and thinking, pushing themselves outside their usual ways of doing so, taking on more responsibility for their own learning, we were able to make genuine discoveries along with them, and their understandings contributed to ours. Working along with students in this way allowed us (as it allowed our students) to articulate and share our own thinking processes, to feel more secure about what we were doing, to trust their evolving understanding as well as ours, to be passionate about our work.

Thus, we have discovered that, in addition to the principles of pedagogy, language, and intellectual development that we embrace, and in concert with the patience, the willingness to take risks, the structures and multiple engagements that we have found to be essential to our work as learning teachers, there is another element without which it would all be to no avail. We must allow ourselves to care about our students and their learning in very personal and unguarded ways: we must acknowledge the enormous personal stake that we have in their growth and success, and they must know that. Ultimately, it is when we allow ourselves to be caught and held by our students that we are able to stop our flapping, find our way, and discover our own competence.

Bibliography

Achebe, Chinua. [1962] 1986. *Things Fall Apart*. African Writers Series. Oxford, UK: Heinemann. Distributed in the US by Heinemann, Portsmouth, NH.

Angelou, Maya. 1971. *I Know Why the Caged Bird Sings*. New York: Bantam.

Applebee, Arthur. 1981. *Writing in the Secondary School: English and the Content Areas*. NCTE Research Report #21. Urbana, IL: National Council of Teachers of English.

Austin, J. L. 1975. *How to Do Things with Words*. Cambridge, MA: Harvard University Press.

Bakhtin, M. M. 1981. *The Dialogic Imagination*. Austin: University of Texas Press.

Bartholomae, David. 1980. "The Study of Error." *College Composition and Communication* 31, 3, 253–69.

———. 1986. "Inventing the University." *Journal of Basic Writing* 5, 1, 4–3.

Bartholomae, David, and Anthony Petrosky. 1990. *Ways of Reading*. Boston: Bedford Books.

Bateson, Mary Catherine. 1984. *With a Daughter's Eye*. New York: William Morrow.

Belenky, Mary F., Beth Clinchy, Nancy Goldberger, and Jill Tarule. 1986. *Women's Ways of Knowing: The Development of Self, Voice, and Mind*. New York: Basic Books.

Berthoff, Ann. 1988. *Forming/Thinking/Writing*, 2d ed. Portsmouth, NH: Boynton/Cook.

Bloom, Allan. 1987. *The Closing of the American Mind*. New York: Simon and Schuster.

Britton, James. 1987. *Prospect and Retrospect: Selected Essays*. Portsmouth, NH: Heinemann.

Britton, James, Tony Burgess, Nancy Martin, Alex McLeod, and Harold Rosen. 1975. *The Development of Writing Abilities (11–18)*. London: Macmillan Education.

Bruner, Jerome. 1983. *Child's Talk: Learning to Use Language*. New York: Norton.

———. 1986. *Actual Minds, Possible Worlds*. Cambridge, MA: Harvard University Press.

Chafe, Wallace. 1982. "Integration and Involvement in Speaking, Writing, and Oral Literature." In *Spoken and Written Language*. Ed. Deborah Tannen. Norwood, NJ: Ablex.

Corder, S. Pit. 1981. *Error Analysis and Interlanguage.* Oxford, UK: Oxford University Press.

Duckworth, Eleanor. 1987. "The Language and Thought of Piaget, and Some Comments on Learning to Spell." In *The Having of Wonderful Ideas and Other Essays on Teaching and Learning.* New York: Teachers College Press.

Elbow, Peter. 1991. "Reflections on Academic Discourse: How It Relates to Freshmen and Colleagues." *College English* 53, 2, 135–55.

Farb, Peter. 1974. *Word Play: What Happens When People Talk.* New York: Knopf.

Farrell, Thomas. 1983. "IQ and Standard English." *College Composition and Communication* 34, 4, 470–84.

Frank, Anne. 1985. *The Diary of a Young Girl.* New York: Penguin.

Freedman, Samuel. 1990. *Small Victories.* New York: Harper and Row.

Freire, Paulo. 1970. *Pedagogy of the Oppressed.* New York: Continuum.

———. 1973. *Education for Critical Consciousness.* New York: Seabury.

———. 1985. *The Politics of Education: Culture, Power, and Liberation.* South Hadley, MA: Bergin & Garvey.

Fugard, Athol. 1984. *Master Harold and the Boys.* New York: Penguin.

Fulwiler, Toby. 1986. "The Argument for Writing Across the Curriculum." In *Writing Across the Disciplines: Theory into Practice.* Ed. Art Young and Toby Fulwiler. Portsmouth, NH: Boynton/Cook.

Gass, William H. 1985. *Habitations of the Word: Essays.* New York: Simon and Schuster.

Gee, James. 1985. "The Narrativization of Experience in the Oral Style." *Journal of Education* 167, 1, 9–35.

———. 1989. "What Is Literacy?" *Journal of Education* 171, 1, 18–25.

Geertz, Clifford. 1973. *The Interpretation of Cultures.* New York: Basic Books.

Gilligan, Carol. 1982. *In a Different Voice.* Cambridge, MA: Harvard University Press.

Groden, Suzy, Eleanor Kutz, and Vivian Zamel. 1987. "Students as Ethnographers: Investigating Language Use as a Way to Learn to Use the Language." *The Writing Instructor* 6 (May), 132–40.

Heath, Shirley Brice. 1983. *Ways with Words: Language, Life, and Work in Communities and Classrooms.* Cambridge, UK: Cambridge University Press.

Heath, Shirley Brice, and Amanda Branscombe. 1985. "Intelligent Writing in an Audience Community." In *The Acquisition of Written Language: Revision and Response.* Ed. S. W. Freedman. Norwood, NJ: Ablex, 3-32.

Hirsch, E. D., Jr. 1987. *Cultural Literacy: What Every American Needs to Know.* Boston, Houghton Mifflin.

Hoffman, Eva. 1990. *Lost in Translation.* New York: Viking Penguin.

Hymes, Dell. 1972. "Toward Ethnographies of Communication: An Analysis of Communicative Events." In *Language and Social Context.* Ed. P. P. Giglioli. Harmondsworth, UK: Penguin.

Kingston, Maxine Hong. 1977. *Woman Warrior: Memoirs of a Girlhood.* New York: Random House.

Kohlberg, Lawrence. 1976. "Moral Stages and Moralization: The Cognitive-Developmental Approach." In *Moral Development and Behavior: Theory, Research and Social Issues.* Ed. Thomas Likona. New York: Holt, Rinehart and Winston.

Krashen, Stephen. 1982. *Second Language Acquisition and Second Language Learning.* Oxford, UK: Pergamon.

Kutz, Eleanor. 1986. "Students' Language and Academic Discourse: Interlanguage as Middle Ground." *College English* 48, 4, 385–96.

Kutz, Eleanor, and Hephzibah Roskelly. 1991. *An Unquiet Pedagogy: Transforming Practice in the English Classroom.* Portsmouth, N.H.: Boynton/Cook.

Labov, William. 1972. *Language in the Inner City: Studies in the Black English Vernacular.* Philadelphia: University of Pennsylvania Press. Includes "The Logic of Non-Standard English."

Lessing, Doris. 1981. "The Old Chief Mshlanga." In *African Stories.* New York: Touchstone.

Marshall, Paule. 1988. "Poets in the Kitchen." In *The Borzoi College Reader.* Ed. Charles Muscatine and Marlene Griffith. New York: McGraw-Hill, 133–40.

Mead, Margaret. 1964. "Discussion Seminar on Language Teaching." In *Approaches to Semiotics.* Ed. Thomas A. Sebeok, Alfred S. Hayes, and Mary Catherine Bateson. The Hague: Mouton.

Morrison, Toni. 1974. *Sula.* New York: Knopf.

Nieto, Sonia. 1992. *Affirming Diversity.* White Plains, NY: Longman.

Olson, David. 1977. "From Utterance to Text: The Bias of Language in Speech and Writing." *Harvard Educational Review* 47, 3, 257–81.

Perry, William G. 1970. *Forms of Intellectual and Ethical Development in the College Years: A Schema.* New York: Holt, Rinehart and Winston.

Piaget, Jean. 1959. *The Language and Thought of the Child.* London: Routledge and Kegan Paul.

———. 1968. *Six Psychological Studies.* New York: Vintage.

Potok, Chaim. 1967. *The Chosen.* New York: Ballantine Books.

Rodriguez, Richard. 1982. *The Hunger of Memory.* Boston: Godine.

Rose, Mike. 1989. *Lives on the Boundary.* New York: Penguin.

Sapir, Edward. 1921. *Language: An Introduction to Speech.* New York: Harcourt, Brace and World.

———. 1949. *Culture, Language and Personality.* Berkeley: University of California Press.

Scollon, Ronald, and Suzanne Scollon. 1981. *Narrative, Literacy and Face in Interethnic Communication.* Norwood, N.J.: Ablex.

Scribner, Sylvia, and Michael Cole. 1981. *The Psychology of Literacy.* Cambridge, MA: Harvard University Press.

Searle, John. 1969. *Speech Acts.* New York: Cambridge University Press.

Shaughnessy, Mina. 1977. *Errors and Expectations: A Guide for the Teacher of Basic Writing.* New York: Oxford University Press.

Shen, Fan. 1989. "The Classroom and the Wider Culture: Identity as a Key to Learning English Composition." *College Composition and Communication* 40, 4, 459–66.

Shostak, Marjorie. 1981. *Nisa: The Life and Words of a !Kung Woman.* New York: Vintage.

Silko, Leslie. 1989. *Storyteller.* Berkeley, CA: Arcade.

Slobin, Dan. 1989. "From the Garden of Eden to the Tower of Babel." In *The Development of Language and Language Researchers.* Ed. Frank Kessel. Hillsdale, NJ: Laurence Erlbaum.

Smith, Frank. 1988. *Understanding Reading.* 4th ed. Hillsdale, NJ: Laurence Erlbaum.

Sommers, Nancy. 1982. "Responding to Student Writing." *College Composition and Communication* 33, 2, 148–56.

Spradley, James. 1979. *The Ethnographic Interview.* New York: Holt, Rinehart and Winston.

Street, Brian V. 1984. *Literacy in Theory and Practice.* New York: Cambridge University Press.

Stubbs, Michael. 1983. *Discourse Analysis: The Sociolinguistic Analysis of Natural Language.* Chicago: University of Chicago Press.

Tannen, Deborah. 1982. "The Oral/Literate Continuum in Discourse." In *Spoken and Written Language.* Ed. Deborah Tannen. Norwood, NJ: Ablex.

Terkel, Studs. 1980. *American Dreams: Lost and Found.* New York: Pantheon.

Vygotsky, Lev. 1962. *Thought and Language.* Ed. and trans. Eugene Hanfamann and Gertrude Vakar. Cambridge, MA: MIT Press.

———. 1978. *Mind in Society: The Development of Higher Order Psychological Processes.* Ed. Michael Cole, Vera John-Steiner, Sylvia Scribner, and Ellen Souberman. Cambridge: Harvard University Press.

Weidenborner, Stephen, and Domenick Caruso. 1990. *Writing Research Papers: A Guide to the Process.* New York: St. Martin's Press.

Whorf, Benjamin Lee. 1965. *Language, Thought and Reality.* Cambridge, MA: MIT Press.

Wong, Nellie. 1984. "When I Was Growing Up." In *This Bridge Called My Back: Writings by Radical Women of Color.* Ed. Cherrie Moraga and Gloria Anzaldua. Latham, NY: Kitchen Table, 7–8.

Zamel, Vivian. 1983. "The Composing Processes of Advanced ESL Students: Six Case Studies." *TESOL Quarterly* 17, 2, 165–87.

———. 1985. "Responding to Student Writing." *TESOL Quarterly* 19, 1, 79–101.

Index